HOW TO DO WHAT YOU LOVE FOR A LIVING

HOW TO DO WHAT YOU LOVE FOR A LIVING

Nancy Anderson

MJF BOOKS
NEW YORK

Published by MJF Books
Fine Communications
Two Lincoln Square
60 West 66th Street
New York, NY 10023

How to Do What You Love for a Living

Library of Congress Card Catalog # 99-74097
ISBN 1-56731-317-5

This edition published by arrangement with New World Library.
Typography: Stephanie Eichleay

This book was originally published by New World Library as *Work with Passion*.

Manufactured in the United States of America on acid-free paper

10 9 8 7 6 5 4 3 2

Dedication

For my brother and my sister everywhere,
that you may bring forth your hidden light,
and show it to a waiting world.

CONTENTS

FOREWORD TO THE SECOND EDITION

When my publisher suggested I revise *Work with Passion*, I was reluctant to go back over what I thought was done. That night I had a dream in which I walked through a large, two-story house, sturdy, but needing work. "What do you need to do to this place?" asked the woman with me, obviously my intuitive self, since she always asks the right question. "Well," I said, "I need to open up the front and let in more light — the back needs work, too, but that should not take too long."

The next day I began remodeling *Work with Passion* (and myself). I expanded the preface and the autobiography outline, and included the insights I gained following publication. I rewrote a few parts in the back of the book, and added a chapter on entrepreneurship for readers whose passion is independence.

Work with Passion was challenged when it first appeared in 1984, the middle of the so-called greed decade, as if greed were new to humankind. The concept of the book was interpreted by some to mean that all one has to do is what one loves and the money will come. Not true.

This book makes it clear that freedom is the result of self-discipline, and of values that strike a happy balance between the material and the spiritual.

PREFACE

"The world will never be happy until all men have the souls of artists — I mean when they take pleasure in their jobs."

— Auguste Rodin

This book was written to help you live the life you were born to live — a life that works in the true sense of the word "works." When your life works, your life comes together, with a harmonious balance among all its facets: your work, your family, your loves, your finances, and your mental and spiritual growth.

We are all in this life to learn our lessons, sometimes in painful ways. But learning can be fun, full of humor and joy, when we follow wise advice. "How can that be?" you ask. "My life is far from what I want it to be. How is it possible to laugh and enjoy myself in the midst of so much evidence that life is one long struggle? What can your book say that dozens of other self-help books haven't said? I've read all of those and I'm still not satisfied."

Well, perhaps the answers for you are within these pages. I approach you the same way I approached the men and women who asked me for direction in their careers and businesses. In each case, I outlined the same steps to take — and the steps worked. I talk to you personally in this book, as if you are in front of me, a style that personalizes the problem you are trying to solve: What is your best niche in life? Where can you be most successful?

You will be most successful when you are connected emotionally to your daily tasks, and to the people you serve. If you are a flower arranger, or any other worker, the love affair between you and your product or service makes itself known to your customers, who are magnetized by the feeling and effort you put into your work. How do you make this connection between you and your work — and make a living from it?

First, you must eliminate the distractions in your life: bad habits that are harmful to your mental and physical health, possessions you do not need, empty socializing, and entanglement with "friends" and family members that drains your energy. When you empty your life you may find that you are doing what is right for you, but you are not risking emotional contact with others, leaving you feeling isolated and alone. You may be doing too much, or you may be with the wrong people, or in the wrong setting, or your money and power goals may be taking precedence over feelings. The chapters in this book help you clarify what action is right for you, whether a simple adjustment is necessary, or a radical change.

I use many sources to make the steps to power as clear as possible. There are numerous written exercises for you to do, the same exercises I use with my clients. Additionally, there are many personal success stories. We all love to hear success stories. Have you ever noticed how you feel thrilled when you hear about a person's victory over adversity? If you feel discouraged, you will find within these pages dozens of people who felt the same way. They are ordinary. But they found they could do extraordinary things, once they listened to their feelings.

As you read, you will observe the focus is not on "how-to" as much as "how-to-do." You will learn how to reproduce powerful behavior — through exercises, reading, thinking, feeling — and as a result, changes will take place in your life.

Change begins with a desire for change — a new job, more fulfilling work, or your own business. In the process of helping my clients achieve their objectives, I came to see how crucial to their successes were faith, belief, and imagination — their passion! In each chapter of the book you will find a "passion secret." When you understand all ten secrets, you too will be the powerful actor, not the passive reactor.

Most self-help books focus on techniques, information, and other external sources. This book, however, insists that you first focus internally before focusing on external marketing techniques. Unlike most products, you were conditioned to respond to life and work by the people who brought you into the world, and by the people who gave birth to your parents. Add to those powerful influences your peers, your teachers, and your culture as a whole and you have some idea of the forces that impinge upon one human life. Confronting those forces is my work; my most effective tool is my client's autobiography, written as outlined in Chapter One.

Over the years, I have noticed a theme that runs through every story: an intense struggle between the part of the self who wants to be free (the Victor), and the part of the self who wants to be enslaved (the Victim). The manner in which the battle is fought determines the outcome: Are we honest, or do we deny what we do not want to hear? The clients of mine who work through the autobiography with minds open to the truth, and to the changes that follow illumination, move quickly into the Victor role. In many cases, clarity comes to them without having to work through each chapter in the book. The process is not necessariily linear, but it always starts with the autobiography.

A look back at your family, then, is the first step to knowing yourself, and to discovering the block to your passion. As you write, try to understand, not blame, the influences that shaped your character: economic, social, political, and religious. Pay particularly close attention to your relationship with your father or, more accurately, with the Father within, the taskmaster who makes you do it right, whatever "it" is. If your human father did not master the work he loved, the entire family suffered from his lack of discipline, his anger at himself and life, often expressed in abusive ways. This missing father syndrome, so prevalent in our culture, is a metaphor for lack of focus, instability you may need to confront in yourself.

Your mother is important, too, since she taught you, by example, how to respond to your father, and to authority in general. If she worked outside the home, she gave you another example to follow, or ignore, depending upon how she reacted to the demands of her work and to authority figures. The solution to your career problem is to see both parents as they were, not as you wanted them to be, and to see in what way you copy them, or *repeat your response to them* with men and women who remind you of them. When your perception is clear — and this may take awhile — you alter the behavior that does not work and your career (and life) moves forward.

Self-scrutiny takes great courage, since what we see initially can be ugly: our darker motives of greed, lust, sloth, anger, pride, and jealousy. If we look without judgment, however, we gain insight and power over what formerly controlled us. From a more balanced perspective, we see the lighter side of our personality: our humor, compassion, generosity, wisdom, patience, and love.

You may need professional help as you bring the hidden parts of yourself and the characters in your story to the surface, such as a challenging counselor or a support group to keep you on track. Like Sleeping Beauty's castle, the Self is covered over with brambles and weeds, the ideas and beliefs you accepted that smother authentic life. The Prince is the part of you who hacks his way through all obstacles to his Princess — the struggle as important as the reward. Thus it is with finding the work you love: you will succeed if it is in harmony with this inner self. If the work you choose is not in harmony with your deepest values, you will fail, no matter how much money you make. Or, you will sabotage the work so that you can get out of it. Far better to choose work that makes you grow.

I would like to be there when the light of understanding goes on for you, as I know it will. In whatever way it does, I congratulate you and wish you the most powerful life you can have!

HOW TO READ THIS BOOK

Read all the way through the book before you begin writing out the exercises. As you read, absorb the concepts, look where you are led, what you are shown. Let at least two weeks go by before you begin to read again. This time, stop to do the assignments. If you are an independent thinker, you will want to know about the results of so much hard work. Finishing the book before you write will show you the results, the happy ending.

HOW TO FIND YOUR PASSION AND YOUR POWER

Do you love your work? Are you as happy to see Monday morning come around as you are Friday morning? Do you have satisfying job relationships, friends with whom you work and play? Do you make all the money you want? Do you admire your boss and the philosophy of your company? Do you go home at night with a peaceful feeling of accomplishment, looking forward to a new day of challenge, variety, and excitement? Do you identify with the product or service that your company or firm sells? Do you enjoy the business you own? Do you have security, recognition, and advancement potential? Does your private life work?

If you answered "no" to any of the above questions, then my response to you is the one I give to my clients as we begin the months of work to find their right niche: You *can* love your work. You can have a life full of adventure and satisfaction. There are many choices and opportunities. You literally do not have enough time in this life to do all the exciting things you could do. So in order to get what you want, we must begin with *you*. You must know yourself, your uniqueness, your strengths, and what you do naturally, easily, without effort. You may need to go to school to learn the *technical* application of this natural talent, but you do not need to change drastically, drop out, or get fired to create the results you want.

People come into my office with many concerns about their lives and careers. They are dissatisfied with their present situations. Their creativity is stifled. They do not know what kind of job or business is best for them. They do not like their supervisor, or they are disenchanted with corporate politics and structure. Perhaps they feel a general boredom; they need a new challenge but cannot, for one reason or another, focus on exactly which steps to take to solve their career problems. Frequently, they want to be making more money or getting more benefits. Most of all, they want to advance, to grow, to make contributions for which they receive genuine recognition from their peers and their employers, or employees.

A typical conversation in our first meeting may include any or all of the following. I ask, "What brings you here to my office?"

Response: "I feel stifled, unappreciated. My employees and customers are draining me. My associates' attitudes are poor, my boss is not a leader I admire, I can't seem to get my ideas across, and top management doesn't really care about the employees. We're just faces at desks to them. The job (or business) I'd like is unavailable to me. I have background, training, and experience, but I can't put my skills to full use. I know I have potential but I can't seem to be able to develop it so I can be appreciated and rewarded the way I want to be."

"What have you tried to do on your own to solve your problem?" I ask.

Some of the responses include, "I've been thinking about changing my career for months. I've tried to talk to my boss and others where I work, but nothing has changed. I made up a resume and answered ads, even sent out a few to companies."

I ask what the results have been and they respond, "Not many.

I've had a few interviews, but either they're not what I want or I'm not what they want. I'm doing something wrong. The whole process has affected everything else in my life, too. I'm not much fun to be around right now, and my home life isn't the greatest. My family (or wife, husband, or lover) can't be of much help; they have their own problems to think about. I know there's something out there that I can really get my teeth into, but what and where? I don't know the market; I don't know where I fit."

Fortunately, I have digested the first section of my client's autobiography before we meet, a revealing study of family beliefs about money, work, sex (including gender beliefs), and religion. The client's current situation often reflects an early struggle fought between and among childhood characters. As we work through the story, I encourage my clients to use their current jobs or businesses to correct behavior learned in this early setting.

"You'll find the answer when the Self is remodeled," I say. "And the result will probably surprise both of us."

DISCOVERING YOUR NEEDS

The right "fit" in a job comes when the work satisfies *your inner needs*. A need is a force, a wanting, a passion that may or may not be conscious. This desire runs through every life, but it often gets thwarted when we ignore our feelings. When the work you do satisfies this desire you will feel happy again. If your current job or business is not meeting this need, you try to make up for it on the weekend, with hobbies, friends, perhaps overindulgence in drink or other escapes. By noon on Monday, you are deflated, counting the days until next Friday. You wonder if this is all there is to your life.

When you begin looking for the right environment, it helps to think about nature's way. You do not find a pine tree in the middle of the Mohave Desert. If you are constantly wanting to run things yourself, and have always done so since your flower was a tiny bud, then do not plant yourself in a big corporation. Look at small businesses, under twenty employees.

You will know your environment is right when you sense the pleasant growth of yourself: you are glad to be learning what you are learning and you like the other flowers around you. The gardener (yourself, the owner, boss, supervisor) gives you just the right challenge, does not overwater (rescue) you, does not expose you to too much sun (overexpectations), does not undernourish you (with no praise, or plenty of criticism).

Let us assume, then, that you need replanting — you are a seedling that is not coming along as it should. *The environment in which you can flourish is available to you.* Remember this statement; say it every day. What needs to be unearthed is your unique personal power. Before you move to a new environment, you must think about this natural power of yours, and then direct it toward appreciative soil.

Human beings are wonderful. We are also despicable. But I believe in the human spirit and its will to survive even the most brutal circumstances. Over the years, I have seen men and women achieve power over their lives rather than living as victims. They discovered that when they did the work they loved, all else in life fell into place. Like these clients, when you do well in your life's work — whatever that is — you feel well. Your sense of personal worth is keen, and you then see the personal worth of others. *It is through the dignity of the work we do that we achieve self-esteem in life.*

Helping individuals discover the right path for them allows me to do what I do best: first, heal the heart and clear the mind, and second, design a marketing strategy. For some clients, the main career or life problem is one of focus, knowing what choice is best for them (and what choices are not). For others, the problem is how to make contacts and develop strategy: the approach, the follow up, and other job-search techniques. For all my clients, success comes when they connect with their feelings. I am able to assist them in making this vital connection because they trust me enough to reveal the truth about themselves and what they truly want. (*Passion clue*: If you are *embarrassed* about something, you are close to your passion! This may not be obvious at first — but think about it.) The purpose of this book is to help you make that emotional connection in your life, too.

YOUR MIND AND HEART CREATE YOUR EXPERIENCE OF LIFE

When you know exactly what you want and have the emotional strength to go after it, your mind and heart work together as you give your plan enough time to come into being. The combination of mind and emotions is powerful; it creates your experience of life, good and bad.

Our educational system and the majority of our relationships with other people concentrate on *thinking*, cause and effect: if this, then that. This concept is linear, rational, orderly, predictable, logical, and analytical. It is what is popularly called "left-brain thinking," since, in most people, this type of thinking has been demonstrated to take place in the left hemisphere of the cerebral cortex. The function of the left side of the brain is to put the events we observe in order. The principle of rationality eliminated superstition and excessive emotion; rationality brought us the scientific and industrial revolutions. However, this emphasis on our rational abilities was often at the expense of our imaginative, feeling, and creative abilities.

In our rapidly changing world, *alternative* thinking is urgently required. Like the human body, the social and cultural body experiences pain during periods of rapid change and growth (for example, dealing with dramatic changes in the once-solid family unit, or the breakdown in the public school system). When new solutions to problems are needed, people are forced to tap a different source — their creativity — which is right-brain thinking.

CREATIVE THINKING

Imagination, creativity, alternative ways of thinking — these are all functions of the right side of the brain. The right brain is intuitional, irrational, nonlinear, *feeling*, creative, and innovative. Some have described the left and right brain as, respectively, male and female, the yang and yin. From the right side of the brain come hunches, insights, irrational thoughts, flashes of inspiration. That information is then processed by the left side of the brain, which is very strongly developed in most of us. The exchange occurs rapidly, in milliseconds. For example, if your feelings are dominated by the thinking side of your brain, you might fantasize about some lovely thing you have always wanted, and then your intellect steps in and says, "Don't be a fool — you can't have that!" So you stop dreaming.

The result is that instincts, first feelings (need I say passions?) about an event, can be repressed and stifled. In the end, rigidity of thinking can occur. The ideal state is a balance between the two modes of thought, an ability to go beyond the either/or, left/right syndrome. When the mind is balanced, the mind is open to the heart, the heart open to the mind.

Few of us are taught anything in school or at home about creative thinking. On the contrary, we are usually rewarded for being similar to some external model, whether it is at home, school, or work. When were you taught about the power of your mind, and that thoughts are things? Who gave you the magic keys to powerful living: spontaneity, flexibility, and following your heart's desire?

If you are like most people, you have a sense of limitation — and you developed it early on in your life. Your genius — and we all have this — began to be stifled the first time you had a sense of knowing what you could not possibly know rationally (you were too young, too uneducated, too *something*). Because then you believed it was impossible to know the "unknowable," you cut off your genius, suppressing it and limiting yourself. And in the process you capped your passions. Those strong natural impulses are still within. You and I will bring them out of hiding, revealing the creative spirit within you.

You may believe that a project like attaining passion in work will not happen overnight. You are right. However, what *can* change overnight, and literally transform your life, is your attitude, your way of looking at a problem. This change can come from a dream, a conversation, or any event that suddenly plunges you into awareness — you "see the light." First, you must have a strong desire to change. Then your attitude makes a shift, although it may take some time to bring the new goal into being — a new job or your own business, for example.

Since I do not have you in front of me to talk to you about your thoughts and feelings, I will use the individual experiences of other people throughout the book to illustrate how their desire to change led to a more passionate and powerful life.

PASSION AND POWER

Passion is intense emotional excitement. It is a feeling that comes to those who feel intensely about some object, person, ideal, or belief. Human passions are released to create both good and evil. There are many examples in history that show the difference one passionate person can make. Every love story, every major change in history — social, economic, philosophical, and artistic — came about because of the participation of *passionate* individuals.

We all have the capacity to feel intense emotional excitement. However, few of us *act* on our passions. We bury our passion because, among other reasons, we were ridiculed early in life because our enthusiasm was not backed up with expertise. Or, you may have submerged your natural passions as a child around adults who submerged their own passions. As soon as you give yourself permission to feel whatever you feel, that power will resurface, surprising all who "knew you when." Then you will take action on those feelings.

Power is defined in *Webster's New World Dictionary* as *the ability to take action*. As an adult, you know that your decisions are your choices. It is no longer necessary to do anything you hate — you can choose to do only what you truly love to do. That is power.

Since power is a word that has many negative connotations, keep in mind its spiritual meaning: a force that is internal, not affected by external reality. You may think that presidents, kings, and wealthy people have such power. They may, and they may not. The power I describe can change your experience of the world, and life. You no longer feel trapped like you did as a child when you felt the very real restriction of your authority figures. You know how to control your impulses, risking the rebellion of the hostile forces within you. You are patient, you know that time reveals true wisdom.

MATURE POWER

I want to add a few kind words here for parents, teachers, and other parental authority figures who may feel offended by my references to typical child-rearing practices: While you had authority and an awesome responsibility, you did the best you could or, in some cases, less than your best. If this book stirs up feelings of remorse, make amends. If, on the other hand, you realize some of your actions were wiser than you knew, commend yourself. My point in this section is that the past is not the focus of power: "*The present moment is the point of power.*"[1] Our lives are renewable, from moment to moment.

Power is the ability to act, rather than power over something or someone. Action, putting our passions to work, requires several preliminary steps. *The first step* is to know yourself — to have mental clarity. "Well, that's easy," you say, "I know myself, let's get on to the next step." Surprisingly, most people, even highly paid professionals, do not really know themselves. Here we are speaking of knowing ourselves completely, in the past, present, and future. Why am I here? Where am I going? What do I want to do with my life? Knowing the answer to these questions gives your life focus and power.

How do you find the answers? The good news is that you already know — you have that information inside you! The bad news is that your internal information is hidden behind layers of fear and disbelief. Fear and disbelief are the reverse sides of the coins labeled action and faith. Fears are irrational emotions that keep us from freeing our passions and achieving power. *Half of the first step to power comes from acknowledging your fears* — the fears that stand between the person you are today and the powerful person you will be in the future. These fears were instilled in you as you grew up, given to you (many times unintentionally) by your parents, siblings, authority figures, and peers.

THE SIX GHOSTS OF FEAR

There are six basic fears, according to Napoleon Hill, author of the now-classic book, *Think and Grow Rich.*[2] Hill calls the fears "ghosts." These ghosts of fear are:

1. Fear of poverty.
2. Fear of criticism.
3. Fear of ill health.
4. Fear of loss of love.
5. Fear of old age.
6. Fear of death.

Study the following symptoms carefully, taking note of any you are troubled with. These are your enemies, and they are sometimes elusive: as they fight for existence, they tend to resist scrutiny.

Fear of Poverty

Fear of poverty is the worst of fears, and it has several symptoms: indifference, worry, indecision, overcaution, and procrastination. Fear of poverty is not limited to "poor" people — it can be a very real "ghost" even for people who have a great deal of money.

One of my young clients, John, had over $50,000 in the bank and a steady stream of income from an inheritance and investments. Yet he feared losing it. He was immobilized, and his career choices seemed limited. He worried, procrastinated, and refused to take risks.

"John," I asked, "what do you want to do with your time each day, now that you do not have to work?" John responded, "Everything I think of loses interest for me after an initial investigation. Being someone's employee doesn't appeal to me — I know how independent I am. The other alternative is to invest in a business, as a partner. The question is, what business? I don't want to use my money to buy a job."

"Why do you have to use your money? What do you really want to do? Figure that out first — not the money question. It is likely that once you've done some research and figured out how you can involve yourself in a project that excites you, your money will be a side issue."

It turned out that John was fascinated with race cars. He had raced Formula V Fords as a hobby and the thrill of the track showed in his eyes as he talked about it. He still worked with Formula team members on occasion. I suggested that he talk to people in racing who were professionals, and learn what the income possibilities were. He did. The process of investigation took weeks, but he found his answer — and was he excited when he came in!

"Nancy, this is it! I learned that I have all the skills and knowledge I need to organize and run a successful racing team. Organizing the team comes first. Preparing a cost/benefit presentation is next. Finally, I will approach businesses whose sales would increase as a result of sponsoring our cars. Their name and logo would be on the cars and their prospective clients could be brought to the track. They watch an exciting race, and identify with the company in an atmosphere that brings them to their feet. All this helps companies sell their product or service to special customers — those who respond to speed and drama."

A year later, I went to John's first regional race and met his teammates. They had three beautiful royal blue cars, several sponsors, and lots of enthusiasm. The race was an exciting triumph. John did not finish first, but he was on his way. We shook hands and planned the next race date.

"Nancy, the best part about this year is that I discovered a way to keep my savings and investments and earn the income I need in another way. As I talked to people on the advice calls I made, I discovered they had needs I could fill. For example, some wanted leasing arrangements — they were new drivers who wanted to lease a race car to learn to drive. Others needed a good mechanic. I know how to repair those cars, and I earned good money doing it. I see now that a year ago I was concentrating on *loss*. As soon as I concentrated on *gain*, my income increased," John said. He added that the Indianapolis 500 was his ultimate goal.

John solved specific problems — repair and leasing. And he lost his fear of poverty because he knew how well he could repair and lease race cars, his *passion*. It had never occurred to him that he could make money at what he loved, for he thought — like so many others — that he could not successfully combine fun and profit.

This belief comes from the old-fashioned Puritan work ethic — the idea that work and life are not supposed to be pleasurable and that rewards come in an afterlife. "Pleasure" is seductive, sinful, irresponsible — the "devil's lure." Have fun in work? Just be glad you have a job, say the cynical disbelievers. Today we live in an era that rewards happy productive living, and yet most people are not happy in their work.

Fear of Criticism

Fear of criticism brings self-consciousness, lack of initiative, lack of ambition, and an inferiority complex. Fear of criticism quite possibly is the most damaging and prevalent fear in our culture. Concern about what other people think about us is instilled in us quite early by well-meaning (and some not so well-meaning!) parents, friends, teachers, and peers.

Picture a bright, pretty, intelligent young woman with talent in the graphic arts. Sharon had run her own free-lance business ever since she was a teenager, yet she was gripped with fear of criticism. She had finally overcome the fear of rejection in her work because she knew she needed only a few clients to make a profit. Yet certain nagging self-doubts remained.

"You handle your business problems so well, Sharon. Where is this fear coming from?" I asked.

"No matter what I do, my father and stepmother still think I'm flaky. They always ask, 'Why don't you settle down and get a real job?' (You see how others can discourage your passion?) And my best friend seems to think I'm battling hopeless odds. She says that because there is so much competition, I shouldn't expect to be successful."

How many times have you been discouraged by friends and family, who throw boulders of criticism in your path? You are often most stymied by those closest to you — a reflection of your own (unconscious) mental attitude. In Sharon's case, once she took action her fear decreased, as did her patience with people who criticized her. She found other characters to fill her life, self-employed men and women she met at entrepreneurial gatherings.

Most fears are *beliefs* about reality, not reality itself. Healthy fear protects us from harm. Unhealthy fear is based on false evidence.

Fear of Ill Health

Fear of ill health causes hypochondria, lack of exercise (you believe you may overtax yourself), susceptibility (you think you may catch something, and you do), self-coddling, and intemperance. Keeping your body active is a surefire way to keep your mind alert. Especially during the time of career change, a self-initiated training program will release tension, improve your overall self-confidence, and increase your energy. I always insist that my clients exercise regularly.

Fear of Loss of Love

Fear of loss of love — one of the most tragic fears — brings jealousy, faultfinding, possessiveness, clinging, and even gambling (to buy the love you want so badly). Fearing loss of love comes from the belief that you can "lose" love. Actually, once you have felt love, at any time, *you get to keep that experience forever*. You add the experience of one love to another, opening new doors to more love. You will know if you are free from this fear when you can love *yourself* at all times. Until then, you need outside verification.

Loving means caring about and supporting a person without expecting a payoff, which is no easy feat. Very few of us were around that kind of unconditional love in early childhood. If we are very fortunate, we have one or two people in our lives who want us to be happy, with no conditions on what that happiness is. No matter what your situation is, resolve that you will love yourself enough to love your work.

Fear of Old Age

Fear of old age involves denial of age, apologies for one's age, and thinking of oneself as slipping or declining in some way. This fear kills off initiative, imagination, and self-reliance. This fear comes from the belief that getting "older" is a diminishing experience. *Not true!*

For a woman, fear of old age is often connected to strong traditional security needs. A woman is taught that her physical allure attracts a man, whom she needs for economic support. If she starts looking "old," she fears her man will discard her for a younger woman, and she will lose her "security." Fear of old age involves an acute sense of loss — loss of the *power to attract.*

A wise woman moving into maturity will see that movement as an achievement. The mature woman adds depth of experience to her personality. Her inner self radiates wisdom, joy, beauty, appreciation, kindness — her mind probes for the meaning behind her own and others' experience. Who would not want to appreciate and love such a woman?

Today, any woman, no matter what her age, can look good. Exercise, nutrition, clothes, makeup, color coordination — all can be developed to enhance a woman's natural attributes. The outer person is a reflection of the inner person: balanced intellect, sensuality, and spirituality. Every year brings more to her — more life, more wonder, more experience. The wise woman uses these riches to her advantage, becoming more powerful and influential — truly the backbone of civilization.

For a man, the fear of old age is connected to a fear of loss of his independence and power. A man fears his fellows will best him, take away what he has or, worse, show him up. Much of a man's fear is sexually connected, as is the woman's, but with a more competitive edge. The man who is moving into his mature years would do well to read biographies of famous men. He may be startled to discover how many of them came into their greatest productivity late in their lives (and to learn how many were influenced by the kind of woman described above!).

The truly mature man radiates strength and vitality, a vitality that comes from an appreciation of daily life. He is curious, perceptive, knowledgeable, affectionate, and warm. Believing in himself, he believes in others. He does not take life or himself too seriously, and laughs easily. The man who is mature savors life, lingers over it. He recognizes the value of quiet reflection; alone and away from others, he balances and weighs his days. As a result, he is the source of balance and encouragement for others.

As with all of the six basic fears, which vanish once we understand them, the fear of old age disappears when one realizes that each stage of life is as necessary and beautiful as is each season of the earth. Each season has its own purpose and loveliness. The autumn and winter of one's life are preparation for the new birth to come, the transformation nature always promises.

Fear of Death

Fear of death causes preoccupation with the idea of death, fostering lack of purpose and concentration on what you cannot control.

One of my young clients feared death because her father died suddenly, without warning, when she was a teenager. He had been a strong influence on her and her family — the center of their lives, financially and emotionally. His death was a trauma that continued to affect her life. At thirty-one, Annette's scattered life history since his death had been a testimony to her lack of purpose. She had gone from one experience to another: jobs, lovers, a marriage, and finally a devastating divorce. Her autobiography was two hundred handwritten pages that released the pent-up feelings she had felt since she was a teenager.

The section on her father's death was the longest; she described her grief for pages and pages. To her, his death was a personal affront. "Why? Why?" she asked, repeatedly.

"Annette, the loss of your father put you and your family on your own, a change that forced all of you to grow. Your lack of focus and erratic life are a rebellion against what was best for you in the long run."

"I didn't know until I began writing about him how much anger was inside me. I cried and cried but I kept on writing," she said, crying as she said it.

"Grief has stages, and you have reached the final stage, acceptance of what is. Now, what is for today? You are alive, so live!" I encouraged her.

Annette found others who had lost a parent; she learned that she was not alone. She talked about death, even her own. She realized that her father's overprotective attitude fostered dependence, not independence. Then, much to my dismay, Annette initiated a pregnancy by the older man she dated. They married, and she had another child, ensuring the father figure she lost. Time will tell if she fights her way to independence. Sometimes we all take a long detour from that road.

The remainder of this chapter prepares you to write your own autobiography. As you write your story, you will discover the source of any fears that have interfered with your passion. You will also discover your strengths, your courage. As the star of your story, you will see your character absorb the influence of your environment, and you will learn that most of your fears are a child's illusions, based on decisions you made a long time ago.

WRITING YOUR LIFE STORY

The written autobiography is extremely effective when done with self-discipline and enthusiasm. Each person reacts differently to the assignment — "I'm not a writer!" "What has that got to do with a job?" "How do I have time to do that with all the other demands in my life?"

I have had clients get so upset about the assignment that they have stopped right there. It is amazing how people will walk away from personal power.

Passion Secret #1:
The first step to power is clarity.

Why is writing an autobiography so important? Notice I said "writing." Writing forces you to hold still and think, which is why I do not recommend a taped autobiography. Writing down on paper what you have thought, felt, and experienced makes those thoughts, feelings, and experiences real. In addition, you see the uniqueness of your personal history when you put it in writing. Taking the time and energy to complete such a project gives you a new understanding of your life.

All of us have an incomplete picture of the past. We have memories that float up into our consciousness from time to time, but we have little sense of how a memory and the event that triggered it ties into our life as a whole.

Seeing our lives as a unified whole is difficult. Each day there are so many demands and distractions: family, job, bills, problems, all so immediate. Philosophers concerned with this problem — from Plato to Descartes to Sartre — designed belief systems whereby human experience would be understandable. Beginning with William James in the late nineteenth century, a new way of looking at human experience emerged. James was a pragmatist; he believed that you can change your life by changing your experience. For example, you do not sing because you are happy, you are happy *because* you sing. If you act cheerfully, you will be cheerful. When you *act as if*, it will come about. The technique of *acting as if* works. In other words, what you think about and concentrate on *becomes* your experience. The following story illustrates this concept.

MARK'S STORY

One of my younger clients, whom I will call Mark, was concerned because he had no professional work experience and yet he wanted to start out on a job as a manager. He came to my office with a three-page resume in his hands, nervous and unsure of his future. Mark had just finished college with a bachelor's degree in Business Administration. He had mailed dozens of resumes, had problems getting interviews and, if he was interviewed, he would hear the same line: "You don't have any experience." Mark was discouraged by this "Catch-22" situation: How could he get experience if no one would hire him?

We began work by focusing on his abilities and achievements, on what he did naturally and easily. Mark had worked his way through college helping manage a delicatessen. "Did you do anything to increase efficiency and profits in the deli?" I asked. After puzzling for awhile, he said, "Well, I moved the mayonnaise closer to the mustard!" What a good time-motion idea!

Then he remembered an even better idea — he had introduced a new sandwich that became a daily best-seller. And his willingness to stay late when business was good showed his initiative. Very quickly, we catalogued his many marketable strengths and abilities. By consciously recalling his strengths, Mark came to view himself as an *experienced manager*. From then on, he presented himself as a confident, aware self-starter — and soon he got exactly the job he wanted. Interestingly, the man who hired him said his decision was based on Mark's self-assured presentation.

Since Mark's passion was automobiles, we found a tire company through our marketing survey that had the training program and the potential for growth that he needed.

The manager who interviewed Mark liked his thoughtful approach letter (which we will deal with later, in Chapter Seven) and his thorough research on the company. He was flattered, and considered himself fortunate to have a person with Mark's initiative. Mark performed beautifully in his new job — in one year, he rose to a managerial position.

We develop a commitment to whatever we have spent time on: the more time, the stronger the commitment. If we spend our time worrying about failure, that is what we manifest in our lives. When Mark changed his thinking about himself, his experience changed. His first important step was to focus on an alternative way of thinking. You too can accomplish this necessary change, by using the specific techniques covered in each chapter in this book. In addition to learning *to use* these tools, you will learn how to recognize and tap the valuable resources of your childhood — awareness, spontaneity, innovation.

Spontaneity and *flexibility* are two words that define the experience of having real personal power. When your mind is open and free of judgment, it has one of the tools of childhood at its disposal — awareness. To look at things with a detached view opens the door not only to emotional adventure, but also to innovation, to change, to alternative modes of thought and action. Think of Edison, Einstein, Picasso (to name only three), who unlocked their power and genius by remaining open to fresh possibilities. Be flexible, spontaneous — do not tie yourself into only one way of thinking and doing. Instead of fearing any event in your life (especially failure), try viewing your experience with detachment, as if you had no stake in the outcome. Then the solution will come tumbling out of hiding.

WRITING EXERCISES

Since the first step to power is clarity, let us prepare for the writing of your autobiography. Taking time out to write may appear boring, especially when you want to read this book, get results quickly, and get it over with! But once you spend time with yourself, you will get to like it more and more. When you become acquainted with yourself you find out how complicated you are. I ask my clients if they have ever spent twenty-four hours completely alone with no plans — and very few say yes! If this overly-scheduled life is like yours, how are you ever going to know yourself? Rest assured, once you slow down the pace of your life you will never go back to hectic living. You will be much more productive as a result of the calm, quiet moments you spend when it looks like you are not doing anything.

THREE SAMPLE WRITING EXERCISES

Self-Description Exercise

Write a few paragraphs of self-description, as this client did. (My comments are in parentheses to illustrate what his self-image shows.)

"Basically, I find this is a difficult thing to do. (An honest beginning!) So, I'd say it is one of my personal traits that I don't do well focusing on myself.

"My personal qualities: I consider myself to be bright, giving, sometimes to the point of negating the need 'to get'. (He knew he gave more than he received and by expressing this was releasing his feelings about that trait. A healthy and accurate picture will emerge as he takes responsibility for that self-defeating behavior.) I am self-motivated in most things, although of late a sense of not knowing what I want has been getting in the way of motivation. (Apathy is the result of lack of focus.)

"In the physical sense, I am a fighter for the things I want out of life as well as quite spoiled regarding comfort, possessions, and lifestyle. (Here you see conflict. On the one hand, he fights for the good things; on the other hand, he feels 'spoiled' because he has so much. I had asked him why he felt spoiled — he earned it; that is a big difference. Does he feel guilty because he got what he worked for? This is an example of fear of criticism; somehow we should feel guilty when we get what we want.)

"Physically — although I was lectured not to think about this as a kid (can you see the parental message, 'Don't be proud of your body'?), I would say I am way above average. I take the time to keep myself looking good. I know how to dress well although I often go out of my way to 'dress down' in order to blend in more. So, I would simply say on a physical level I look very good and know how to use my looks, although I am constantly aware of being careful not to let my looks play too major a role in my life. (The words of a man who has balanced the gift of attractiveness with appreciation of that gift and its limits.)

"On the mental/emotional level, I'm a constant flip-flop. I have trained my mind to observe and see and feel. But at the same time, I am my own worst enemy. I often take all of the knowledge I've gained and use it negatively; I'm always analyzing things, with sometimes too high a level of consciousness. However, I am also very aware when I have let things 'flow,' using all my intuition as a positive force. This feeling is much more desirable and I work at that level most of the time. I do consider myself emotionally stable as a general rule and limit my less positive times to when I'm alone." (This whole paragraph shows how his mind works — sifting, balancing, seeking awareness. The client was a highly successful restaurateur who built an outstanding restaurant from scratch, never having had previous experience in that field. Highly creative and intuitive, he used his imagination to create exactly what he wanted — a restaurant of his own that would serve superb cuisine.)

Others' Description Exercise

Next, describe how others see you. What picture do you think others have of you? The same client's example looked like this:

"Mostly my impressions of what others perceive come from what other people tell me. (This is how we all learn about ourselves. That is why it is so important to have accurate mirrors in our lives, people who will reflect back to us images that correspond to reality. It is very rare to have accurate mirrors. Most people, particularly our families, are biased.) I often am told, 'You're nothing like what I expected you to be.' It seems I give the impression of being very aloof. Sometimes I'm described as looking mean, and I even hear comments about 'those eyes'. (He has very penetrating blue eyes.) So it often seems that others see my moods and changes reflected through my mannerisms. I'm seen as self-assured, bordering on indifferent. Or if I'm feeling good, I'm seen as having a twinkle in my eye and sort of a devil-may-care attitude."

Balanced Description Exercise

Finally, describe your *balanced self*. What qualities do you want to enhance?

Again, the same client said: "If I were the person I'd like to be all the time, I'd be quite a bit looser with myself than I am. I truly prefer the more relaxed me. I would like to fine-tune my 'consciousness' level so it wouldn't send me into a pensive state but rather would keep me on a 'high' which I get glimpses of quite regularly. (He is talking about the sense of well-being you feel when everything goes well — you hear, see, say, and do all with ease. It is the feeling of always being in the right place at the right time, a high aspiration, but attainable with mental discipline.)

"I'd like very much to truly trust all the knowledge I've gained. I know for a fact that I function at my best when I'm in a 'flow pattern' rather than on a 'stop and go' trip. It also is clear that people respond to me best when I'm in one of my relaxed periods." (The 'period' he describes is one that is free of the six basic fears. It is a mental state that comes from the belief that everything is all right, life has meaning, and our lives are significant.)

Another client of mine found so much difference between how he perceived himself and the description of his balanced self that it disturbed him. Balance was unattainable, he said. I asked why.

"Well, look at the words: 'I am calm, financially secure' — that's the opposite of what I am!" he said.

His self-image was pretty bad. "Joe," I said, "are you *afraid* to be calm and financially secure?" He hesitated. "You've answered my question," I said.

You may find you do not really want to be balanced, in your most private thoughts. There is so much in our past training that causes us to cast a wary eye toward success of any kind. Too much creature comfort might be bad for us. This is the long-suffering view of life, the fear that without struggle, what would life mean? In Joe's case, his self-image gradually began to conform to a balanced image. First, he had to see that his beliefs interfered with any possibility of changing his picture of himself.

If there is something in your past that troubles you, guilt may interfere with a positive self-image. Perhaps you hurt someone, or did something that makes you feel uneasy. Or perhaps you have not admitted to yourself how much someone hurt you. These old, unfinished situations can keep us from experiencing happiness in the present.

Awareness of what we think and feel comes in several stages: *denial*, intentional or unintentional; *shock*, when someone or something breaks through our denial; *anger* or *remorse*, depending on whether we were the transgressor or transgressed against; *action*, internal and external change in attitude and behavior; *forgiveness* and, finally, *detachment:* psychological freedom.

With freedom as your reward you can see why it is important to sit down and take inventory of past actions. Next, *make amends*. You can do this in person or in a letter or telephone call. If you were the injured party, approach the other person and express your concern. This gives the person an opportunity to heal the wound he or she caused you.

If this is not advisable, write down your thoughts in a letter. Imagine that the other person has apologized, forgive him or her, and throw away the letter. Forgiveness is a courageous act and, in the end, you are the greatest beneficiary. (*Passion Clue:* The truly passionate feel sorrow and remorse for their transgressions, and they are not afraid to confront those who have hurt them. Remember, passion is intense feeling.)

Emotional pain does not end with one, two, or even a dozen attempts — consciousness takes *work*. But one day, you will feel all you need to feel about the past. You will no longer discuss it, or repeat your old mistakes.

FOUR WARM-UP WRITING EXERCISES

I recommend that you get a pen and paper — or a typewriter or computer, if that is easier for you — and work through the four exercises that follow. You can also use a cassette tape recorder for these first preliminary attempts at recall. Your own voice is a good teacher and clarifier. (Do not, however, tape your autobiography which will come later. You will shortcut the process that only writing can best serve — developing clarity of expression.)

The suggested questions for each exercise are designed to get you started. Add any stimulating ideas of your own that come up. Do not take these exercises too seriously — have fun with them!

Describe a Success or Failure

Pick an incident in your life when you were either a success or a failure. Think about the incident, and then write about it. Look at the language you use. Did you picture yourself as passive or active?

Your Picture of Yourself

You have a current picture of yourself. Do you see yourself as unique or special? How do you feel about your personality? Do you like what you see in the mirror today? Do you like your hair, eyes, walk — your body design? Do you like your thoughts, hopes, goals, and aspirations? Do you appreciate all the good things you say and do each day? What about your work? Do you think you do it well, whatever it is?

How Others View You

What is the picture others have of you? Do they see you as you see yourself? Think about your answers. What do others think about your physical self, your personality? Do they like you? Do they think you are optimistic, depressed, cautious, adventurous, funny, competent, incompetent? A good father, mother, sister, brother, wife, lover? Do they like to be around you? Do they show how they appreciate you? Are they uncertain about what and who you are? Do they trust you, think you are sincere? Do they tell you what they think and feel about you?

Your Balanced Self

Picture your *balanced self*. Are you very different from your first picture? How so? What would you change? By whose standards are you measuring yourself? Your standards, others' — your parents'? Is your balanced body different from your present one? What about your attitude, friends, work, income? What similarities are there between balance and what you see now? Who can verify these similarities for you?

CAPTURING YOUR EARLIEST MEMORIES

After you have done the preliminary writing exercises, you are ready to begin writing your autobiography. Feelings of the past recalled in the present will give you great insight into several important areas for power-building: your values, needs, goals, characteristic behavior; in other words, your view of your unique existence!

Many of your values were formed by early childhood experiences. Your views of success were solidified as you moved through the educational process — a process that included experiences with family, friends, and outside activities, as well as school.

Let the memories come, whatever they are. There is no such thing as a "good" or "bad" autobiography. It is your experience, so naturally it is good. What we are after is how you responded to your past and the people in it. Writing your autobiography can help you discover those powerful feelings.

Your autobiography has two parts: Part One includes your family origins; Part Two covers the remainder of your life. Describe in detail the experiences you feel are important. Include significant people who aided or assisted in your growth.

Read through the following suggested outline for your autobiography. The questions will help you get all the events in chronological order — and your answers can be very revealing.

Avoid substances that block feeling as you write: alcohol, cigarettes, excessive food, or any activity that distracts you from the task at hand. Your goal is to know what you feel so that you can make wise choices. Exercise, eat well, rest when you get tired.

PART ONE — YOUR GRANDPARENTS AND PARENTS

What did your grandparents believe about money, work, sex (including gender beliefs), and religion? If you do not know the answers, ask your parents or a relative or extrapolate from your parents' beliefs. Many of my clients are surprised by what they never knew about the past, simply because they never asked! Next, describe how your grandparents brought up your parents. For example, did they grow up in the city or the country? Were there many children or just a few? What was positive about the grandparents' marriage?

Once you introduce your parents into the story, *call them by their first names all the way through the story*. This technique gives you emotional objectivity, and creates a new category for them in your mind. My clients call their parents by their first names in our sessions, too, a startling concept at first, even sacrilegious for some. If they persist, they soon see a change in the way they relate to their parents, and to authority figures who may be standing in for the parents.

Additionally, if there is dependence between and among family members, I request a three- to six-month moratorium on contact: no phone calls, no letters, no social interaction. Time apart gives everyone a chance to break old habits, and to clarify values, which, in the end, determine with whom we feel at home. Much creative energy is wasted in entanglement with the family, which is not the same as genuine relatedness.

According to Robert Firestone, author of *The Fantasy Bond, Effects of Psychological Defenses on Interpersonal Relations*, grown-up children's entanglement with parents and siblings, and parents' entanglement with these children, is rooted in the fear of death. Unlike "the genuine companionship and closeness that occurs in families that do *not* have dishonest or neurotic dependency ties, real togetherness is replaced by special attention, intrusiveness, and possessiveness on the part of parents and their children. Children and their parents come to expect this kind of counterfeit 'love'."

Firestone believes that the reluctance on the part of therapists and others to disturb these bonds is because of "the fear of breaking into one of the strongest and most effective defenses against death anxiety."

Fear of death is inherent in being alive, "it is mankind's 'incurable' neurosis," says Dr. Firestone. To remove this fear, we fixate on fantasy love and "withhold our feelings for the things that remind us of our mortality."[3]

Working with passion, then, will stir up fear of death, since when we care deeply about our work, we simultaneously know that it is finite, like our own human lives. The alternative is to live in bondage to parents and children, or their substitutes, to maintain a sense of security. But it is false security, since time moves forward whether or not we believe it is moving forward. Without deep feeling, we come to the end of our lives never having lived, never having risked the unknown.

In his essay on the difference between him and Sigmund Freud, the Swiss psychiatrist Carl Jung said the only way out of the biological bondage to our parents and our offspring is a through a spiritual leap, the intuited recognition that we are souls on a journey through life, unattached and free:

> There is nothing that can free us from the familial bond except that opposite urge of life, the spirit. It is not the children of the flesh, but the "children of God," who know freedom. . . . We moderns are faced with the necessity of rediscovering the life of the spirit; we must experience it anew for ourselves.[4]

As you grow in spiritual strength, you will find entanglement with the family constrictive and a waste of creative energy, based as it is on the fear of being alone in the world. This is not to say that children do not need the base camp a good family provides. But you are not a child — you are an adult, one who is trying to find the work you love. Rest assured, if your family shares your values they will remain an integral part of your life. If, on the other hand, they do not share your values, trying to force closeness leads to endless conflict. As thoughtfully as possible, go your separate way: live and let live, the most loving relationship of all.

The next step in your autobiography is to describe how your parents met. That meeting begins the theme of their partnership. Were they equally matched? Did he do what he wanted to do? Did she? What was going on in their marriage before you were born? Were there other siblings before you? How did they react to your birth?

Next, we turn to you when you were a baby, coming into a personal and collective tidal wave.

PART TWO — BIRTH THROUGH SCHOOL YEARS

Pre-School Years

Where were you born and under what circumstances? Was it in a hospital or at home? Was the birth easy, difficult? Were you first-born, second, or when? (Infancy is extremely important. Find out what kind of baby you were from your family. Go through old photographs and select a picture of yourself. Keep it near you from now on. This person is still you, the little child who is part of your personality. Looking at this child every day will be a reminder of your innocence, curiosity, and belief in the future. The you of long ago will encourage the grown-up you of today.) Did you have both parents throughout your life? Was your early life comfortable and predictable? Was it full of change, moving, and upsets? Were your parents happy with each other and their life? Did they love you and tell you so? How? Did your family express their feelings? Was there laughter in your home? Did you tell your family you loved them? How important was love in your life? Where did it come from?

How did you know you were special or not special? What were your brothers and sisters like? Did you like them? Did they like you? How about other relatives? Did you identify with your father or with your mother? Did you have an adult outside the family who took an interest in you? Was she or he an influence on you? How? Were either of your parents alcoholic? How did this affect you at that young age?

Did you have friends when you were young? What special things did you like to do? What made you feel lonely or unappreciated? How did you know when you had succeeded? Failed? What happened — how were you praised or reprimanded? What was considered "good" or "bad"? Did you have pets? If so, what kind?

These are pre-school influences. Can you see how important each influence can be to the development of the character in your story? Developing a good story depends on the consistent behavior of the main character in the plot. The best books hold our interest because of the characters — their unique and consistent reactions to events. Be generous with details; little things that come to mind can be quite enlightening. We are looking at your story to know what *you have experienced* so far. Let us go on to your school years.

Socialization

Where and when did you go to school? Were you glad to go or sad? Afraid? Did you feel encouragement from home? Did your parents like school? What did they tell you about school? Did you go first or did your siblings go before you? How did you get to school — bus, bicycle, car, or walking? Who went with you? What was your first reaction to your teacher? Your classmates? Did you learn easily? What subjects gave you trouble? When did you do well and why? Did you make new friends quickly? Did you ever take them home? What did your parents think of your friends? Did you ever run away from home?

If there was alcoholism in your family, how did it affect you during those years? If not at this point, did it later on? (Do not underestimate the impact of alcohol on your life. Unless you have extensive education about this problem, the emotional legacy left to you by family and friends who drank excessively can be devastating. Detail any problems you had with alcohol or drugs in the teenage and adult sections of your autobiography.)

What teachers influenced you the most? Good or bad? What were your grades like? What did your parents and teachers think about your school work? What did you think about yourself in relation to the other students? What sports or extracurricular activities did you participate in? Why? Did you feel prepared to go on to each grade? How did you feel when you left grade school? What did you look like? Were you tall for your age, medium, or short? What effect did that have with your peers? Were you admired or ignored? How did you get the attention you wanted at school? Did you have crushes, did you notice the opposite sex? Did they notice you? Did you win any awards? Were you quiet or outgoing?

Your character is pretty well jelled now. The socialization process has had an effect. You are about twelve years old now and coming into puberty. Surges of hormones are changing your whole world. This is a very impressionable time for you. The next five years of junior high and high school will accelerate feelings to the breaking point. Now is when you either open up or close off your feelings. Peer pressure is enormous. Your conformity, or lack of it, to the nature of your peers is extremely important. How did you conform? Who were your peers? Did you rebel against your parents?

Junior and Senior High

Describe how you felt about junior high and high school — excited, scared, bored? Where did you go to school? Did you stay in the same town? Did your family move in these years? Did you adapt to the work? What were the teachers like? Did you take the classes you wanted? Who counseled you about school? Did you have college in mind?

Did you have a close friend to talk things over with? Did you have a girlfriend or boyfriend? Several? What was your earliest sexual experience? How did you feel about your sexuality? Others'? Were you ever caught masturbating? What was said? Did you have an adult to talk to about sex? List any early sexual activity and describe how you felt about it (whether homosexual, heterosexual, or incestuous). When you come to your teenage and adult years, make a similar list. Who made you feel good about being sexual and passionate? Who teased or ridiculed you? Who said it was bad? Did you have trouble getting up in the morning? What time of day did you feel most alert? Was it always the same time of day? Did you go to school events, like football or basketball games? Did you have school heroes?

What books did you read for fun? What movies did you like, what celebrities? Did you have any heroes or heroines? Did you spend time alone with your thoughts? Were you busy, always into some activity? Were you taught anything about how the mind works, what creativity is? Did you feel in control of your life? Out of control? Who inspired you? What was happening in the country and the world that held your interest?

Were your parents active in your school life? How active were you in student government? How much did you participate in school clubs, drama, or singing groups? Did you ever work with your hands — pottery, art, or woodwork? Did you excel at this? Did you work at part-time jobs? During school? In the summer? When did you first earn money? Was your work behavior similar to either parent? Did you receive any memorable advice, correction, or support? At this point in the story, take two weeks off from writing.

These years solidified many attitudes and interests of yours. You tried and rejected many self-pictures. Remember how you copied the latest fads after studying them with magnifying intensity: clothes, walks, jokes, mannerisms, dances, cars, dates — the focus was *external*, watching to see what was acceptable, what "they" thought. "They" usually meant four or five of your friends and their friends. A small but critical sample for formation of your character.

You also may have begun to limit your possibilities. You heard many stories about "what life is" and accepted some of them as true. You narrowed your paths and perhaps began to stop dreaming and envisioning. The confusion about your identity increased if you placed more limitations upon yourself. Study your character now, at eighteen years old. What was your self-image after socialization? You are looking for consistency of character, a natural *tendency of behavior* that is by now predictable. Look at what choices you made about your friends, your family, your loves, your work, and/or future college plans.

The Time of Choice

What direction did you have in your senior year in high school? What were you planning to do when you got out? Is that what you did? What did your close friends do? Did you think about moving away from home early? Did you want to stay home while you worked or went to school? How did you feel at your graduation and other senior-class activities? Did you take an active role in the events? What did you enjoy the most about your senior week?

Did you finish high school? If you quit, why? What did others think about your leaving? What did you do?

What did you do the summer after high school — work, play, or prepare for college? Where were you? Who did you spend time with? If you had no plans for college, what did you plan — and why? Who did you want to be like? Who did you not want to be like? Did anyone advise you on a career that would be right for you? Who told you what you did well? What did you settle for? Did you pick the college you went to? Why? Did you have help with finances? What did your parents think about higher education? Were you encouraged by them to go as far as you wanted? If not, who gave you encouragement to go to college?

In your work — whatever it was to this point — what did you do? What was your relationship to your bosses? How did you get along with co-workers, with customers? In all of your school and work life, how did you relate to authority figures — teachers, principals, counselors, bosses, government employees, business owners?

How did you spend your money? Did you save any that you earned? Did you buy your own clothes or your own car? Did you travel? If so, where did you go?

At college, did you choose your major, or did someone else design your course of study? Did you have financial aid, scholarships? How and why did you pick the courses of study? What classes did you like and not like? How did you feel about your college life — did you feel like a part of the campus? What was your greatest success? Your greatest failure? Did you meet significant people? Have they stayed in your life? What professors made the greatest impression on you? Why? How did they reward your efforts? Did you take part in campus life — sports, clubs, class activities? Did you have an active social life? What made you laugh? Were you serious or detached about being in school? What were your grades like? Did they move up, down, or stay the same?

Did you notice any big emotional shifts in your attitude toward life in general? Did you ever have a friend betray you, lie to you? How did that affect you? Did you question what you were being taught? Did you take part in any campus rebellion? What were the issues? What happened? Who were the student leaders you admired? Were you one of them? Did you ever feel like quitting? Did you? What happened then? Did you go back and finish? How old were you when you were in college? When you graduated? In your senior year did you begin a job search? Who and what did you consider? Were you recruited? By whom? Did you feel happy to leave college? How would you summarize your college years — fulfilling, empty, or exciting?

Did you marry or get engaged? Did you pick a person who turned out to be a replica of either parent? Did this choice force your growth, or encourage old patterns of behavior? Take another break from writing at this point. Exercise, eat healthy food, get plenty of rest. By now you will be amazed by the discoveries you are making about yourself and the characters in your story, and surprised by how much energy writing an autobiography requires.

PART THREE — ON YOUR OWN

Young Adulthood

Now you are about twenty-two years old. Look at your main character in your story. What is different? What is the same? How have the values changed? As you observe the unfolding story, can you see any repetition of patterns — behavior that coincides with your early years? Were your beliefs in flux? Were you confused about your future? Did you have a sense of direction? You were ready to be on your own then. Did you feel prepared for the challenge? Did you fall in love? Did you marry? As a man or a woman, how did that event change your goals? Many of us find that when we look back over those early decisions, there was a feeling of being caught up in circumstances beyond our understanding and control. Did you feel like that?

Your character is moving into adulthood now. What is he or she like — self-confident, insecure, or on a firm path? Changing towns, jobs, relationships? Where were you living and with whom? Who were the most significant people in your life? If you were in a new job, how did that come about? Did you like it? Were you making enough money? Were you and your spouse or lover sharing expenses? Were you working? Where?

What kinds of friends did you have? Were they supportive? In your family life, did you stay in contact with your parents and other relatives? Were they involved in your life? Did they help you financially? Did you buy a home or rent one? Did you have children? What effect did they have on your life? How did becoming a parent affect your self-image? Did you take fathering or mothering seriously? You may have had several children. If so, did you have a favorite? If a boy or girl, which was easier to know and enjoy? How would you describe your family life — smooth, difficult, or a mixture of the two?

My Life Today

End your story with today's summary, personally and professionally. Where are you now? Why? What work are you doing? Is it satisfying? Is your social life pleasing? Summarize your sexual experiences from high school until now. Do you have friends? Do you have honest relationships with family members? Do you laugh frequently?

What *fascinates* you? *(Passion clue!)* What books do you read? What is your boss like? Are you in business for yourself? Do you want to be? If you have children, are they in school and living at home? Did your life "turn out" the way you thought it would? How does it differ from your expectations? Does your story in any way resemble your favorite fairy tale from your childhood? Or the story of your favorite hero or heroine?

What about money? Do you handle it well? Are you in debt? If so, how long would it take you to get out of debt? If you are burdened by possessions you do not need, sell them or give them away — scale down your life so that you can maneuver. Record every penny you spend, save what you can. When you have six months' living expenses saved, then is the time to invest in some conservative plan. Until then, make do with what you have. Most people believe if they had all the money they needed, they would do what they love. The process is just the opposite, as you will learn in Chapter Three.

Once you start your autobiography, the memories will come as a flood. The dam of fear eliminated, you will see your conditioning, your loves, your hates, your indifference, your irresponsibility, your sexuality, your humor. At this point I wish I could tell you about all the wonderful autobiographies I have read. I have laughed, cried, felt dismay, admiration, and sheer joy over the capacity we all have to experience life's ups and downs and survive them. Your story, told with complete openness, is a valuable document — something for you to treasure.

A word about love and anger: once you have identified what you are angry about, you will see that behind your anger is disappointed love. Realize that you only "hate" that person or that group because they failed to be what you expected them to be. Anger at others dissolves with understanding, then is replaced by forgiveness, although you may not have contact again. What is important is that you *care (passion clue!)* as much as you do. You are capable of intense feelings.

You will probably have about fifty pages when you are finished, more if you are inclined to write. Read your story over slowly. Try to imagine the outcome as if it happened to someone else — you will be more understanding and compassionate. Looking at your story as if it were another's will give you the chance to act as an editor, not a writer. These are two different skills. It is a rare writer who can edit his or her own work. You are too close to it, too emotionally involved.

Ask these questions: Did this character accept the misinformation he or she got? What beliefs are outmoded? How much of what happened in the past still decides the present? See if you can identify any patterns and reactions that are learned behavior. The following story illustrates a client's old behavior pattern that interfered with his career.

FRANK'S STORY

One of my clients, Frank, had at age forty a repetitive job pattern in his career as a printing executive. He performed well in whatever job he took, up to a certain point. Then conflicts would arise. The problem always revolved around an intensely personal clash with his superior, after which he would quit or get fired. Add to the turmoil a well-developed case of hypertension: Frank was mad most of the time! "When I'm not kicking dogs, I'm thinking about it," he laughed. His sense of humor had kept him functional, but that was all.

Going over his autobiography, I discovered a significant series of events. Frank was the second son following behind a brother who excelled in everything: school, sports, and social life. The father was a perfectionist — exacting and successful. He often made comparisons between Frank and his older brother. Frank remembered one in particular. "Why can't you be like your brother? He does everything so easily; you always do it the hard way." Whatever Frank did, it was never quite good enough; he always missed the mark.

Frank spent a great deal of time trying to meet his father's unreasonable standards. Seldom did he hear praise (one never gets enough praise). His accomplishments came as a result of fear, fear of reprisal. Frank also became conditioned to be the person doomed to fail — fulfilling his father's unfortunate prophesies. His self-esteem dwindled.

I asked Frank if he saw any similarities between the relationship with his father and the bosses he had chosen. The pattern began with his expectations of failure, not success. Or, if success came, it had unpleasant strings attached. He felt that even when you win — at building a business for example — you lose personally in some way.

Frank was startled to see that his bosses were, on the whole, unpredictable, judging, and hard to please, just like his father.

"Could you possibly be choosing to work for your father?" I said. "If so, you'll never make it."

"You're right," he said. "I can see that I believe I'm really not that great!"

All of Frank's problems were not solved with this information about his early experiences, but a light of recognition went on for him. From that base, we worked together until he began to think about gaining approval rather than disapproval. For Frank, the fear of criticism brought him exactly what he feared the most. The happy ending to Frank's story is that he now enjoys a prestigious position and loves the independence that goes with it. In a recent conversation, Frank was buoyant and optimistic.

"I'm having a great time over here," he said. Then he lowered his voice, conspiratorially. "It's a piece of cake," he admitted. We both laughed, remembering the times when Frank saw life as one long struggle.

FIND TIME TO BE ALONE

We can all benefit by finding more time to be alone. We learn to sit down, to hold still, and to reflect. Try to find some time each day — even just a few minutes — to be alone with your own thoughts.

At first, you might notice a reluctance to even sit down alone. You might find diversions, relish interruptions, run errands, do chores. You might even read something and then move about — restless, maybe even annoyed. Good. That means that you have been inoculated with new information and it has gotten under your skin. Almost all of my clients experience feelings of restlessness when they begin contemplating the changes they are about to set in motion.

The Western world is an extroverted culture, one that rewards external activity. If you are an introvert, as about twenty-five percent of us are (according to David Kiersey and Marilyn Bates, authors of *Please Understand Me: Character and Temperament Types*[5]), time alone gives you the chance to recharge. If you are an extrovert, as about seventy-five percent of us are supposed to be (although I believe much of this is conditioned), you recharge around people. Just make sure you do not use talking to people as a substitute for the hard work of writing and processing what you write. Unlike talk, which can be forgotten over time, our words in print are a permanent record of what we thought at the time. Writing an autobiography is the ultimate act of courage, said one of my clients. She was a court reporter, someone who knew the power of testimony in print.

Remember, the first step to power is the experience of clarity. Just before the moment of clarity — the "Ah-ha!" — comes the greatest confusion. So if you feel "stirred up," or puzzled about how this introspection will produce results out there in the world, congratulate yourself. You are beginning to understand the first step to power: you are beginning to know yourself.

DESCRIPTIVE TRAITS EXERCISE: ANOTHER PERSON

In this descriptive traits exercise (the first of two), you are asked to evaluate someone close to you, such as a friend, spouse, boss, or teacher. Does your rating of your friend match his or her own self-image? You might ask the person if it does (provided your relationship is close and supportive). This exercise will give you perspective about someone else's self-image.

Circle the word from each of the comparisons listed under Descriptive Trait Choice that most aptly describes the other person most of the time. For example, is he or she more agreeable or more resistant?

After you have completed this, rate the person for each word you have chosen on a scale from 1 to 10. Keep in mind that the selection of number 1 on the scale would indicate that you feel this is one of the person's more minor traits, a selection of number 2 would indicate a greater degree of intensity, and so on up the scale, with a selection of number 10 indicating you feel this is one of his or her major traits. The purpose of rating someone else is to give you practice in assessing others — a preparation for assessing yourself.

DESCRIPTIVE TRAIT CHOICE	MINOR TRAIT									MAJOR TRAIT
Agreeable/Resistant	1	2	3	4	5	6	7	8	9	10
Boastful/Modest	1	2	3	4	5	6	7	8	9	10
Courageous/Timid	1	2	3	4	5	6	7	8	9	10
Controlled/Impulsive	1	2	3	4	5	6	7	8	9	10
Emotionally stable/Easily upset	1	2	3	4	5	6	7	8	9	10
Flexible/Rigid	1	2	3	4	5	6	7	8	9	10
Energetic/Slow	1	2	3	4	5	6	7	8	9	10
Introvert/Extrovert	1	2	3	4	5	6	7	8	9	10
Leader/Follower	1	2	3	4	5	6	7	8	9	10
Objective/Subjective	1	2	3	4	5	6	7	8	9	10
Passive/Aggressive	1	2	3	4	5	6	7	8	9	10
Quick to anger/Slow to anger	1	2	3	4	5	6	7	8	9	10
Reflective/Superficial	1	2	3	4	5	6	7	8	9	10
Self-assured/Insecure	1	2	3	4	5	6	7	8	9	10
Sociable/Loner	1	2	3	4	5	6	7	8	9	10
Sophisticated/Naive	1	2	3	4	5	6	7	8	9	10
Tolerant/Judgmental	1	2	3	4	5	6	7	8	9	10

DESCRIPTIVE TRAITS EXERCISE:
YOURSELF

In this second exercise you are asked to complete the descriptive traits exercise on yourself. Does your rating match your self-image and autobiography? You can also have several close friends or business associates evaluate you, using a copy of the chart. This can be helpful and revealing, as it is a source of additional information about how others view you, and it can be compared to your own self-image.

Circle the word from each of the comparisons listed under Descriptive Trait Choice that most aptly describes you most of the time. For example, are you more agreeable or more resistant?

After you have completed this, then rate yourself for each word you have chosen on a scale from 1 to 10. Again, keep in mind that the selection of number 1 on the scale would indicate that you feel this is one of your more minor traits, a selection of number 2 would indicate a greater degree of intensity, and so on up the scale, with a selection of number 10 indicating you feel this is one of your major traits.

DESCRIPTIVE TRAIT CHOICE	MINOR TRAIT								MAJOR TRAIT	
Agreeable/Resistant	1	2	3	4	5	6	7	8	9	10
Boastful/Modest	1	2	3	4	5	6	7	8	9	10
Courageous/Timid	1	2	3	4	5	6	7	8	9	10
Controlled/Impulsive	1	2	3	4	5	6	7	8	9	10
Emotionally stable/Easily upset	1	2	3	4	5	6	7	8	9	10
Flexible/Rigid	1	2	3	4	5	6	7	8	9	10
Energetic/Slow	1	2	3	4	5	6	7	8	9	10
Introvert/Extrovert	1	2	3	4	5	6	7	8	9	10
Leader/Follower	1	2	3	4	5	6	7	8	9	10
Objective/Subjective	1	2	3	4	5	6	7	8	9	10
Passive/Aggressive	1	2	3	4	5	6	7	8	9	10
Quick to anger/Slow to anger	1	2	3	4	5	6	7	8	9	10
Reflective/Superficial	1	2	3	4	5	6	7	8	9	10
Self-assured/Insecure	1	2	3	4	5	6	7	8	9	10
Sociable/Loner	1	2	3	4	5	6	7	8	9	10
Sophisticated/Naive	1	2	3	4	5	6	7	8	9	10
Tolerant/Judgmental	1	2	3	4	5	6	7	8	9	10

HOW DO YOU FEEL ABOUT YOURSELF?

The questions asked in this section should be answered quickly, without too much thought. Notice how far back in time your successful experiences go. If you find yourself seeing success as very recent, like today, you are on the right track. You are living in the now of your life. Watch for passion clues in what you choose to write about.

1. I felt really good when ______________________________

____

____

2. I was most successful when ______________________________

____

____

3. It felt good to me when someone said to me that ____________

____

____

4. The most successful part of my past was ____________________

____

____

5. The best thing that ever happened to me was _______________

____

____

6. I was happiest when ____

____

____

7. The best period of my life was ____________________________

____

____

Passion Clues to the Above:

1. Were you alone most of the time?
2. Were you physically active — indoors, outdoors?
3. What was there about the event that is a pattern for you now?
4. What qualities were you expressing (perseverance, determination, self-control, self-confidence)?

Study these events carefully and look for the *symbols* each example represents in your overall life at the time.

SUMMARY

Passion Secret #1: The first step to power is clarity.

1. Write about an incident in your life when you were successful (or were a failure, if you wish). This is the first of four warm-up writing exercises to help you achieve more clarity.
2. Write a few paragraphs of self-description. How do you see yourself? Describe your personal qualities, your physical, mental, and emotional self. This is your second warm-up writing exercise.
3. As your third exercise, describe how others see you. What image do you think others have of you?
4. Finally, describe your balanced self. What aspects do you want to enhance to achieve this balance?
5. Writing your autobiography is an extremely valuable exercise. It helps you achieve clarity.
6. As you write a summary of your life to this point, notice your earliest memories. Who was there and what happened? Take your character through your life. Part One covers your family background and relationships — particularly a solid word sketch of both grandparents and parents.
7. Part Two of your autobiography takes you through the

remainder of your career. Pay close attention to the word sketches you draw of significant people who aided or assisted in your growth, or who injured you. Recalling these people and events is not always pleasant.

8. Descriptive traits exercises: In the first exercise you are asked to evaluate someone close to you; in the second exercise, focus on yourself.
9. Complete the blanks in the exercise, How Do You Feel About Yourself? Cross-check your other work. Evaluate the results — is there harmony among all, or differences? Is your focus on the past or the present?

2

ARE YOU GOOD ENOUGH AS YOU ARE?

The second step on the way to unlocking the door to your passion and power begins with *acceptance of yourself as you are*. With Step One, through the autobiography and other exercises, you saw the sweep of past events in chronological order. If you want to change the ending of your story, you are ready for Step Two: self-acceptance.

The glimpses you have of your past as shown in your autobiography allow you to see your belief system in various stages of entrenchment. In some cases, you may need a crowbar to dislodge the settled cement of misinformation. Your beliefs may be standing in the way of your passion. In this chapter, we will examine both global history and your personal history to discover the truth about yourself and your times.

Remember, you are learning the secrets of personal power. This is the same energy (passion) that guides and directs very successful people. Like any "secret," the information is only somewhat difficult to discover, not unknowable. You cannot lose your personal power. Your power and awareness may get submerged for a time; your light, your enthusiasm, may go underground. How do you bring those passions to the surface? You must *coax the unconscious mind* to release the information to your conscious mind; you will then begin to deal with this information.

The barrier to this process is the belief that the conscious mind is separated from the unconscious mind. Actually, the human psyche has an efficient feedback system between the conscious and unconscious mind. The way in and out of the rich storehouse of creativity, the unconscious, is *through the imagination*. The imagination is a bridge: it takes you from one place to another, from one belief to another.[1]

If you can imagine what you want, these images will "build the bridge." For most people, the lack of a sense of personal power begins with faulty beliefs. For example, you believe you do not measure up to your father's ideal image. But what you *are* is good enough; it is your father's beliefs you need to examine and your response to him. When Frank (in Chapter One) altered his beliefs about himself vis à vis his father, his daily experience changed. Work became a "piece of cake."

KNIGHTS AND MAIDENS

One of my clients had always wanted to be the white knight, the savior, the hero who swoops in with shining armor — teeth flashing and sword cutting through the brambles to victory. The result: the maiden swoons with delirious relief, the dragon tippy-toes off to the cave, and the other knights gnash their collective teeth in envious admiration.

The desire to be the rescuer, the hero, is a pattern that limits many men and some women. The image of the hero who fixes others' lives is based on assumptions of superiority and inferiority. When we are children, we are taught that society consists of a *hierarchy* and that people are positioned like rungs on a ladder, some higher, some lower. There are authority figures — most commonly the father — who know best and keep order. (Whether they actually do or not is irrelevant.)

When we become adults, we see our fellow human beings as individuals, first and foremost. This requires a mind that rejects hierarchical and stereotypical thinking. Some examples of this kind of flexible thinking: the parent who realizes his child is an individual quite apart from himself; the man who understands that a woman is a human being, not an idealized image; the woman who believes a man is sensitive and caring, as well as competent. Hierarchical thinking limits our own and others' development. Men and women will become cooperative equals when each gives up attitudes of superiority and inferiority, such as the man believing that his rational mind is superior to the woman's mind, and that she is more sensitive than him.

As children, we are dependent on those in control; as adults we need to become truly independent. This drive for independent choice-making is at the root of political and religious freedom. The concept of individual responsibility rejects the notion that outside authority exists: no man or woman has the right or the ability to direct my life. I direct my own life. This is the mark of a grown-up society, as it is the mark of a grown-up person, one who is no longer dependent. Thus, the purpose of authority in our lives is to outgrow it.

One of the problems with the previously mentioned white-knight-on-a-white-horse image is that it destroys the confidence of the person receiving the "help." Resentment builds, initiative is weakened. "Well, why don't you do it? You always know how to do everything," says the helpee. In addition, the knight (who is only human, after all) gets tired of carrying the whole load. And being the great provider, though it is well-intended, leads to a form of emotional slavery and dependence for the one who is "helped."

Carl Jung said that within each of us is a male and female component: the *anima* (female), and the *animus* (male). Women need to make friends with their animus, to learn to act overtly, rather than project this part of themselves onto the men in their lives. Conversely, men need to express their emotional side, the anima, rather than depend on women to do their feeling for them. Men who reject emotions fear their own anima, according to Jung. This repression of feelings can result in a man's sense of discomfort with women, and women with him. Once our internal male and female co-exist peacefully, we become balanced; we feel, we perceive — and we act and do. When each side of our psyche is active, we are whole, united, the ultimate goal of a fully lived life.

Society needs individuals who balance the orderly, rational, left-brain thinking — which implemented the industrial and scientific revolutions — *and* the creative, intuitive, right-brain thinking to solve the pressing problems that those revolutions created.

In the past, scientific analysis reduced everything to empirical definition, to what could be known through the five senses. If you could not "see" data through a microscope, or hear, taste, touch, or smell it, it was considered nonexistent. However, hunches, insights, intuition, experiments in parapsychology, the revelations of mystics — all point toward knowledge available to us beyond the five senses. Executives at the highest level have told me that their most crucial decisions are made at a "gut feeling" level. Naturally enough, businesspeople, educators, and scientists are reluctant to reveal the mechanics of such decisions, fearing they will appear to sound "illogical."

Many women fear the responsibility of power; it is safer to step back and act merely as a support system for others. However, they grow to resent the men who get to have all the fun that goes with being in control. Until women as a group and as individuals realize that they are equally responsible with men for the "maiden" image, ambivalence will prevail: the uncertainty and conflict about who they are and what they want holds them back, not obstacles in the outside world. Remember, *power is the ability to take action, to influence,* and must be accompanied by the willingness to assume the responsibility that goes with power.

The knight and the maiden of the past both agreed to their roles. He achieved his goals through visible confrontation. She achieved her goals through how well she could motivate him. Her power was covert, his was overt. He was powerful; she was a step removed from power, and was angry about it. Today a woman who wants to slay a dragon can go out and get her own.

Equal partnerships are based on trust; like foxhole buddies, you watch out for each other in danger and work as a team to achieve objectives. Never does it occur to you to compete in your partner's special arena. In fact, admiration and respect for the individuality of your partner guides your every interaction. This dynamic is the most beautiful human relationship. Each unit is independent of the other, but linked toward a common objective. It is *shared* power: two minds working in harmony.

When the common goal is no longer shared, relationships end. The powerful person accepts the consequences and moves on. When change comes, however, we feel pain, a normal reaction to loss. Who could want divorce? Who enjoys a broken partnership? The anxiety, hurt, and anger are searing and disruptive. Yet, many divorced people (myself included) who are asked years later, "Would you go through it again today?" respond "Yes." The change was necessary for personal growth, and we see life after divorce as wiser, future choices based on what we learned from our experience.

LIMITED CHOICES — PLENTIFUL CHOICES

A society is largely a reflection of the belief systems of that society. In Alvin Toffler's book, *The Third Wave,*[2] he discusses Western society, describing it as a series of "waves." The first wave, agrarian society, was composed of small units — the villages. The power structure, which was local, was defined by land and position of birth. The thinking was geared to the power structure — hierarchial and authoritarian.

The second wave of civilization, according to Toffler, brought an end to the former local power structure. The industrial revolution and resulting technological growth changed civilization and gave a factory-like definition to life: schools, families, and work meshed to the gears of production. Standardization, specialization, synchronization, concentration, maximization, centralization — all these led men into second wave "centralized" thinking, while the women stayed behind in the first wave. The wife "produced" for her family, not for the larger market. Toffler explains his theory further:

> As the husband, by and large, marched off to do the direct economic work, the wife generally stayed behind to do the indirect economic work. The man took responsibility for the historically more advanced form of work; the woman was left behind to take care of the older, more backward form of work. He moved, as it were, into the future; she remained in the past.
>
> This division produced a split in personality and inner life. The public or collective nature of factory and office, the need for coordination and integration, brought with it an emphasis on objective analysis and objective relationships. Men, prepared from boyhood for their role in the shop, where they would move in a world of interdependencies, were encouraged to become 'objective'. Women, prepared from birth for the tasks of reproduction, child-rearing, and household drudgery, performed to a considerable degree in social isolation, were taught to be 'subjective' — and were frequently regarded as incapable of the kind of rational, analytic thought that supposedly went with objectivity. Not

> surprisingly, women who did leave the relative isolation of the household to engage in interdependent production were often accused of having been defeminized, of having grown cold, tough, and — objective.

Sexual differences and sex role stereotypes, moreover, were sharpened by the misleading identification of men with production and women with consumption, even though men also consumed and women also produced. In short, while women were oppressed long before the Second Wave began to roll across the earth, the modern 'battle of the sexes' can be traced in large measure to the conflict between two workstyles, and beyond that to the divorce of production and consumption. The split economy deepened the sexual split as well.[3]

Toffler says that our present social turmoil can be reduced if we shift from second wave thinking to third wave thinking. He echoes my earlier statement in this chapter and elsewhere that acceptance of reality *as it is* speeds growth and understanding. When we hold on to the past because we think that is the only way to live, we automatically hold back our comprehension of the future — a better and more diverse future.

LANCELOT AND GUINEVERE IN THE TWENTY-FIRST CENTURY

The Lancelot of the twenty-first century is a fuller person than the Camelot character of the past. He laughs, cries, and feels more. Sometimes he notices that he does not really want to slay the dragon anymore. (He has slain enough already.) As for maidens and kings and jealous knights, Lance changed their roles, too. He peoples his life with real friends, rather than the one-dimensional heroes and cowards of a childhood fairy tale.

As we grew up, we heard many stories about how to be successful. A woman's best chance, we were told, was to be born well or to marry well. So she learned to play the maiden. A man was taught to believe that life, at best, is a defensive struggle in which you try to win more than you lose. So he learned to play Lance. However, the future holds many alternatives. When we are tolerant of differences and respect an individual's right to make choices, it increases our awareness and creates harmony. A civilization in which only one way of living is accepted brings repression and authoritarian rule. Similarly, when you tolerate only *one way* for yourself, you diminish the opportunities available to you in a free society. You have closed the door to alternatives and to growth.

RECASTING YOUR OWN STORY

In order to recast your own story, begin thinking about the times in your life when a "happy ending" came about. You may have to practice remembering success. Most people have a very hard time recalling when things went right. If you do not believe it, ask a friend or co-worker two questions: (1) How did you succeed this week? and (2) How did you fail this week? First, they will say, "Succeed? What do you mean succeed?" This unfortunate commitment to looking at the bad side of life also exists in television, newspapers, books, magazines — much of the time the focus is on calamity or, at best, adversity. It is true that human beings are fascinated with *conflict*. The best stories — the classics — have many conflicts, antagonists, protagonists, and a supporting cast. But the best stories also *resolve* the conflicts, in one way or another.

You will notice that I use stories to illustrate how passion and power work in people's lives. I continue to use those illustrations throughout the book because I want you to get a "feel" for your life as a story.

Stop now in your reading and make a list of powerful people you know personally, or have at least met in person. What do they do for a living? Are they intensely excited about what they do? What kinds of people do they have in their lives? Do you think they know themselves? If so, what do they know? Do they accept themselves as they are? Remember, power is the ability to take action. Consider the actions they take — with themselves, with others. Do they have "happy endings" in the stories of their lives? Keep in mind that a happy ending is a state of being in which the mind is quiet and tranquil, focused in the moment.

Study your list. If you list only two or three people, then your picture of power will need more illustrations. Also add to the list people you do not know personally. Be careful here, because what looks like power from a distance can really be powerlessness. Keep in mind the definition of power.

When you accept yourself it is because you have taken the time to know that self *as it is*, not merely as you want it to be, or as you were taught it should be. Self-definition begins with an honest evaluation of the past, and a comparison of the past and present. As you do the assignments in the book, do not compare yourself to an ideal. Doing so sabotages your path to personal power, since your power lies in your uniqueness.

Passion Secret #2:
Powerful people do not want to be like anyone else.

Powerful people do not reject any part of their experience. I cannot overemphasize the necessity of self-acceptance. You must have a genuine appreciation of your individuality if you are going to make an impact on your life and on those around you. Anytime you are tempted to compare your experience of life to another's experience, ask yourself this question: Can any human experience diminish the importance of mine? The answer is: It cannot, unless you permit it to.

Mental tyranny is as effective as political tyranny in its ability to limit choices and development. If you believe that you are trapped — that it is only rich people, corporation presidents, and political figures who have power, the ability to take action — you are tyrannizing yourself. *You* are the dictator you dislike, the one who tells you what to do with every waking hour, what to think, and what to say.

JIM'S STORY

One client was so embroiled in proving he was "right" and his ex-wife was "wrong," that he sent her child support checks late and wrote her name in the tiniest of letters.

"You're trying to eliminate her, Jim," I said.

"You're right; as far as I'm concerned, she doesn't exist," he said bitterly. We had been wrestling with his anger for weeks and the anger was showing in the interviewing process. I had heard from a prospective employer that he thought Jim had a bad attitude, and though he thought Jim was technically qualified, the employer hesitated to hire him.

"How do you know he has a bad attitude?" I had asked.

"Well, he was stiff with his answers about his past job. He's defensive about that period of his work life. It made me wonder what happened. I just got the impression he was mad, and tense, and would have trouble with his co-workers." He explained that Jim needed more maturity before he could be a good manager.

I told Jim what was said and he was surprised.

"I had no problem with my last job. It was my divorce that made me angry," he said.

"It's still making you angry, and it's noticeable," I said. "When are you going to confront your own responsibility for the break-up? It's been five years. When you write her name so the bank teller can't read it, you think you are controlling her still, getting back at her, and making her nonexistent. Actually, she exists and she's controlling you so much now that you won't even get the job you want," I said.

Jim was quiet. He did not like what he heard. He looked uncomfortable. "How do I stop feeling angry?" he asked.

"First, you've got to admit you used anger to fuel anger, to be the victim."

I knew he had lived as a victim for so long it was going to be hard for him to change his mind.

"I always felt so powerless every month when I wrote that check to her. I am still mad that I have to give her money. She left me for someone else and I got hurt," he said. "I'm still living in the past, dragging around a dead carcass, thinking each month about the whole marriage and divorce," he added.

Jim was so committed to anger and revenge that those feelings spilled over into his present life. What employer wants to put a time bomb on the work site?

Jim defused his anger when he ceased to see himself as the wronged victim. The attitude change gave him control over his life. Today, Jim is employed by a computer firm. He said to me, laughing, "They said they hired me because of my good attitude."

WHAT'S YOUR PLEASURE?

The following assignments are designed to help you learn about your pleasures. Take a few minutes and think about what you do when no one tells you what to do. When left alone you gravitate to certain activities, books, reveries. The following exercise shows you what you do when you are "working" at what you like. (You will need several sheets of paper to complete this exercise and the ones that follow.)

Focus on pleasure in this assignment — the times in your life when you were enjoying yourself. Begin with a definition of the word "pleasure." What thoughts does this word bring to your mind? Most of us think work and pleasure are antonyms, not synonyms. You will find that this exercise gives you a fresh way of looking at work. You have never analyzed your happy times, you just had them. *Spontaneous, joyful times hold the keys to our natural strengths.* From analysis of pleasurable moments, you will discover your strengths, those qualities that allow you to perform effortlessly and naturally. Use big, positive, cheerful words to describe your pleasures. Also ask yourself why you remember these particular events. The answer to "why" is a direction signal that gives you an insight into your own behavior, and the pattern of choices you developed when you were younger.

1. Pleasures in school. When did you feel the sense of accomplishment that came from doing well at what you liked? How about extracurricular activities? What did you like? What fascinated you?

____

____

2. Pleasures in hobbies or special interests. Again you enjoyed these times; no one had to motivate you.

____

____

3. Pleasures that you felt when you received results from tests: educational, psychological, or other.

____

____

WORK-RELATED PLEASURE

This section focuses on work-related pleasure.

1. There were times, on the jobs you have had, or the businesses you have run, when your pleasurable accomplishments *reduced costs* and *increased income*. For example, did your *ability to laugh* increase rapport with a customer so much that they bought more? Was your *curiosity* responsible for discovering a costly error? The italicized words are strengths — marketable qualities that make businesses work better. You may not have even been aware that these were valuable qualities, because they are so much a part of you. In fact, your chief strengths are your unconscious ones; you are so good at them that you do not have to think about them. This assignment forces you to think about them. What have been your most pleasurable accomplishments on the jobs you've had?

____

____

2. When did you solve problems and have fun doing it? (Problems can involve people, data, or objects.)

____

____

3. When did you improve efficiency because you were relaxed and enjoying yourself? This could be something quite simple — perhaps you saw a better way to stack things, or an easier way to get a job done. Your decision made your work and others' easier and even more enjoyable.

____

____

4. Comment on the pleasure you felt in developing new ways to market the products or services your company sold. Your ideas need not have been put into effect, but list any times when you came up with imaginative improvements that you knew would work. "Marketing" can apply to a nonbusiness setting, in which you propose new projects, ideas, and contacts.

____

____

EDUCATIONAL SKILL GRID

1. From the work pleasures you wrote about, select the words that refer to your natural strengths, such as optimism, organization, problem solving, communication, writing, reading, speaking, perseverance, analysis. These words illustrate what you do and how you act when you enjoy yourself the most. You will probably have ten to twenty words that keep cropping up as you write about those pleasurable times in your life. These words should be listed across the top of your educational skill grid, as in the sample that follows.
2. Next, look at your most pleasurable classes in high school or college. You may want to list your classes in chronological order, as the Educational Skill Grid sample shows, checking where you were using your strengths. Or, you may want to look at your transcript, pull out your favorite classes, and write down the reasons why you liked them so much. Choose the paragraph technique or the grid technique, whichever best helps you discover what you do when you are enjoying yourself.

List any course or subject you were taught outside of school as well — in seminars, training programs, or home study courses. You will see several key words recurring repeatedly, signalling your strengths.

3. Ask yourself if others agreed with you about these strengths. Did you hear from teachers or classmates that you were, for example, analytical, original, hard-working, creative? (Again, choose the words that reflect your individual abilities.)

SAMPLE EDUCATIONAL SKILL GRID

	Analysis	Problem Solving	Communication	Organization
1. Intro Chemistry	X	X		X
2. Human Sexuality	X		X	
3. Fundamentals of Music	X			X
4. Concert Choir	X			
5. English Composition	X		X	X
6. Elementary German	X	X		
7. Conversational German	X	X		
8. General Psychology	X	X	X	X
9. Language Lab (German)	X			X
10. Elementary Speech	X		X	X
11. Intermediate Algebra	X	X		X
12. Physical Education				
13. Work Experience I	X	X		X
14. Work Experience II	X	X		X
15. Elementary Algebra	X	X		X
16. Continue as above				
Totals	**14**	**8**	**4**	**10**

SAMPLE EDUCATIONAL SKILL GRID

STRENGTHS I SEE	VERIFICATION
	Who agreed with you about these strengths? Write a short paragraph.
1. ANALYSIS (Example)	1. Professors gave me high grades and praise. Other students complimented me on my papers. I received the most praise for my accurate analysis.
2. COMMUNICATIONS (Example)	2. In class response, I contributed, answering questions. I spoke when called on without fear. My papers were well researched and written; my teacher read part of my paper to the class.
3. Continue as above	3. Continue as above
4.	4.
5.	5.
6.	6.

SAMPLE WORK SKILL GRID

As in the previous education-oriented work, focus on your pleasurable strengths. These are far more important than your job title or function! Make a list of your jobs, beginning with your most recent position. Choose the technique you want to use, either the grid or the paragraph form.

What part of each job was pleasurable? You liked doing it — so you did it well. Notice the patterns.

As before, who agreed with you, noticed that you were enjoying yourself?

STRENGTHS	ANALYSIS	COMMUNICATION	ORGANIZATION	ETC.
1. Job A	X		X	
2. Job B	X	X		
3. Job C	X		X	
4. Continue as above				
TOTAL	3	1	2	

WORK SKILL GRID — STRENGTHS

Rank your strengths in the order of ability and frequency of use. You will list your top five strengths at the end of the chapter.

STRENGTHS I SEE	VERIFICATION
1. ANALYSIS (Example)	1. Salesmen relied on me for data and told me how helpful my work was to their success.
2. Continue as above	2.
3.	3.
4.	4.
5.	5.
6.	6.
7.	7.
8.	8
9.	9.
etc.	etc.

DEFINE YOUR ASSETS

Your assets are your natural resources — gifts granted you at birth — your height, weight, smile, posture, bone structure, and mental and emotional inclinations.

Think carefully and prepare an extensive list of your personal assets. Do not confuse strengths (you've already done those!) with your assets. Your strengths are the result of individual effort and interest; your assets are your natural abilities and gifts.

Your List

1.
2.
3.
4.
5.
6.
7.
8.
9.
10.
11.
12.

etc. (As many as there are!)

Next, have someone who knows you well prepare a similar list. Ask this person: From your perspective, what assets do I possess? Better yet, ask several friends to respond. They will enjoy doing it and you might gain some insights!

Your Friend's Copy

You are being asked to assist in an exercise of perception. A large part of self-awareness is based on how others see us. Think carefully about the individual's characteristics.

Assets may be defined as natural resources, gifts granted to each person at birth. For example, height, weight, smile, posture, bone structure, and mental and emotional inclinations are all assets. List the person's assets in column one.

Strengths are the result of individual effort and interest. Do not confuse assets with strengths. Strengths include measurable abilities like perception, organization, analysis, management, writing, communicating, and teaching. Every person has many strengths. List the strengths you see in column two.

Assets

1.
2.
3.
4.
5.
6.
7.
8.
9. etc. (As many as there are!)

Strengths

1.
2.
3.
4.
5.
6.
7.
8.
9. etc. (As many as there are!)

VALUES

Of all human activities, your work has the greatest potential to satisfy your basic needs. It follows that accurate self-knowledge precedes job choice; in fact, it defines the job choice. When you know yourself, you will be able to choose a position through which you become truly fulfilled.

Needs and values are sometimes hard to distinguish. A need is a strong force, an emotional desire. A value is a need transformed into a concept by which you interpret your world and by which you live. Your goal is to discover how your particular set of values harmonize with each other.

By careful observation of your behavior, your values may be identified, analyzed, and verified. Some values are conscious and easily identifiable; others are unconscious and require more work to bring them to the surface. In the following exercise are listed fifteen values that you may be concerned with in a work setting.[4]

Respond to the following items in as much detail as possible in the space provided. Focus on how important each one is to you in a work setting.

1. SECURITY — Freedom from worry, safety, certainty, and similarity between prediction and event.

____

____

2. STATUS — The state or condition of a person in the eyes of others.

____

____

3. COMPENSATION — Equivalent in value or effect for services rendered. Pay or remuneration.

---

4. ACHIEVEMENT — Accomplishment of desired objective; a thing done successfully. Mastery of task, project, or goal.

---

5. ADVANCEMENT — To improve, progress.

---

6. AFFILIATION — Fellow workers or associates, desire to associate with like beings

---

---

7. RECOGNITION — Special notice or attention for individual or team effort.

---

8. AUTHORITY — The power or right to command, direct, and manage.

____

____

9. INDEPENDENCE — Freedom from the control of another.

____

____

10. ALTRUISM — Concern for the welfare of others.

____

____

11. CREATIVITY — Finding new, improved ways to do anything. The urge to innovate and make new combinations.

____

____

12. ETHICAL HARMONY — Important for moral values, environmental concerns, etc. to be reinforced in work setting.

____

____

13. INTELLECTUAL STIMULATION — Mental electricity, the use of special abilities in the environment that encourage, support, and promote thinking.

____

____

14. VARIETY — Diversity of activity, tasks, and people. Wide spectrum of all three.

____

____

15. AESTHETIC — Desire for beauty in work setting and surroundings.

____

____

Select your top five values — choose the ones that are the most important to you. Now that you know your top five strengths and your top five values, you are narrowing your focus to select work settings that provide the rewards for those strengths and values. That is what you market — your strengths, not a job title.

Top Five Values

1.
2.
3.
4.
5.

Top Five Strengths

1.
2.
3.
4.
5.

Now you have the perfect job description for yourself: a business or job that allows you to use your strengths and identify with your values naturally and effortlessly.

SUMMARY

Passion Secret #2:
Powerful people do not want to be like anyone else.

1. In order to discover your passion and release your power, you accept yourself and all your experience as good.
2. Examine yourself and the era in which you live. Set the stage for change — create and continue your life story as you want it to be.
3. Your imagination is the bridge that connects the conscious to the unconscious mind. Learn to visualize what you want.
4. To move into the next phase of your life, reject the need for hierarchical and authoritarian thinking.
5. If a man, are you trying to be the rescuer, like Lance? Do you

see your own woman within? Are you friends with her? Do you admire her sensitivity and compassion? Do you see women as people first? Do you see your mother as a person? Do you admire your masculine self, and the way you take action?

If a woman, are you the "maiden," the one who waits? Do you defer to male authority figures? Are you well acquainted with the male within you? Do you like his passion and drive? Do you see your father as an individual or is he still an authority that you have to please? Could you tell your father what you think? Or do you feel superior to your father? As women (and men), we must become our own mothers and fathers to be truly independent.

6. Male-female stereotypes (aggressive knights and passive maidens) are obsolete. New definitions of male and female include full development of intuitive, "right-brain" thinking and full development of logical, "left-brain" thinking for both sexes. Men and women as equals are true partners, sharing a common goal.
7. Make a list of powerful people you know personally. Who are they? What do they do? Are they passionate?
8. Feel any anger and past resentment that hinder you from realizing your full potential, make your amends, then release them into the wind.
9. The "What's Your Pleasure?" exercise focuses on the times in your life when you were having fun. "Fun" is the key to your passion.
10. The Work-Related Pleasure exercise helps you remember your most pleasurable times in a work setting and discover which of your personal strengths and qualities were responsible for your accomplishments.
11. The Educational Skill Grid helps you pinpoint your natural

abilities. Look at what you have written in your "pleasure assignments" and select the words that refer to your natural strengths to list at the top of your grid.

12. List your most pleasurable classes in high school or college (or in a non-academic setting) on the grid. If you prefer, list them in paragraph form. Choose either the grid technique or the paragraph technique to help you discover when you are enjoying yourself.
13. List your strengths in order of ability. List instructors or others who agreed with you about those strengths.
14. List your strengths in your most recent jobs. Who agreed with you about your abilities?
15. Define your assets — those natural resources given to you at birth.
16. Ask a friend to make a list of both your assets and your strengths.
17. The Values exercise reveals to you the values that are most important to you in a work setting.
18. Select your top five values and your top five strengths and list them. Keep this list handy, as you will need to refer to it in succeeding chapters.

3

HOW TO SET GOALS THAT MATCH YOUR PASSION

The third step to working with passion is to learn how to set goals that are realizable. When you are steadily overcoming your short-term barriers to success, then you gradually gain the necessary stamina for overcoming the long-term barriers to your objectives. Set goals for a six-month period or less. You get more *excited* about an event that is nearer in time. *(Passion clue!)*

People who set goals they can reach can be compared to moving bodies of water. They will reverse course, ebb toward shore, tumble over rocks, form swirling rapids, glide into still lagoons, and even fall hundreds of feet to join with other waters. Ever onward they move, seeking newness, pushing forward to their eventual destiny — a bigger body of water (and a smoother ride).

Passion Secret #3:
Powerful people know that getting there is all the fun.

People who have developed their personal power know how to use their imagination and, for them, daily life is a chance to travel on their journey. Like the force behind a river, they design and carve out their own course. Your own imagination may have brought you a daily existence that is no fun at all. Do you have a chronic shortage of money? Do you have little or no satisfaction in your work? Do you have conflicts you cannot resolve? Few friends? No joyous personal love in your life? If it is any consolation, most people use their imagination to structure the same outcome: no fun, no money, no joy. Yuck! Life becomes a drag — and you become *dispassionate*.

To see your life as a process — a journey — may take awhile. Always be very patient with yourself when you are learning. Some of the ideas in this book you have already heard. In fact, I will say little that you do not already know, intuitively. What you *will* learn in this book is how to use what you already know.

Most people want economic independence as their ultimate goal. True freedom to go where they want, do what they want to when they want to, and answer to no one. Few people accomplish this objective because they do not know how. You might as well begin to learn. The years are going to go by anyway!

The point to remember is that the journey toward any goal is as important as the goal itself. It is not the trophy, but the race; not the quarry, but the chase. If you are not *learning* as you go, *curious* about the next step, *understanding* the process, and *patient* enough to let time be your ally, not your enemy, you still are not accepting yourself as you are! Economic independence is the result of hard work, patience, and doing what you love. The first "law" of having money is to *do what you love*.

JOANNA'S STORY

I would like to tell you about one of my clients who went through this learning process. Her name is Joanna, and she has two advanced degrees in Public Health Administration. Her father was a physician. Both parents encouraged her to pursue a career in health, and paid for her education.

Joanna was successful by all external standards, holding a succession of responsible positions in public health administration. Yet, internally she was dissatisfied, and she had continual conflicts on the job. She had trouble with the bureaucratic form of management. Decisions were made slowly, and her programs were so watered down by the time they were implemented that she felt discouraged most of the time. Joanna came to me wanting a new job, and expressed a strong desire to get out of the medical field entirely. She had no feeling of accomplishment. Obviously, she had been following someone else's passion — her parents'!

"I'm so frustrated that I can't do the kind of supervision I'm capable of," she said. "The agency where I work is a nest of conflict. It's petty and no one focuses on results. I can't stand the delays and the endless meetings. In fact, I never could, but now I have reached my limit. The problem is that I can't imagine what else I can do. I want to change, but how? I want to go somewhere else, but where?"

Making a transition from a solid career to something unknown at age forty scared Joanna. I assured her that she could make such a change, even though it might take time. But first she would have to stay where she was and change her attitude about the present circumstances.

"First things first," I said. "Let's have you spend some time doing some assignments I've designed. Your answers will give me a good idea about the kind of decisions you make easily and also what type of personal relationships in work will bring you satisfaction. Then I'll have specifics to talk to you about."

The completed assignments revealed much about Joanna. She was an independent decision-maker. She was outgoing, venturesome, tough-minded, and self-assured. Her imagination was keen and her intelligence high. Joanna's profile matched those of people who either owned their own businesses or had daily responsibility for decision-making. Obviously, her career position did not fit her personality.

"Perhaps your father, who, as a doctor is an entrepreneur, thought you'd enjoy the medical field but he did not see entrepreneurial qualities in you. His job promotes his independence in the sense of decision-making, but your job doesn't allow you that freedom. You are the type that needs very little structure in a work setting. You enjoy risk-taking and being in charge, so your desire to change was inevitable. The entrepreneur type always has trouble being told what to do," I said.

"I thought something was wrong with me all these years. Others seem to be able to play the political game. I'm always speaking out and getting in trouble for it. What you're saying gives me a sense of relief. I need to be in the private sector, don't I?" she asked.

"It looks like business will give you the rewards you're looking for. The private sector is very good for those who enjoy making their own decisions. It's the personality fit that counts. You are interested in giving service, but perhaps in another way," I answered.

The first step was to identify a transition job, a quasi-public setting for Joanna. She was not ready for a dramatic shift. (Remember Passion Secret number three: *Getting there is all the fun.*) She found an agency that used both private and government funds as income, providing home health and nursing care to low-income families. Joanna was hired to administrate the program and raise funds. As a fund-raiser, she met and talked to many business people over a year's period. She became experienced in sales as she developed her role as the agency marketing director. Joanna now saw herself as an income producer — a new role for her.

"I do fund-raising so easily, and because the program greatly benefits people, it's easy to promote. The past year has confirmed all that you told me it would. I like the variety and challenge of so much contact work. However, I still have problems with my superior. It's a constant struggle to put my ideas into action. She is very moody and the staff is kept in constant turmoil. I just want to do my work but she takes all the fun out of it," Joanna said.

As we talked, I could see she was ready to consider the next step. "Joanna, what do you do when you're not working? What fascinates *you*?" I asked. *(Passion clue!)*

"Oh, that's easy. On weekends I get up at 4:30 in the morning and chop wood. Then I organize my house, the garage, and my yard. I'm so good at this I even do it for my friends. They're always asking me to help them get their homes in order," she replied, becoming very excited.

"Can you see yourself doing this for a living?" I asked.

"What?" she asked, somewhat shocked. "You mean housekeeping?"

"Not just houses. How about businesses, shops, banks, parking lots, all those places that have to be kept clean," I said.

Joanna was silent and thoughtful. Her mental wheels were spinning. "You're talking about my own janitorial business. I never thought about it but it seems very logical. In all my jobs I've focused on time and work management, the efficient way to do things. But, cleaning! My father would have a fit!" she exclaimed.

"Let's explore it, at least. I sense you're not quite where you want to go yet. Don't close off this alternative until you investigate further," I suggested. "Pick out some companies to talk to."

Joanna selected ten janitorial companies of various sizes. Some were large corporations whose accounts were high-rise office buildings. Others were medium-size companies, with both small and large accounts. She also selected local entrepreneurs in her town; one in particular was an older man whose janitorial business had an excellent reputation. After only three meetings, she came in full of excitement and information.

"The cleaning business is booming! All the people I talked to were so enthusiastic about the need for quality service. I was even offered a job with the biggest company in the city. They said they would train me for management!" she exclaimed.

I encouraged Joanna to talk to the local people before she made a decision. "Often the diamonds are right in your own backyard. Let's see what the old pro in your neighborhood has to say," I said.

That meeting changed Joanna's life. It put her on the road to an exciting and prosperous business. John, the owner, was very impressed with Joanna's background and interest. He told her he had been looking for an assistant but had found no one who was willing to work hard and persevere. He mentioned that he would like to retire soon, or only work part time. His cleaning methods were so good that he had more customers than he could handle. John wanted to meet with Joanna again and recommended some articles for her to read in the meantime.

Joanna had evidently found her passion and had a clear picture of what she wanted. "If I want to start my own janitorial business, I must have training. John told me that the most crucial part of the business is in how efficiently you use your time. If you don't know the fast way to clean, you'll go broke. My plan is to reduce my present position at the agency to halftime and spend the other half working with John. The janitorial work is at night so I'll go in to my other job midday. I can raise money in the afternoon and clean out the banks at night!" she laughed.

And that is just what she did. One year later, she quit her agency job and bought the business from John. He stayed on as a consultant until the transition was made. In six months she bought two more businesses, and in her second year she personally netted nearly twice the income she had been making at her old job! More important than the money was the fact that she now had control over her life; she made all the decisions. She learned how to cope with the ups and downs of owning a business, experiencing the normal anxiety and fear that is a part of risk-taking. Joanna had days of discouragement, feeling so tired that she ached all over. She would call me and let out all the frustration. I would always ask, "Well, do you want to quit and return to your old job?"

"No way! I'm just blowing off steam. Be patient with me," she would say.

And her father had a fit! "We didn't raise you and educate you to do cleaning work! How can you turn your back on your training? All those years were a waste," he said. (Note the disapproval — something all too common from relatives and close friends.)

"Joanna, just send him photocopies of your bank deposit slips. He'll come around when he sees how successful and happy you are," I said. And he did come around. Now he brags about her to his friends — "my daughter, the businesswoman," is how he describes her.

Joanna's future is unlimited. She plans to have a company staff of 250, with black-and-white employee uniforms and a fleet of trucks. She has bought sweepers, carpet steam cleaners, and other time-saving equipment. Her accounts are getting bigger and bigger.

"My company's name is now synonymous with quality, just like John's. He trained me well and I'll always be grateful. I want to pass on my knowledge and use my business to train young people in a valuable profession. There's money and satisfaction in dirt, floods, and debris!" she chuckled. Joanna had found her passion.

We can see that Joanna used her natural interest and ability — what she did easily and well — to find her economic and emotional independence. She enjoyed the journey, *learned* as she went, remained *curious* about the next step, *understood* the process, and was *patient* enough to let time be her ally.

HOW TO GET RICH

Joanna exemplifies the secret of becoming rich: do what you love.

She followed the proven two-stage process for attaining wealth. Stage One begins the process with the involvement in and satisfaction of doing work that you love. Stage Two begins when you reap the natural result of your passion: financial success. This formula for making money is not generally known, except to those wealthy individuals who have made their fortunes.

Gaylon Greer, in his column on personal financial planning, "How Did the Rich Get That Way?," discusses the formula that leads to wealth. Greer paraphrases the conclusions from Srully Blotnick's book, *Getting Rich Your Own Way!*[1], which chronicles a twenty-year research study of a large cross-section of middle class workers.

> Mr. Blotnick found that the people in his study who achieved great wealth did so in two distinct stages. In the first stage, those who eventually became millionaires were not investors in the conventional sense of the term. During this stage their major investments were in themselves. This dedication paid so handsomely that they became active investors out of necessity. By this point they had accumulated so much wealth it could not effectively be invested in themselves, and hence they turned to more conventional investment outlets.
>
> During the first stage, Mr. Blotnick found, those who eventually became rich were so profoundly absorbed in their work that they persisted and eventually excelled at it. Yet, few stayed with the line of activity that characterized their early attempts to carve a career. They were willing to try new approaches, to shift mental gears and go where their occupational inclinations led them. . . . They accumulated a vast reservoir of knowledge and experience that would eventually bear extravagant dividends. In Mr. Blotnick's words, "They accidentally invested in themselves." Throughout this extended period, they remained profoundly absorbed in their work. They had little time for or interest in outside investment activities. . . . After many years of relatively modest earnings, they typically took yet another fateful step into a new undertaking. . . . In other words, carefully planned career moves . . . led to eventual

> movement from the first stage to the second stage.
>
> A characteristic goal of those who failed in their quest for riches (ninety-two percent of the participants) was to someday make enough money so that they could quit their job and do "what I really want to do." Their attempts to accomplish this goal involved seeking "get rich quick" formulas that would rescue them from what they viewed as occupational drudgery. In effect, they tried to achieve the second stage success as investors first, in order to finance their quest for activities they would find deeply absorbing, which is Stage One.[2]

Greer and Blotnick agree with the first law of money: Do what you love; the money will come if you follow your heart. I will add that you must do it long enough, as Joanna did.

SETTING GOALS

Now, let us talk about how to set goals you can reach — goals that match your current passions. Do this exercise as a preliminary step in goal-setting: think of your life as if it were already completed, as if you would be able to instantly replay your life script in reverse. Sit down somewhere, alone with no distractions. Write or think about your epitaph. How do you want to be remembered? By whom? Some examples of epitaphs follow:

"Jack truly did live by his rule of life: 'Go as far as you can; get everything you want. Never step on anyone to get there.' With this as a guide, he lived a fulfilling, exciting, and rewarding life."

"__________ was a loving husband/wife, good parent, wise, successful, and kind. ____________ was the best kind of friend, one you could always count on. _________ gave and received in equal measure."

"Don't forget how I stumbled and danced; how I struggled and succeeded; how I loved and shared; how I ranted, raved, and sang. I leave you my smile, my energy, my photographs, and my caring."

An epitaph written with a three-year time projection gives you the chance to become all that you want to be. Write yours as if you were to die three years from now.

Exercise 1: Write Your Epitaph

Take a few minutes right now. Quickly write four or five sentences that will appropriately summarize the life you would like to have lived. Use the following space to practice:

____

____

____

____

DEFINE YOUR GOALS IN WRITING

If you are not (1) where you want to be in life, (2) doing what you want to do, and (3) earning your true potential, you probably need to take a look at the way you have set your goals, personally and professionally. You may be requesting what is not in your present best interests. Shakespeare said it best:

> ". . . We, ignorant of ourselves,
> Beg often our own harms, which the wise powers
> Deny us for our own good; so find we profit
> By losing of our prayers."
>
> — *Antony and Cleopatra* (II.i.5-8)

Defining your goals is an essential part of reaching them. A client of mine desperately wanted a new job but did not know how to describe or define what he wanted. He worked for a large computer company in the cash management division. As we began working together, all Paul could tell me was what he was dissatisfied with.

"I struggle to go to work every day. I don't like what I'm doing; it's so boring," Paul said. He did know he wanted more money and more recognition. I found out that Paul had strong communication skills which were not necessary in his current job. His greatest personal satisfaction in his school and career activities appeared to be the times when he used his writing and speaking ability in making group presentations.

"Paul, your natural skills and abilities will bring you the greatest financial reward. Why not state them as a basic feature of your new job? You may feel, as many people do, that work is supposed to be a struggle. Can't you imagine a job that is enjoyable, accomplished with ease, and one in which you're making all the money you want?" I asked.

"I've always known I was a good communicator, but my college degrees are financial. I guess I discounted my natural abilities because I couldn't imagine anyone paying me to use those skills," he said. He was not aware of the passion/work connection precisely because it was so effortless for him to communicate well.

Paul's ultimate written goal was very specific, and met three necessary criteria for success: it was *measurable, internally motivated*, and he alone was *responsible* for its achievement. His goal read: "I, Paul, deserve to be independently wealthy. I have a new and exciting job in which I use my written, verbal, and financial skills. I work in the city of my choice, make over $100,000 a year, and provide a service to both private and corporate clients that improves their financial position. I organize and conduct financial planning seminars once a month. These seminars provide useful information and also act as advertising for my services. I have able partners who work well with me. I am creative, dynamic, and mentally alert. My business is a success because it provides a genuine service and it is in harmony with my needs and values. It is my passion!"

A statement such as Paul's is called an *affirmation*. It is written in the *present* tense. No "shoulds," "mights," or "maybes" are allowed. Writing your goals in affirmation form is a powerful technique that works when your goals are authentically what you want, especially if you will plan your goals so that they can be achieved within a time frame of from six to eight months. This keeps you focused on what you can actually envision. Goals set too far in the future may not be what you really want, anyway.

Six months later, after many meetings — not job interviews — with men and women in the financial planning field, Paul had accepted a position. His new job with an experienced company provides a training base for his ultimate venture. He is learning a new business, and in return, his communication skills meet the needs of his new company.

"They told me it was my ability to make presentations that convinced them to hire me. Of course, my financial skills were important to them, but they wanted someone who could organize and set up seminars. That's a cinch for me!" he laughed.

Goals are the very basis of success. Success is defined as the realization of any worthy goal. If you have run into trouble with your goal-setting, it may be because you do not know what you really want. That determination is a process in and of itself which involves honest introspection and value clarification. Once you do know what you want, those wants must be articulated in a very special way — clearly, distinctly, with a sharp definition that meets the three goal-setting criteria of *measurement, motivation, and responsibility.*

The most successful companies know how to set realistic and measurable goals. They know where they want to go and why. At the same time they are flexible and responsive to changing conditions. Their products are known, their markets are defined, and a staff is selected to carry out marketing strategy and follow-up. Few businesspeople would try to sell a product without measuring the market, the competition, and the sales team. Personal success can be the result of similar accurate measurement. You have to set goals that are *measurable*.

MEASURING YOUR GOALS

Let us say that one of your goals is to earn more money. How do you measure "more money"? How much is it, exactly? When do you want it? Are you in a position where your goal can be accomplished? What service are you prepared to provide in return? You are going to have to increase your productivity. How do you plan to do that? For whom, and under what circumstances? Is your money goal one that will allow you to "do what you really want to do"? If so, remember the formula for making money: do what you love, *first*.

With specific information, you can project likely outcomes. Now you are ready to write a measurable goal using the affirmation technique. For example: "I make $________ as my total annual compensation, which includes salary, bonuses, and perks. In exchange, I perform these services. . . ."

Write a personal detailed outline of the time, effort, and service you will exchange for the money you seek. Measure your goal; define it. Describe it in the greatest detail so that you can smell it, see it, and taste it. Your imagination is a wonderful mental gift given freely to you. If you use it to improve your value, the money or reward you seek will follow.

INTERNAL MOTIVATION

Managing yourself is very much like managing a business. There are fundamentals to observe. Once the objectives or goals are defined and measured, you must decide if your goal is *internally motivated*. Just as Joanna was unable to find satisfaction at her old job, you cannot persuade yourself to work for rewards that are not genuine.

Enough has been discovered about human motivation in the last twenty-five years to show that attainment of inner satisfaction — "self-actualization," as the psychologist and author Abraham Maslow called it — depends on authenticity. The coach of a top-functioning basketball team assumes that each player is on the court because he wants to be there. Good competitors and managers understand internal motivations and, as a result, they practice self-correction. If a particular action continues to bring the same undesired results, the action is changed! Internal motivation is connected to how *intense* your feelings are about achieving an objective. Make your objectives realistic. Practice in achieving small passionate goals prepares you for achieving larger ones. For example, if you envision a trip to Greece as a long-term goal, go to Greek restaurants, learn the language, locate some Greek immigrants, take a course in mythology or Greek architecture. You may "accidentally" find your passion!

Finding out what motivates you is related to discovering your natural interests — your passions. You will gravitate toward your interests because they are connected with desire, want, longing. All individual needs begin with desire. What do you want more than anything else? Position, prestige, achievement, wealth, power, recognition? These needs and values are a few of the motivators that can be satisfied in varying ways. Refer to the values exercise you completed in Chapter Two and take a look at your values. People who love their work find it life-giving, natural, and enjoyable. Your work should be as natural as your play.

If you find that you are living your life to suit an external source — family, friends, boss — consider the likelihood that your completion of their goals for you will continue to bring an empty, hollow feeling. That is because it is their passion, not yours, that propels you! Passion is intensely personal.

INDIVIDUAL RESPONSIBILITY

Once your personal goals are measurable, specific, and authentically motivated, you are ready to check the final criterion, responsibility. You and only you must be *responsible* for the completion of your goal. If reaching your goal relies on the actions of others, then your chances of success are minimized. You cannot control the behavior of others; state your goals in a way that concentrates on how your own efforts can bring about the desired end.

To say, "I want a promotion in six months" can trigger trouble. You are relying on the behavior of a whole chain of individuals whose approval you must gain. If six months go by and you do not get the promotion, you become reluctant to set any further goals. You feel discouraged. The same goal (expressed in the present tense) might read, "I am making the necessary improvements in my performance that lead to promotion. At the same time, I am examining alternatives in the job market and investigating other firms who will reward the increased value of my performance." In this way you achieve your goal whether or not you receive the promotion, and do not miss out on the satisfaction and encouragement gained by reaching it. Achieving our goals initially gives us the encouragement to set even greater ones.

Your goals and the definition of them must be clear, or else your mind will not know how to focus, how to eliminate the unnecessary information that can obstruct your target. The mind is like the good earth, reproducing faithfully what is planted. Given good growing weather, the farmer knows to expect corn if that is what he plants. Your mind will reproduce whatever you think about in great detail. What a valuable resource!

Think for a moment. You are unique. Unlike a business which must specialize, you have a wealth and diversity of products in your skills and abilities — all of which are highly marketable. You are not threatened by supply shortages, inflation, or markets drying up — you are the dream of every enterprise! The strengths you possess will allow you to achieve your goals if you know how to market them effectively. I will show you how to do this in the succeeding chapters.

A SAMPLE BUSINESS PLAN

You must have a business plan before you begin any enterprise, including goal-setting. Otherwise, your business — you — will have only a haphazard marketing strategy. Allow your interests totally free play. If you had all the money you needed, what would you do? With whom would you spend your time? Where would you live?

Separate all your wants into categories — financial, personal, professional, and family. Focus on the next six to eight months. Analyze carefully how you word your goals. My clients start out by misstating most of their wants. For example, a goal stating a request for a new job might read: "I want to make more money, have a new job, and achieve greater recognition in my field." However, an accurately stated goal would read:

"I, ____________________, deserve to be as successful as I desire. I make $____________ a year with $ ____________ medical coverage, $ _________ insurance, $ ____________ bonus, and vacation time of ______________. In return, I provide my services of __________________, ______________________ and ____________________, for which I am paid. I solve problems for people. First, I increase my sense of self-worth with an accurate analysis of what I do best, easily and naturally. I read, go to seminars, and increase my circle of contacts. I look within my company to see if internal problems interest me. I also talk to other companies whose product or service interests me. In this way, others know about me and what I can do for them. I achieve recognition because I first recognize myself as worthwhile and capable. I assume all the responsibility for marketing my special talents."

Note: all is written in the present tense; this is the *affirmation* technique illustrated earlier.

Now, let us write out a six-month "want" list. You are going to imagine all the things you would like to have during the next six months.

Exercise 2: Write a Six-Month Want List

Begin with a writing pad, a pen, and a *completely open mind.* Write down everything you want, from a new toothbrush, to a new job, to peace of mind. Write quickly, freely; go as far as you can. Put the list down and then walk around. Have lunch, let your mind wander, let go of your limitations. Think about the next six months ahead of you.

Now, come back to your master list and add all the other things you want. Most people have twenty to thirty wants. There is no limit, however!

Exercise 3: Your "Ten Most Wanted" List

Next, break down your master list to the top ten wants. Try not to "lump" your wants. If a new car is one of your wants and a trip across the United States is another, do not combine them. A car and a trip are two different things. Put your number one want at the top of the list. Then the second, and so on.

Read over your top ten wants carefully and make any necessary adjustments. Now, write out a full paragraph describing each want as if you *already* have it. For example, a want that specifies a new wardrobe will read: "I, *(your name)*, have a new wardrobe. I appreciate my appearance, like my body, and always look exactly the way I want to look. I have three suits — grey, blue, and casual. I have matching shirts and ties (or scarves) and three pairs of dress shoes. I have two pairs of designer jeans, three casual shirts, two sweaters, and three pairs of casual shoes. I have a beige raincoat and a casual coat for hikes, beaches, etc. I look good always."

The technique of *acting as if* works. The "law of interest" is activated because you are now focused, narrowing down what interests you. You are talking only in the present tense. Do not have "should," "ought," "will," or "perhaps" in your paragraphs. If you use those words, you will not feel you deserve to get what you want. And, guess what? You will not get it! Remember, your mind is like the earth, it will reproduce what you plant.

After you have completed writing a paragraph for each want in a very specific way, describing it in as much detail as possible, read each paragraph out loud to yourself. How does it sound? Is it authentic; do you really want what you hear? Your tone of voice as you read will give you the answer. If your voice is unsure or it wavers, think again about your want. You will have to suspend disbelief while you are doing the exercise. Can you feel any *excitement* while you're writing or reading? *(Passion clue!)*

I have used the word "wants" in this section deliberately because I have found that people will allow their imagination freer reign when they conceive of a "want" rather than a goal. However, your top ten "wants" are really your "goals."

Next, read your want list to a trusted, supportive friend. Their reaction is not as important as yours is while you are reading it. Are you nervous, unsure? You may surprise yourself with your own assertion. Great! You are halfway there. Now, *tape* this list of thoroughly articulated wants. (If you do not have a cassette player, get one. They are inexpensive.) Play the tape every morning and night for twenty-one days. It takes about three weeks for the subconscious mind to "lock in" new beliefs. Do not worry and fuss about how these wants will come to you. You are only concentrating now on focusing your mind. Soon you will be aware of information, events, and people who will help you bring all your wants into existence. You will be activating the "law of interest" which I discuss in the next section.

Do not be afraid to rewrite and reset your priorities. You can change your wants until they are exact. You will soon notice a focusing effect in your life. Next, tell your rewritten goals again to someone close whom you can trust. This person could be an impartial, objective listener — a knowledgeable professional. Whoever you choose should be committed to the success of your quest. In my own experience with clients, I have found that the most valuable service I can offer them is an objectivity coupled with professional commitment. Clarity of thinking precedes right action and provides an excellent motivational environment.

THE "LAW OF INTEREST"

Once you begin formulating goals, you set in motion the "law of interest," a law that draws information to you, seemingly from nowhere. This law works because you are open, sincere with yourself, receptive, and stimulated. You are picking up information that was always there; you simply were not aware of it before, because the law of interest was not activated. Suddenly, you begin to see articles and books relating to your goals; you hear relevant conversations, and even find new ways of doing the same activity. For example, did you ever notice that once you learn a new word, it seems to pop up everywhere? Once you focus on an area, you attune yourself in a way so that you become fully receptive to information of concern to you.

PERSEVERANCE BRINGS SUCCESS

The achievement of your goals and the acquisition of what you want rest upon your willingness to persist in your efforts. Sadly enough, fear of the unknown keeps many people trapped right where they are in life. Psychologists say that most people prefer what is familiar, even if a situation is extremely stressful — rather a known devil than an unknown one. That is because change requires new combinations of thinking and behavior that can be threatening not only to the person making the changes, but also to others in the same environment.

I recommend vigorous daily exercise to aid you in developing the perseverance necessary to follow through, if discouragement threatens to thwart your goals.

Getting your heart's desire really begins with you: you must want the change. The achievement of the desired change comes to pass with the *action* you take, a steady progression toward the realization of your goals. You can control what you think about. Manage *your* thoughts, measure the goals you want, make them your goals and no one else's, and consider it your responsibility to attain your objectives.

If you manage your assets well, you are a growth enterprise. Your bottom line, the most tangible reward of all, is inner satisfaction — a reward that is measured not only in terms of dollars, but also in terms of creativity, productivity, and better relationships.

COLLAGE ASSIGNMENT

Go to an art supply store and buy a piece of picture matboard and a glue stick. Pick your favorite color for the matboard. Then cut out pictures from magazines and newspapers that reflect you and what you like. For example, you may choose beautiful scenery, stylish clothing, children playing, food — whatever appeals to you.

Arrange the final selection of cut-out pictures on the matboard. Leave it overnight. The next day, see if you still like the arrangement — if not, change it. Then coat the backs of the pictures with the glue stick and press into place.

Every client of mine does this assignment with great emotion. It is fun, enlightening, and a creative way to get to know more about what your passion is. Your passion will be on the collage, symbolized perhaps, but it will be there. After six months, look at your collage again, with fresh appreciation. You will be surprised how far ahead of you your unconscious mind was.

EAVILY
RMED

SAMPLE COLLAGE

The powerful man who created the sample collage did not see himself as powerful when we began work. An introvert in an extroverted corporate world, he spent 99 percent of his time managing others. His autobiography made it clear that he was conditioned to believe he was anti-social if he wanted to be alone. Exhausted from over-stimulation, the collage shows he longed for rest, beauty, solitude, and affection. Tears came to his eyes when I told him there was nothing wrong with him except when he betrayed his needs in order to please others.

Today he has his own computer programming and consulting business. He works at home, at his own pace, in beautiful surroundings, his Golden Retriever at his side. As his friend wrote to him, his hobby of body building is a good metaphor for his strength, "a fair reflection of the mental and spiritual 'iron' you've pumped into your recovery [from alcohol and drugs], your career, and your personality. You inspire me to take what I have and transform it into what I need and want to be."

SUMMARY

Passion Secret #3:
Powerful people know that getting there is all the fun.

1. Learn as you go.
2. Be curious about the next step.
3. Be understanding of the process.
4. Be patient enough to let time be your ally, not your enemy.
5. Write your epitaph in an affectionate manner. How were people affected by this person? What did you do while you were here?
6. Write a six-month want list.

7. Write your "ten most wanted" list. Write a paragraph (using the affirmation technique) about each want. Tape this list.
8. Check your want list against the three goal-setting criteria: measurement, motivation, responsibility.
9. Rewrite and retape your list if necessary.
10. Spend five to ten minutes a day (for twenty-one days) listening to, reading, and thinking about your wants. Allow no distractions during this time. Make sure your voice on the tape is full of emotion, excitement, and enthusiasm. Let your mind envision the want as you listen to the tape. You will love the sound of your own voice!
11. Be sure you stay in shape physically. Vigorous exercise helps you develop the perseverance necessary for your inevitable success.
12. Make a collage. See what part of your life — your mind, body, heart, or intuition — is emphasized by the images you choose. Sometimes we are starved for one or more of the above; for example, we need rest. Then the collage will reflect quiet images, with lots of space between the pictures. If stimulation is the need, hot colors and motion will attract you. If affection is the theme, you will choose puppy dogs and babies — soft, cuddly images to express your love. If there is spiritual hunger, you will be drawn to clouds, the sky, angels, great religious art — all these images point to heaven.

CONTACTS: HOW TO FIND PEOPLE WHOSE PASSION MATCHES YOURS

Take a deep breath. Think about all the work you have done. By now you are bound to feel like talking to others, to someone "out there." You are right. It is time now to take Step Four: finding the people who can assist you in achieving your goals — people who are excited about your passion. Whatever your goals, the achievement of them will take the willing cooperation of others, and you must know how to select your contacts wisely.

Passion Secret #4:
Powerful people always have other powerful people help them achieve their goals.

How is this done — and why? First, look at your list of goals. How will the accomplishment of those goals help others? Who will benefit besides yourself? Let us assume one of your goals is to make more money, say $10,000 more a year. What will your increased productivity do to increase others' income, productivity, or self-esteem?

Are you beginning to get the idea that your gain will be someone else's gain, too? Can you see a connection between what you want and what others want? People cooperate with people for mutual gain in a trade-off situation. In business terms, it is called a cost/benefit transaction. What it costs me to help you must be worth the price, whether it is my time, money, or effort.

When you meet with people to achieve something you want, you will feel more confident if you remember that you have three specific assets to offer. These assets are:

1. Your *skills and abilities*. From your work in Chapter Two, you have your five top strengths clearly defined.
2. Your *values*. Knowing what you value, what you have a strong desire for, gives you a measuring device. Do your values match theirs? (You listed your values in Chapter Two.)
3. Your *personality*. Each of us has special qualities, mannerisms, and magnetism that are marketable because the particular combination of our individual characteristics is unique. Movie stars and entertainers are highly paid because of their almost magical projection of personality. Perhaps you have heard of "million dollar" personalities. Singers, dancers, actors, and comedians all use a pleasing personality to inspire and entertain others. The more harmonious (not servile) your personality, the more you can accomplish — and better yet, *the more you can get others to accomplish what you want*. (A negative attitude toward others can never bring success.)

HOW TO SPOT LEADERSHIP QUALITIES

Leadership of yourself — knowing what you want and implementing the steps to achieve that goal — is exactly like leadership of others. Napoleon Hill, in *Think and Grow Rich*,[1] lists eleven important factors in leadership. These are important for you to consider not only for your own benefit, but for the purpose of assessing those people you will be meeting as you pursue your interests.

Study the following characteristics very carefully. They describe the qualities of the people you are looking for, to guide you as you discover your passion. Individuals who display these eleven traits are models for you to learn from. In your future meetings with others, you will know very quickly if the person you are talking to meets these criteria of leadership.

1. *Unwavering courage* based on knowledge of self, and of one's occupation. No follower wishes to be dominated by a leader who lacks self-confidence and courage. No intelligent follower will be dominated by such a leader very long.
2. *Self-control.* The man or woman who cannot control him- or herself can never control others. Self-control sets a strong example for one's followers, which the more intelligent emulate.
3. *A keen sense of justice.* Without a sense of fairness and justice, no leader can command and retain the respect of his or her followers.
4. *Definiteness of decision.* The person who wavers in his or her decisions shows that he or she is not confident, and cannot lead others successfully.
5. *Definiteness of plans.* The successful leader must plan his or her work, and *work his or her plan.* A leader who moves by guesswork without practical, definite plans is comparable to a ship without a rudder. Sooner or later he or she will land on the rocks.
6. *The habit of doing more than paid for.* One of the penalties of leadership is the necessity of willingness, on the part of the leader, to do more than he or she requires of followers.

7. *A pleasing personality*. No slovenly, careless person can become a successful leader. Leadership calls for respect. Followers will not respect a leader who does not grade high on all of the factors of a pleasing personality.
8. *Sympathy and understanding*. The successful leader must be in sympathy with followers. Moreover, he or she must understand them and their problems.
9. *Mastery of detail*. Successful leadership calls for mastery of the details of the leader's position.
10. *Willingness to assume full responsibility*. The successful leader must be willing to assume responsibility for the mistakes and shortcomings of followers. If the leader tries to shift this responsibility, he or she will not remain the leader. If a follower makes a mistake, and shows himself incompetent, the leader must take responsibility for the failure.
11. *Cooperation*. The successful leader must understand and apply the principle of cooperative effort and be able to induce his or her followers to do the same. Leadership calls for power, and power calls for cooperation.

Copy this list and carry it with you. Few men and women have mastered all eleven factors. Do not waste your time with guides who do not display at least a majority of these characteristics. The passionate, powerful men and women of the world are in every field imaginable. The steps you will be taking will lead you to these people. On the way you will meet those who do not measure up, but do not let mediocre people discourage you. You now have a measuring device to assess the person in front of you.

FOCUS ON THE ADVENTURE AHEAD

As you prepare for the next step, it may help to think about the future in the following way. Focus on:

1. How you really want to spend your time.
2. What specific goals you wish to achieve.
3. The type of company and the kind of people you wish to work with.

So far, the work you have done in the previous chapters has been "internal," focusing on yourself. Since it is now time to venture out into the world, here is an advanced "lesson" about getting things done through other people: once you have answered the three questions above, help comes seemingly from nowhere. You think about what you want, believe it fully, and it *becomes reality*.

As you begin to become conscious of your power, be patient. To learn and understand these concepts and techniques is like learning a new dance. For awhile you just do the steps. And you might falter, stumble, and even decide you do not really want to dance. As I said in an earlier chapter, getting ready to change is unsettling, in and of itself. The process of change is like travel in a foreign country. While you are in your hotel room, in territory that is familiar to you, you feel safe. As soon as you venture forth outside — a new place with a new language — you feel more on edge. That is because you do not know the protocol, the cultural cues, and the rules of the social road, so to speak. No wonder travel can be emotionally exhausting.

The experience of personal growth places you in a foreign land. It is new, unknown (this is a biggie!), and you feel wary on all fronts. Most people will stay where they are — emotionally and geographically — rather than introduce change into their lives. Change usually is *forced* upon us, and the natural tendency is to resist it. That is one reason why I wrote this book, to let people know that change can be exciting, fulfilling. Clients kept saying, "Nancy, if I'd only known this years ago! Can't you tell more people that they can get what they want?" This book is my attempt to give you the inspiration that will guide you to your full destiny in your work. I believe with my whole heart that when you work with love, *all* your life begins to balance.

This is a noble objective, worth trying for with all your might.

JANE'S STORY

I will never forget one client who had completed her "internal" work. She knew her strengths, but just froze when it was time to go "out in the world." In order to postpone the inevitable meetings with others, she invented every excuse imaginable, from illness to being too busy. She was so good at stalling her own ascent to power that she derailed her personal power train for four months. Finally Jane ran out of excuses.

"I eventually told myself that if I keep on grumbling and complaining, I'm never going to get anywhere," she said. "If I don't go and talk to people, I'll do just what my father did — give up!" (She had discovered this pattern in her autobiography.)

At this time Jane wanted to find a position in which she could use her negotiating skills. She also wanted more intellectual stimulation than she had in her present job. "I'm good at resolving conflicts. I'm always asked to mediate between opposing factions in my company," she said in one of our sessions.

Because of her natural interpersonal skills, Jane was able to resolve some problems between her manager, a fast-paced Easterner transplanted to California, and the representatives from the home office which was located in the Midwest. Jane, born and reared in the Midwest, understood the ways of business in both areas, as well as the pace of the relatively low-keyed Californians. She also helped to foster a more congenial atmosphere in her office.

"Our manager is never right in his approach to people," Jane told me. "He acts like he's still in New York — barking orders, wanting everyone to jump fast and work long, hard hours. And he thinks everyone in the Midwest office is a hick. Our office is not performing as it should and he says it's because we don't know how to work. Actually, believe it or not, he's a good manager — but he hasn't changed his pace and his New York thinking.

"Fortunately, I resolved some conflicts when I was sent to the Midwest home office for leadership training. While I was there, I tactfully presented the whole scenario to the regional manager, who understood the personality problems. He flew out to California and became better acquainted with my manager. In their discussions they resolved the interoffice problems and it was decided that in the near future my manager would fly to the Midwest office to meet the staff. During the time the regional manager was in California, I suggested that we all get together socially at my home to have a casual Sunday afternoon barbecue. My manager relaxed and really got to know us as people. Many of the staff told him that day how much they liked the chance to get acquainted. Since then, the whole atmosphere in the office has changed. I'd like to use that negotiating ability of mine all the time. I like being a troubleshooter, particularly with *people* trouble," Jane said. She had found her passion.

We picked several industries that interested Jane, and followed up by selecting some target companies — small, medium, and large. We called the companies for annual reports, articles, brochures — whatever information was available to the public. Next, we read some trade magazines to become generally informed about the various industries and their companies, products, and key people. We also made a list of people Jane already knew.

Contacts are considered by most people to be "something everyone else has but me." When I work on this assignment with clients, I concentrate on defining relationships (contacts) and help them discover how many contacts already exist in their lives. Most powerful people effortlessly tap the considerable resources their friends and associates have to offer. And they, in return, function willingly as a resource tool for others.

A contact is anyone with whom you have a mutual interest. It takes time to build relationships, but you can easily activate new ones if you keep in mind the concept of *mutuality*. Mutuality is a *similarity of interest*, of passions. When you discover your pressing desire, you can be assured that it is a desire that others share.

The "old boys' network" is nothing more than mutuality at work. You can build your own network even if you are in a brand new city. It will take time, but the months and years are going to go by anyway. You might as well be making contacts! If you are receptive, every person you meet can open new doors of experience to you.

Jane made a list of her personal contacts, anyone with whom she had a mutual interest. She was amazed that she had a list of over forty people. "Even my therapist knows people in my areas of interest!" she remarked.

Jane began with a contact list of twenty-six people, drawing from her personal list and the companies she had targeted. Her next step was to get the names of the individuals in the companies who supervised the areas of her interest — arbitration and personnel relations.

When Jane called one company and asked for the person in charge of personnel relations, she was connected to the secretary of the vice-president of personnel. Jane asked her some questions about negotiation and labor relations, finding the secretary to be quite helpful and informative. Jane discovered that her calls to companies built her confidence and developed her ability to clearly state what she wanted. As she talked to more and more people, she became more assured over the telephone and was not thrown by a few negative reactions.

"This process is just like sales. I'm rejected occasionally, but so far I'm batting .800! People are great if you're honest and open. I've had good calls with several people. I can hardly wait to meet these people in person," she said.

The next step was to work on a draft of what I call an approach letter. (This letter is covered in detail in Chapter Seven.) Written correctly, a personal letter to someone with whom you can demonstrate a mutual interest is a powerful marketing tool. Remember, you are now in a marketing phase — you are implementing your plan through other people. Marketing simply means making a sale, this for that: mutuality. At this point, you are marketing yourself.

Keep in mind that you are learning to exercise your power (which you have always had). Any fears that you have, such as fear of failure or criticism, will be what you will learn about first. Meeting people with similar interests will take away much of your fear. This is a good time to recall situations in your past that you were apprehensive about, but which turned out well. (How about that party you went to where you did not know anyone — and wound up having a wonderful time!)

Confidence and fear are two positions a person can act from in any given situation. In living a full life, we will face uncomfortable situations from time to time. Courage to take action in the face of our fear not only enriches us, but also elevates our lives, putting us into the heroic mold. We are all capable of great heights. It usually takes a crisis to bring forth our reserves. At this point, when your courage may falter, turn inward. Ask for guidance from your inner self.

Study the lives of successful men and women; read their biographies, especially those of creative people. I suggest you read Konstantin Stanislavsky's *My Life in Art*,[2] a delightful embrace of life, and a good alternative to the puritanical reserve most of us inherited. The Irish thespian, Kenneth Branagh, makes it clear in his autobiography, *Beginning*,[3] that he was not long for organizations. You will enjoy reading about the projects he initiated, the most daring his acclaimed *Henry V*, a study of the dilemma of leadership — and the effect of egocentric leaders on their countries. No book or person offers a perfect model, but reading about another's refusal to settle for anything less than his or her heart's desire will inspire you.

SETTING UP ADVICE CALLS

The next step in the attainment of your goal is the process of setting up "advice calls." The steps of the advice call are covered in detail in Chapter Eight. But now I would like to walk you through Jane's process so you see the result first — where you are headed with the advice call approach.

An advice call is a meeting you arrange with a person who is doing work you are interested in. Before you make an advice call, you will have completed the research on your field of interest, and will have the names of several people to contact, as Jane did. Jane's marketing plan was based on her problem-solving abilities — just as your plan will be based on *your* problem-solving abilities. Every business has problems, either with objects, data, or people. Jobs can be defined as ways to solve business problems.

Whether part of your marketing plan includes finding a new job or improving the one you have, the advice call approach reaps great rewards. Talking to people about their business problems gives you a clear view of how much the world needs problem-solvers of all kinds. You may be wondering how you can solve problems for a stranger. However, the advice call makes it possible to turn strangers into friends and business associates. (You presently have advice calls all the time. You just have not called these conversations by the name, "advice calls.")

Jane wrote several letters using the "approach letter" format (outlined in Chapter Seven). She followed up with phone calls and scheduled several meetings. I had advised her to avoid "stacking" the meetings.

"At first, one meeting a day, twice a week is enough," I said. "You need time in between the advice calls to digest what you've learned. Be sure to come in after the meetings so that we can review them and go over your technique. With each meeting, your knowledge of the field increases. You carry that accumulated knowledge to your next meeting so that you're not always beginning again. For instance, after you meet with the first two personnel specialists, your third will sense your awareness and will find you to be quite knowledgeable. As a result, your questions and your dialogue together will be more focused and detailed. You'll sound more like an equal," I said.

Jane soon learned how mutuality of interest works. Her meetings went very well, and she was especially excited about one company who wrote insurance policies for shipping firms — the supercarriers that keep international trade active. Jane, in her research, had chosen shipping as a category of interest.

"I've always been fascinated *(see the passion and interest clue?)* with ocean traveling and trade. Something about the water and boats.. Even when I was very small, the fantasy books I liked the best were always about big boats and long ocean journeys," she said.

Here is an example of an early natural interest, a yearning, if you will, to know more about a subject. We rarely see how these interests can connect with our careers, and sometimes they do not. They become our hobbies, our spare time fascinations. But Jane was able (through the same exercises you are doing in this book) to *connect* an interest with her skills and experience. Although international trade is a typically male field, we have seen that Jane is comfortable working with men both in a negotiating capacity and also in the technical area of insurance.

Jane firmly believed that she could succeed in shipping and insurance. That belief came about when her faith and imagination were activated. She pictured herself in a job *before* she had it, using all the details and information she had gathered on her advice calls.

The large insurance company that was Jane's target had an extensive training program. The vice-president in charge of the shipping underwriting met with her for over an hour, answering all her questions. He then told her about the company's training program and asked her if she would be interested in taking it.

"I think you'd have a clear idea of the career path you're on after six months of class and field work. You'd be paid while you're in training, of course, but considering what you've told me, that would be just a start. We really need people with your background," he said. He understood her strengths and recognized her initiative by the thoroughness of her approach to him.

Before Jane made her decision, she met with two employees first — one in the training program and one who had gone on to work in the field. She kept the vice-president posted on the meetings, wrote each person a thank-you letter, and then followed up with a summary letter to the vice-president, stating her impressions. In her final meeting with the vice-president, she was hired and began the training program, which she is using as a stepping stone in her career.

"My goal is to be the most knowledgeable woman on the West Coast in the field of shipping insurance. I've enrolled in law school part-time for the fall program and plan to specialize in maritime law. I'm so excited. I can now see *exactly* where all my skills will be used," she said.

It is evident that Jane is actively creating her future. She finally found her passion — her fascination with ships — and combined it with her natural abilities. Jane released the power she already possessed. Her productivity and creativity increased, and everyone benefitted, particularly the man who hired her.

SUSAN'S STORY

In many cases the solution to another's problem is the solution to your own, as in the following client's story.

Susan was a professional therapist with a Ph.D. in Counseling. She had made quite a mark in her field, excelling in graduate school and later in her career. She built a private practice which concentrated on family problems. She had also worked as a director of Goodwill Industries and similar nonprofit organizations. Susan was a specialist in both administration (group interaction) and personnel (one-on-one interaction). She solved knotty problems on a daily basis. When she began working with me, her desire was to make more money and change her environment.

"I've worked long and hard with very needy people. I have the social worker syndrome. It's time for me to leave while I'm still effective. A 'helper' job is notorious for burnout. You start feeling contempt for clients who are always in emotional trouble. I want a different kind of reward now — money and status," she said.

For many of us, it is hard to make a statement of intent that involves money and status. It is embarrassing to openly state we actually *like* what we have been conditioned to think of as "not nice." Topics we are embarrassed to discuss can be very illuminating if we examine them closely. Underneath the uncomfortable feeling may lie a passion. One day I asked Susan to state verbally her top five strengths (in my sessions with clients I emphasize the importance of articulating their strengths, values, and goals).

"Well, I'm good at communicating, both in writing and speaking. I'm great at organization. . . ." Susan paused and looked toward the door of my office.

"What's wrong?" I asked.

"You know, Nancy, I can just see my mother standing there saying, 'Now Susan, two's enough, don't be such a braggart!'"

We both broke into laughter, and even I could see the judging parent standing there, shaking her finger at a child's attempt at self-affirmation. "Our shyness is the result of early criticism given freely when adults think we get too uppity: 'Too big for our britches' is the usual phrase," I said.

Parents can unknowingly place a limitation on creativity that can last a lifetime. Here was Susan, forty years old, recalling old dialogue in a crucial moment. Her training and education had not removed her childhood admonitions. But we laughed and went on with the exercise.

"All right," she said. "To tell the truth I'm a master at communication. I speak clearly, listen to all that's said, and even hear between the spoken lines for real feelings; I organize my time and my work naturally and efficiently; I analyze problems effortlessly, separating things logically; I synthesize data into general concepts, but can extract the crucial points quickly so that right action can be taken; I have good judgment and trust my instincts with people and situations," she said. She was sitting erect and poised, and her tone was reflective and positive.

"Those are outstanding marketable strengths, Susan. Those are what you do naturally, effortlessly. Employers are desperate for employees like yourself," I said.

Susan's next step was to choose a field to explore, and she selected executive recruiting. Both the money and the status were there. She learned that a good recruiter needs communication skills and, above all, must be a sensitive listener, registering all the information that an employer needs to solve his or her problems. A recruiter has to be organized and adept at analyzing and synthesizing enormous amounts of data. Finally, the recruitment of executive candidates requires good judgment, an ability to "read" people and make accurate decisions about them.

The fit was perfect. After several meetings, Susan not only had the job offer she wanted — *she had created the job*. She convinced the executive recruiting firm that she would be an asset. In her former jobs she had been responsible for recruitment. Yet, in her advice calls she focused on her strengths, not her previous job functions. Her employer felt she was qualified to do the work because he had the same strengths, so necessary for success in that field. Their meetings were based on equality, one equal talking to another.

Today, she is one of the best performers in her office and trains new personnel as well. Her income is over $100,000 and rising fast. She now plans to open her own recruiting firm in a year.

"Not bad for someone whose mother encouraged modesty," I said, laughing.

"Nancy, I love what I do. I help so many people — the candidates, their families, and the employers! They think I'm the answer to all their problems. I even gave one my chicken soup recipe the day he called me complaining about a heavy cold!" she laughed. (She got a contract from him, too!)

MOST GOOD JOBS ARE NOT ADVERTISED

The majority of the jobs involving judgment (sometimes called management positions) are never announced, nor are they advertised. Fully eighty-five percent of all good jobs are *never* advertised. Where are they? As we said earlier, the jobs are where the problems are, in the minds of the owner or manager or executive — the decision-maker who is trying to solve his or her problem.

In the advice call you are able to shorten your job search by personally contacting key people in companies that are dynamic growth operations. You state your strengths, ask questions, and at the end of the meeting you obtain the names of other people who are active in your area of interest. That is how Susan found the employer she eventually went to work for. In one of her advice calls Susan had asked about his company, and her contact offered to introduce Susan to him. Several meetings followed during which Susan learned what his goals and values were. They matched her own. With her on the payroll, he now makes more money, and he got a superb trainer as well.

An employer's problem may be (1) a position that needs to be filled, (2) something he or she can specifically define, or (3) a vague feeling that "things" are not going well. When you establish contact through the approach letter and the meeting that follows, you will eventually meet the man or woman whose problems interest you — and they may find that you are the solution to their problems!

RESEARCH ASSIGNMENTS

Properly conducted research can lead you to the kind of work you are *really* interested in. After you have determined your interests, you will be prepared to make your contacts. Let us begin like Jane did. Let your curiosity guide you as you begin the project of looking at general categories of work. A category is a broad term, like art, finance, music, real estate, publishing.

Use the index section of the Yellow Pages in the telephone book. As you look through the index, you will be aware of the tremendous variety of work in the world and you will increase your frame of reference.

Do not analyze what you could do in any of these fields. This is not an analytical assignment, but one designed to open your mind to alternatives. If Susan had begun with limitations (her original job title was a counselor), how could she have imagined herself as an executive recruiter — which comes under the Yellow Pages category of management consulting? She would still be in her old job and hating it!

When a category is of *any interest whatsoever* (do not at this point try to analyze what job you would like to do), just write the category down with the page number. List as many categories as you desire. Eventually you will reduce your initial list to fourteen categories, and then finally to six major areas of interest.

I have included blank forms for you to use, and also samples of finished assignments. After you have completed the survey, go over it in your mind. Think of it, you have looked at the entire world of work! Congratulate yourself on a good day's work.

TIME MANAGEMENT EXERCISES

Before you begin the actual research assignments, it is very valuable to look at the way you are spending your time. I am suggesting here that most of you have more time to do this work than you think. The "time pie" assignments that follow are helpful in discovering how to set aside more time for creativity. If after completing these assignments you find that you are still having difficulty managing your time, consult your local library for books on time management.

Draw two time pies. In the first "pie," segment your time as you are currently using it. How many hours cannot be accounted for?

Where and how are you spending the majority of your time?

First, here is a sample of an imaginary client:

Sample: 24-Hour Time Pie

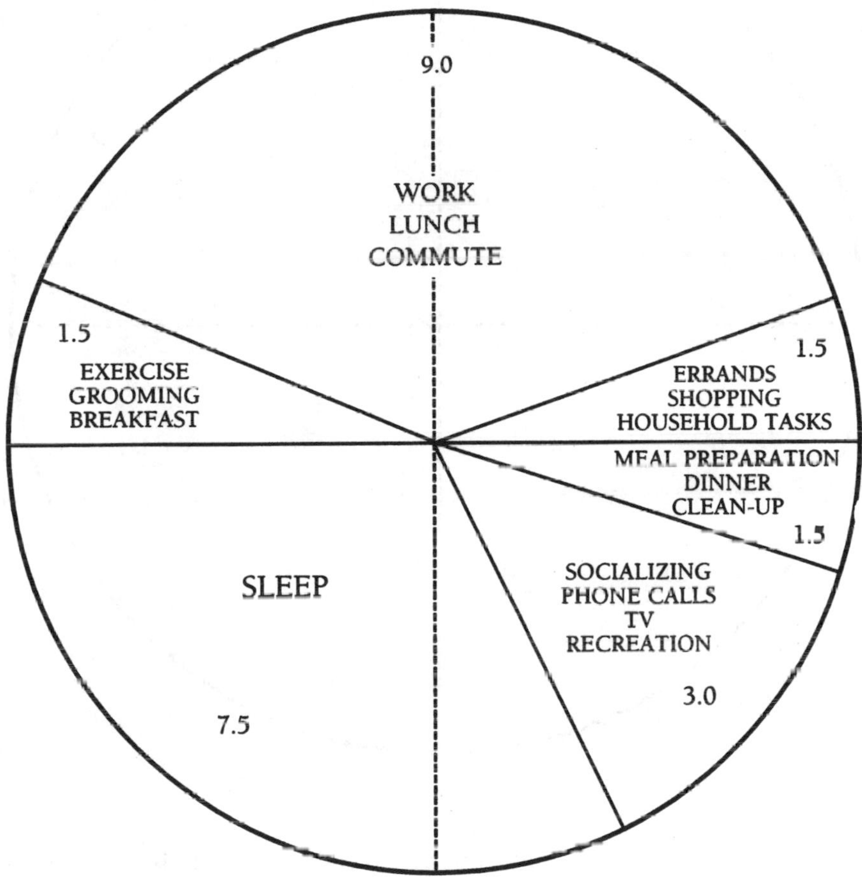

Now, fill in the pie yourself, charting approximately how you spend your average day.

24 Hours As I'm Using Them Now

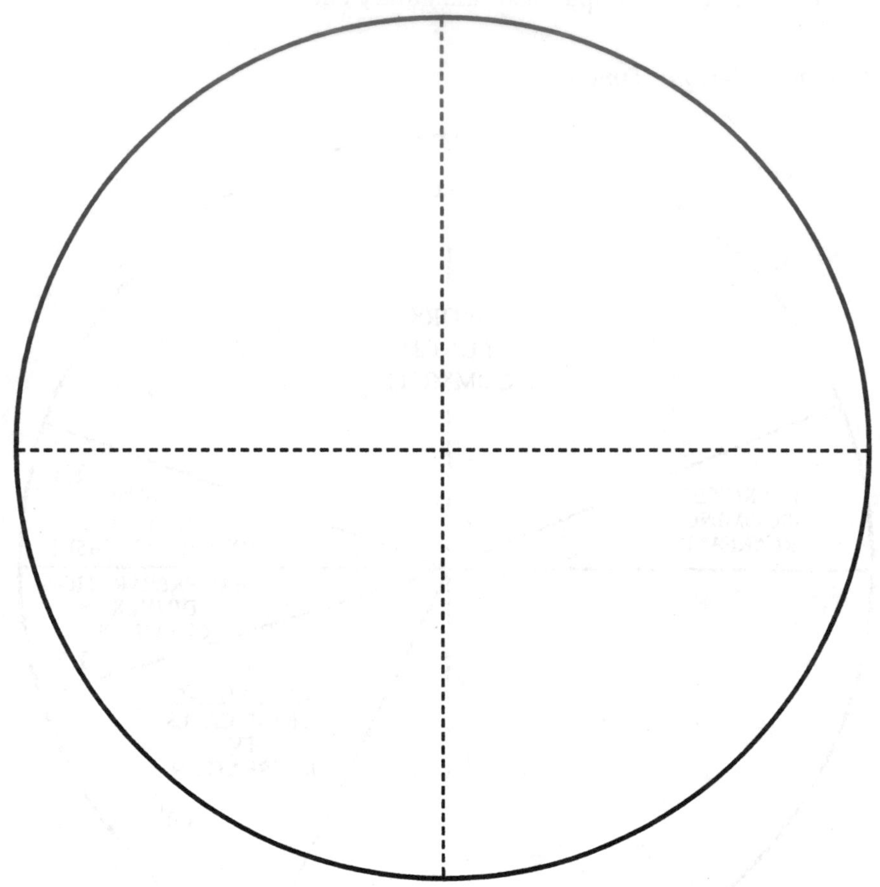

Next, draw a time pie as you would like your time to be ideally spent.

What hours would you change? Why? What would you eliminate? How many hours do you spend on self-improvement? You may find that much of your wasted time is spent with other people. Spend more time alone. Reflective thought is essential to helping you integrate your daily experiences and vital to creating the changes you want to make.

In addition to creating two time pies (one of your present work day, and one of an ideal work day), it is necessary to make two separate time pies for weekends. How do you spend your weekends? Can you plan more time alone? You may discover that you spend a lot of time doing a certain activity. Many hours spent in gardening, reading, or sports, for example, may indicate a passion that is worth investigating. Remember Joanna in Chapter Three, who loved to clean and organize on the weekend?

My Ideal Time Use of 24 Hours

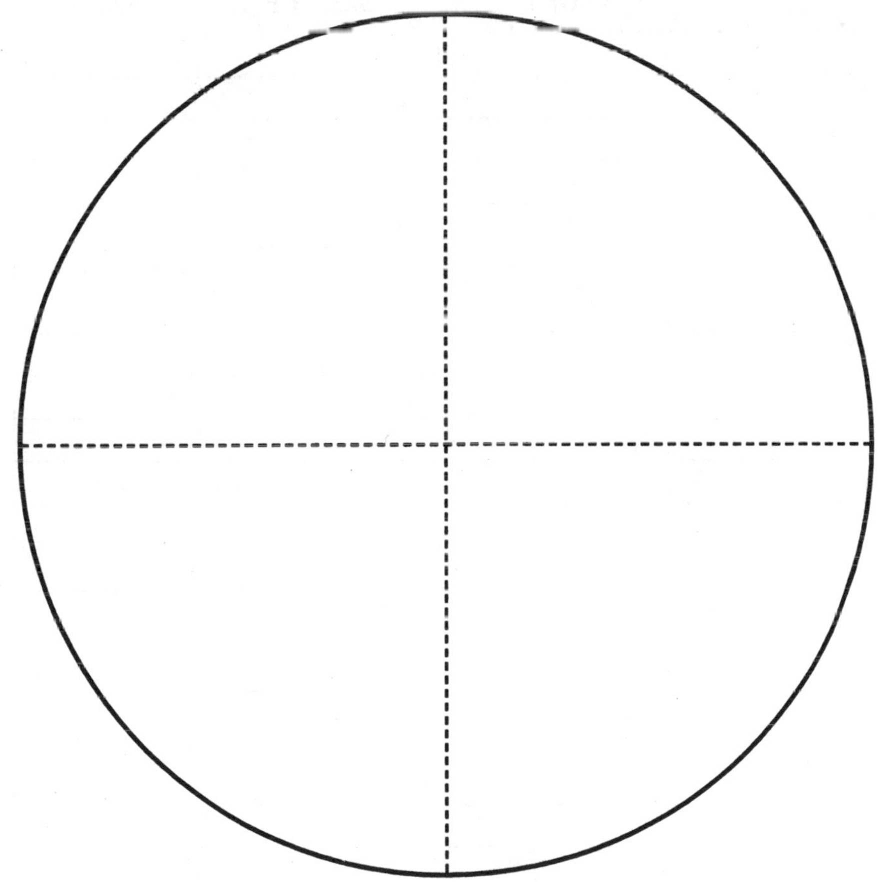

Now you are ready to begin your research assignments. Begin with the index section in your local Yellow Pages in your telephone book. List every category that holds any interest for you on the following chart. Do this exercise in two or three days — A to Z, every category that holds an interest. Do not think about your choice as a job, just as an interest. You will be amazed by the world of work!

YELLOW PAGES ASSIGNMENT WORKSHEET

PRODUCT OR SERVICE	PAGE #	PRODUCT OR SERVICE	PAGE #

YELLOW PAGES ASSIGNMENT WORKSHEET

Break down your master list to a top 14 categories of interest

First Cut — Top 14 Categories

PRODUCT OR SERVICE	PAGE #	PRODUCT OR SERVICE	PAGE #
1.		8.	
2.		9.	
3.		10.	
4.		11.	
5.		12.	
6.		13.	
7.		14.	

Break down your top 14 categories of interest to a top six.

Final Cut — Top 6 Categories

PRODUCT OR SERVICE	PAGE #	PRODUCT OR SERVICE	PAGE #
1.		4.	
2.		5.	
3.		6.	

Note: Be sure to fill in all the blanks on all pages.

YELLOW PAGES ASSIGNMENT SAMPLE

PRODUCT OR SERVICE	PAGE #	PRODUCT OR SERVICE	PAGE #
AIRPORT SERVICE	41	ENTERTAINMENT	657
AIRTOURS ETC.	28	FASHION SHOW PROD.	679
AIR TAXI CHARTER SERV.	35	FOREIGN TRADE CONSULT	720
APPRAISERS	63	FUR DESIGNERS	734
BEACH WEAR	1563	FUR RENTAL	735
BEAUTY CULTURE SCHOOL	276	GOWN, BRIDAL	332
BED & BREAKFAST	291	HOME DECORATORS	882
BOAT CHARTER	306	HOSTESS & HOST	480
BUILDERS	824	CONVENTION/ESCORT	
WOMEN'S CLOTHING	1822	SERV.	659
CONSTRUCTION CONSULT.	334	INTRODUCTION	432
CRUISES	504	JEWELRY BUYERS	915
CUSTOMS CONSULT.	508	MAKE UP STUDIOS	996
COMPUTER DATING	1183	WEDDING CONSULT.	1798
PARTY DECORATING	529	PARTY PLANNING	1177
DIAMOND APPRAISER	63	PERSONAL SHOPPING	
DIAMOND BUYER	558	SERV.	1549
DIAMOND INVESTMENT	560	TOUR & TRAVEL	1703
DISPLAYS, CONV.	480	TRADE SHOWS	567
		WEIGHT CONTROL,	
		REDUCING	1372

YELLOW PAGES ASSIGNMENT SAMPLE

First Cut — Top 14 Categories

PRODUCT OR SERVICE	PAGE #	PRODUCT OR SERVICE	PAGE #
1. Tour & Travel Escort	1703	8. Decorating, Party	882
2. Air Tour	28	9. Diamond, Buyer	558
3. Appraiser	63	10. Display, Conv.	480
4. Beauty Culture School	279	11. Fashion Show Prod.	679
5. Clothing, Women's	1822	12. Hostess & Host	480
6. Cruises	504	13. Party Planning	1177
7. Dating Service	528	14. Weight Reduction	1372

Final Cut — Top 6 Categories

PRODUCT OR SERVICE	PAGE #	PRODUCT OR SERVICE	PAGE #
1. Decorating, Party	882	4. Hostess, Host	480
2. Fashion Show Prod.	679	5. Diamond Buyer	558
3. Tour & Travel	63	6. Weight Reduction	1372

These samples were the work of an actual client of mine. Do you see the pattern that emerged in her passions? She narrowed her areas of interest to several areas. Then she was ready for the next step — talking to people in these areas of interest.

This client is now conducting city tours for tourists and convention attendees and loving it. She enjoys the "show biz" aspect of working in front of the microphone on the tour buses. In addition, she is also doing research on starting her own singles' introduction business.

The other categories on her list turned out to be personal interests: fashion, diamonds, weight reduction, and decorating — all were what she wanted for herself, but not as a full-time activity. As I said in the Preface, you must be connected emotionally to what you do, and to the people you serve, if you are to work with passion. This client values recognition, and her customers give it to her! She, in turn, gives to them an entertaining tour of the city she loves.

COMMUNITY SUPPORT GROUPS

Now is a good time to join together with other people who are doing what you are doing. "Job clubs" — groups of people who are looking for the right work — can be helpful to you. You can even form your own group, with several friends that meet regularly. Check the community announcements in your local paper to look for groups that you can join. You will stay encouraged if you have support, but be selective in your choice of companions — not everyone is able to be your "foxhole buddy."

SUMMARY

Passion Secret #4:
Powerful people always have other powerful people help them achieve their goals.

1. How do you really want to spend your time?
2. What specific goals do you wish to achieve?
3. What types of companies and what kinds of people do you wish to work with?
4. Be *patient* as you begin to learn about your passion.
5. Change is scary at first.
6. Implement your plan in the proper order.
7. Explore your categories of *interest*; allow the "free spirit" within to direct you.
8. Treat your business contacts as carefully as your personal relationships.
9. *Mutuality* runs the world.
10. Keep tabs on your fears; be aware if they are hindering you.
11. Affirm your worth to yourself.
12. Marketing yourself is based on problem-solving.
13. The best jobs are never advertised; they are in the mind of the

man or woman with the problem.

14. Enthusiasm activates curiosity.
15. Look at the world of work comprehensively.
16. As you complete the assignments at the end of this chapter, allow your natural interests free play. Do not be afraid to couple the familiar with the unfamiliar. Use the telephone Yellow Pages indexes. This simple research assignment increases your knowledge of the world of work.
17. Make a list of all the people you already know in your "passion." Can you think of any others who may know people in these fields?
18. Join together with others who are doing what you are doing in a community support group.

5

HOW TO FIND YOUR NICHE

You now have a good understanding of your strengths, values, and interests. You are ready for Step Five to finding your passion: discovering the right work relationship, and the right company size and structure for you.

Passion Secret #5:
Powerful people know how to find their niche.
They follow their passion.

First, let us examine the three types of relationships in any working environment: partnership, team, and solo. Each of us has an individual way of working. Just as flowers prefer certain environments, people flourish in compatible relationships. A blooming flower that is well planted and properly nourished is *working with passion*. Let us find out what kind of environment you will best flourish in — and what relationship type you are most in alignment with.

THE PARTNERSHIP

Would you be happiest in a partnership? Working in tandem with one other person in an equal give-and-take relationship requires two people with great sensitivity and balance. Moreover, a partnership works only if both individuals are mature, self-confident, and happy to see the other become successful. The personality of the partner type displays these characteristics:

1. The partner loves and needs give-and-take feedback in conversation and decision-making processes. ("What do you think?")
2. Forms intimate, long-lasting friendships with a select few. Is equally balanced between liking to be alone and with one other.
3. Finds that *creativity increases* in the confines of a trusted relationship.
4. Is self-reliant (paradoxical, but true).
5. Is an excellent listener. *Enjoys* hearing the partner's ideas and concepts.
6. Likes pooling resources: money, ideas, property, knowledge; feels more powerful with shared riches.
7. Sees relationships as shared independence between equals. Is uncomfortable with authoritarian relationships.
8. Thrives on encouragement from the partner (not necessarily from others).
9. Likes to share risk-taking with the partner.

If the above profile fits you, and your present occupation requires that you work alone or with a team, you have not yet found the right relationship in your work. Other clues that can indicate your "partnership" personality: you married early; you have always had one close friend, even as a child; you share easily with a trusted individual. You are happiest when paired, in romance, in sports, at dinner, etc. Also, you are fascinated with duos of any kind, in love, work, or play. Famous man/woman teams intrigue you, and you would like to be part of one yourself. (Remember these are simply clues, not hard and fast rules.)

A successful partnership involves not only a willingness but a strong desire to include the other. In fact, you perform at your best when creating together. It is a rare and beautiful flower you become if you are a partner type and can find the right partner.

A TEAM ENVIRONMENT

The individual who flourishes in the team environment is a specialist at whatever he or she does. This individual enjoys the camaraderie of the larger group, where decision-making conversation is spread around: Plenty of discussion, consensus agreement, and the group's benefits are all highly regarded by the team type. The team works for each member who is willing to play his or her part and play it well. The team player enjoys the rivalry between and among other departments and companies, valuing the team within the larger framework. The team type personality exhibits these attributes:

1. Loves competition and rivalry as a motivator.
2. Forms many friendships easily. Is gregarious and outgoing.
3. Responds to a good leader. Comfortable with authority figures who are competent.
4. Finds that creativity increases with abundant praise from teammates and leader.
5. Sees relationships as cooperative units within a larger structure.
6. Is conscientious, loyal.
7. Is sociable, likes to belong to clubs, groups, organizations.
8. Likes to be alone about twenty percent of the time. Most of the time, likes companionship.

9. Likes to share risks with team and leader.

As a team type, you wilt without comrades to share your defeats and victories. Loneliness is your biggest fear. You are right at home when your career serves your need for stimulation and excitement. Other clues to the team player: as a child you played with a group of friends; you came from a large family, or you had early positive experiences with large families; you can maintain several relationships at once: lovers, friends, etc. You love team endeavors — in sports, in success stories of large corporations. You prefer to use your talents to help a team win.

The team player thrives in cooperative, competitive, stimulating environments. You are a lusty, hardy, cheerful flower when you are on the right team.

SOLO

Are you happiest when you are completely in charge? Do you like to make all the decisions? The solo type likes to say, "I did that." "That" can be the company he or she builds, or the sale made, or the book written. The key to this personality is the desire to wear all the hats. The solo strongly resists outside influence, does not feel comfortable on teams or in partnerships unless he or she can maintain personal autonomy. Since the solo type needs little group contact for feedback, the tendency is to be a lone wolf. The personality of the solo type displays these qualities:

1. The solo type is resourceful, self-contained. Prefers to make all decisions, likes privacy.
2. Is highly creative, finds that *creativity increases* with freedom! Inventive, imaginative, artistic; a thinking, contemplative mind.
3. Is independent, fiercely so. A risk-taker.
4. Carefully chooses friendships; selects other independent types

for associates and friends.

5. Strongly resists any authority. The more freedom, the better.
6. Enjoys working alone; personal thoughts, ideas, and time to ruminate are precious commodities to the solo type.
7. Sees all relationships as individual, unique, one-on-one.
8. Feels that the act of creation itself is the most important stimulant for further creativity. Takes praise for accomplishment with easy grace. Surprisingly, the truly talented solo is grateful, not arrogant.
9. Picks an independent marriage partner — another solo.

You can see from the above description what a tragedy it is for the solo type to be in a large, highly structured company or organization (unless he or she is president!). If you are a solo, you like to make up the rules as you go. Other clues: As a child you were extremely imaginative, daydreaming a great deal; you had imaginary playmates, pets; you had great powers of concentration; you love nature — being alone in the woods is your idea of heaven; you were on stage alone as a performer; you are drawn to individual sports; the singular, the unique individual, the star fascinates you; you had early experience with entrepreneurism; you made your own money early. You are the flower with a deep tap root, whose blossom permeates society with a lasting, ever-renewing beauty and impact.

These three types — partnership, team, and solo, are *not* mutually exclusive. For example, a solo can work within a partnership if the other individual is similarly iconoclastic and freedom-loving. Such a pair of individuals would not exert control or restriction. The same is true of the team type, with one difference: the solo would probably emerge as the natural leader.

It is not uncommon to be a combination of types — but knowing which type you are *more in alignment with* helps you to define your goals and your passion more accurately. It is rewarding and useful to discover what type you are — you like knowing it, as do others. And this knowledge is essential in helping you to find your "niche."

CHOOSING ALTERNATIVES

Let us assume you presently hold a position in a company but are not totally satisfied with your working environment. You have three alternatives available: (1) you can decide to remain where you are, either in the same position, or in a new one; (2) you can choose another company; (3) you can decide to start your own business, whether in a partnership or on your own. The ideas and techniques discussed so far plus those yet to come enable you to become successful in whatever route you choose — as long as you are choosing it with passion!

Over the past decade, I have noticed a strong trend toward entrepreneurship. Women, especially, are striking out on their own. Yet many people think that owning their own business is an impossible dream. (Not so!) Every client I have worked with scores as being *venturesome* on psychological profile tests. They are risk-takers. You are too, or you would not be reading this book.

If you work for a company, whether large or small, remember that the structure of a full-fledged successful business is an excellent training ground for you, whether you are a career person on the way up or a budding entrepreneur. You learn about what works: what "works" in business is to make a profit. Profits are what make stockholders and owners happy. And profits, wisely invested, produce business expansion and create even more jobs. So here is your first lesson about niches: pick one that works. Stay away from dying industries.

Read the weekly business journals to learn which companies and industries are on their way up, which are solidly entrenched, and which are on their way down. Dying industries are strike-ridden, cumbersome, and out-of-date in their marketing approaches. In your own city you can find small companies whose owners are building their organizations with passion! Check your chamber of commerce

— make some inquiries.

A well-managed business will teach you about pragmatism — a word that means "what works." You will also learn about marketing: the promotion and sale of the product or service is the root of an enterprise — nothing happens until a sale is made. Additionally, you will learn about timing (impatience is the number one problem in business, as one executive told me), finance, politics, and relationships. A poorly managed business will teach you the same lessons, but faster. You will find you do not have to stay around so long to learn them!

PRODUCTIVITY

Without productivity, a business fails. Without productivity, an employee or owner becomes dissatisfied, as well as the customers. Productivity results from genuine interest. Some people are productive no matter where they work because they have an interest in completing whatever they set out to do. They are internally motivated, seeing a task as meaningful in itself. However, the commitment to complete tasks only goes so far with anyone. Beyond that, we all want other rewards, such as financial compensation or personal recognition.

You will be productive if you *love* what you are doing. For example, if you work in a chocolate-chip cookie factory and love chocolate-chip cookies, you will communicate that love to the owner, your co-workers, and the customers. You will all have fun producing a product you love personally. This applies to any product or service. (Did you ever wonder why people who are financially independent continue to work when they really do not have to? The answer is that they are having fun.) *Passion clue*: Ask yourself what product or service you buy that you *love*.

You will know you are productive by your use of the hours you spend working, or by how much you are absent or late. Many people do not enjoy what they are doing so they make the hours go by with endless meetings, coffee breaks, lunches, and daydreaming.

STAY IN THE NICHE YOU LOVE

Sometimes a promotion will *lessen* an employee's productivity. A classic example is someone who performs superbly at a given task and then is promoted to supervise and motivate others who now do what he or she used to do. However, managing others' productivity requires an entirely different set of skills, not necessarily natural for the peak performer. Let us say that you make the best hamburgers in a restaurant, and because you are so skillful, it is now assumed that you should supervise the other hamburger makers. You do not get to do what you love anymore, and the frustration of watching others fumble as they learn drives you crazy. This is a simplified analogy of the chain of promotion in most companies. The end result is called the "Peter Principle," a description of what happens when a person is promoted beyond what he or she does best, and loves best.

We have all been told to be upwardly mobile: "Keep moving, be a comer, run on the fast track." Big companies constantly need managers, and usually they are sought internally first, and then externally only if necessary. Most people naturally want both the prestige of a new title and the opportunity to earn more money. But the chosen individuals often give little thought to whether the new job satisfies their basic needs and values, values that may change as they grow older.

We need to become aware of the multitude of opportunities that surround us. It may be possible to find the right position in your present company. Or you may have to take the time to research other possibilities while still working full time at your job. You should understand that your career growth is not dependent on moving up in your company — it depends only on how effectively you *remove the limitations* that prevent you from discovering your "niche."

JIM'S STORY

Let us look at a few examples of people who removed their limitations, and see how they did it. The first example is a marketing manager I will call Jim, who told me that his most valuable experience occurred when he had to deal with a difficult and conniving associate.

"I couldn't 'read' him. He was friendly to my face, he said I was doing superb work — which I knew I was — and he seemed very happy with me. Then I'd overhear phone conversations where he'd run me down and blame me for every failure in the region," Jim said. He became so ill from an ulcer that he began looking outside the company for a new job.

"Anything was better than being around him. Then I learned he'd been setting me up to be the fall guy in some very unethical dealings he was involved in. That's when the light went on for me. Guys like this are very manipulative, making you always doubt yourself. It was devastating."

Once Jim "read" the destructive manager's game plan, he could outmaneuver him. "It gave me great pleasure to turn the tables on him — not because I wanted to 'get' him, but because I found that when my self esteem returned to normal, I was already one step ahead of him. I could predict what he would do. That felt great!" he said.

There was a happy ending for Jim. After one too many unethical moves, the destructive manager got fired. (Do not count on this to happen for you to be happier — notice that Jim changed his thinking *before* the firing.) He eventually ventured out on his own into a partnership with an old friend who worked in the same company. Later on, Jim went out on his own. Here you see that part of Jim's problem can be traced to lack of self-knowledge; he was a solo-type misplaced in a team and partner environment.

"Now that I look back on it, that experience with the manager — and the partner — was worth the ulcer. Both taught me more about myself than ten personal growth workshops!" he recalled. Here we have a good example of how to turn a problem into an opportunity.

You may find that your niche is in a smaller organization. It is very important to know what size fits your temperament. For Jim, having a partner to have fun with in his new business seemed to be the optimal choice. In the corporation where they formerly worked, they went through many trials together and had developed trust in one another. But his true destiny was being in complete control. As I said earlier, looking at yourself is scary, but the payoff is finding your right niche.

INDIVIDUAL VALUES AND BUSINESS SUCCESS

In his book, *The Entrepreneur's Manual*,[1] Richard White says that the person who succeeds in business must have intellectual honesty — the ability to see things as they are, not as she or he wants them to be. Moreover, the *values* of a person must be in harmony with the venture or it is doomed to failure, no matter how good the product or service, according to White. For example, if a manager of a fine art gallery does not believe in the life-enhancing aesthetic value of painting, sculpture, ceramics, etc., he or she is unlikely to make the gallery a success.

White works as a consultant with venture capitalists, people who represent companies interested in investing their capital in budding enterprises. Because good management of these young companies is crucial to their development, the venture capitalists, who want a handsome return on their investments, research the management team carefully. Before investing money in the venture, the backers evaluate the personal values and maturity of the management staff — if the staff is felt to be unsuitable, the venture capitalists will help the company owners replace them or add other good people. Venture capitalists must be good at spotting when a person's values are at odds with his or her work, or they risk business failure.

Because the world of work is vast, talented people sometimes have difficulty making choices precisely because they are able to do so many things. That is why the work on your needs and values must be continually reviewed (see Chapter Two). Once you have started the process of finding your niche, you become inundated with possibilities. This should remove any fears about scarcity. There are two ways to look at the possibilities on earth: (1) They are contracting and shrinking — therefore my chances are scarce. (2) They are expanding and growing — my chances are based on abundance. Give the process of finding your niche the time it needs to develop. Finding the right job is a lot like romance. You may have to give it several tries before you get it right.

ED'S STORY

"The day came when I said to myself, enough is enough," recalled Ed, formerly a personnel executive with a major bank. Ed, forty, realized he was not having fun anymore — the thrill was gone.

"At first, you think it's the bank's fault, the institution. Now I know better. It was me. I learned I simply had to control more of my own destiny," he said.

Ed recently celebrated his third anniversary in his own consulting business. He says he will never go back to the corporate world. The change was not easy, because Ed had to give up the security of a paycheck and the society of his comrades.

"I planned for over a year to go out on my own. I've been in personnel most of my working life, selecting and directing people. I felt I had the ability to do whatever I wanted, but I had to structure the economics first. Giving up a secure income without a replacement takes some thought," he observed. And his first months were rough and lonely.

"The hardest thing for me at first was the lack of a team. On your own, you are the resource," he said. *(See the solo need outweighing the team need?)*

Finding out what motivates him has been the most exciting part of starting his own business. Ed says that the management consulting activity he is involved in allows him to solve problems in a variety of ways. And the variety really turns him on.

"Just knowing that you can't be sure of the outcome of the meeting with a management team is exciting. Sometimes there are so many problems you hardly know where to begin. I started one project to recruit some staff and wound up structuring and implementing the management team's career path strategy: timing, income, training, everything," he said.

Ed admitted honestly that he had remained in the wrong slot for too long. "The bank is better off with people who want the structure, the security, the organizational backup. That's not for me, not anymore."

Ed said that his next problem will probably be having more business than he can handle! His urge to be his own boss illustrates the cycle of his personal growth, cycles that we all experience.

YOUR NEEDS MAY CHANGE

According to Rich White, the consultant and author mentioned earlier, "A creative worker is troubled when his organization no longer rewards his innovation. Profit maximization is great for the stockholders but can be restrictive for the creative, do-it-yourself-a-different-way types. They get restless, start thinking about change, and usually quit or get fired with fireworks.

"It doesn't matter how much money they're making, either," White says. "If they're not getting their needs met on the job, they'll try to meet them some other way, not always constructively." Ulcers, heart trouble, drinking — it is tragic what happens to people when they do not like the work they are doing. Emotional problems assume reasonable proportions when you love your work. It is amazing how many problems disappear when my clients finally find their niche!

Both Ed and Rich White advise that you remain in your present position as long as possible while you are researching new opportunities, absorbing new ideas, and implementing new goals.

"You learn patience working in an organization. Business is a game and a good one compared to some others. Your decisions and plans may take months, even years. When you get enough confidence in your own decision-making abilities, you'll venture out into no man's land," observes White.

KEVIN'S STORY

Your right niche may be *right where you are.* First you need to define whatever is making you uncomfortable. A social or personal conflict may be the source of your problem, not the job itself. Kevin's situation was a good example — here was a young man who confused his needs. He came to me for help with finding the right niche. At twenty-seven, he did his job well and was moving along fast in his chosen field, selling top of-the-line outdoor sporting equipment.

From my perspective everything in his career path looked fine.

"What's the problem?" I asked.

"I'm running out of time. It seems like I need to think more about the future, and I've noticed I'm not enjoying my work anymore," he said.

I had Kevin do some of the assignments in this book, to reveal more specifically where the trouble was. The results showed enormous anger and resentment. Kevin's drive to change his niche was unusual because he was successful in a field he enjoyed. But we found out that his anger and resentment were the result of his childhood experiences. He told me he was not allowed to pick out the college he went to, and he rarely had the opportunity to make important choices in his life. Yet his assignments showed strong self-reliance in the decision-making area. He was self-sufficient, not group dependent; he was venturesome, not shy. During his childhood his wealthy parents had assumed he needed to be cushioned, and they made nearly all his decisions for him. Kevin complied because he believed then that his parents knew better than he did.

Sometimes parents take away some of the arenas for testing that strengthen young character. Children who do well in adult life often have had early experience in making decisions. They learn first that they can make a decision. Second, they learn not to be *afraid to choose*. Third, they learn that no matter what decision they make, *more good than bad* comes from it. Essentially, you learn to trust yourself and to trust the perfection of your experience, whatever that experience turns out to be.

Kevin also tended to be suspicious, demanding, and impatient. He felt that people were always on the verge of taking advantage of him. His fear about "time running out" was a good indicator of his basic belief about himself: he could not "make it" alone. The fact that he was successful did not affect his belief. He was expecting failure, programming it in fact, and, with his growing suspicion and anger, he was bound to lose what he already had.

The solution for Kevin began as his self-awareness increased. He saw from the results of his assignments that he was self-reliant and did not want anyone making decisions for him. He liked making them for himself. The information showed how he compared to others. An objective analysis, such as Kevin received, showed him that he was unusual and talented. Because he liked his *real* image, his enthusiasm, interest, and faith increased.

Kevin realized that he was mad at his parents (and also at any authority figure) because he thought they never let him make his own choices (the Victim). But he learned that he was capable of choosing wisely, and consequently lost his fear of failure (the Victor). He had been afraid — at a deep level — that he could not make it on his own. How could he disbelieve all the evidence to the contrary in his present job? Because unconsciously he carried a childhood belief that he would get just so far, and then fail. This is an example of the internal struggle between the voices of the Victor and the Victim within each one of us that I discussed in the preface. Sooner or later, one voice wins. In Kevin's case, he resolved the past and the Victor won.

Kevin's niche was right where he was, and he stayed there. He is happy now that he knows his problem was not connected to his job. Many people think their present dissatisfaction means total change is called for. Before you quit your job, analyze your relationships, analyze your own "type." You may find opportunity right where you are! Work management, like life management, is a course that never ends. We all have to continue to go to class, take tests, and discover the answers that work.

JO'S STORY

One woman who discovered that her work was harmonious with her relationship type was Jo, the only female vice-president in a large telephone company. She says the corporate world satisfies her inner needs. Jo likes her job — supervising 18,000 telephone operators — because she gets to take the risks inherent in management, and at the same time work with a team.

"If I had my career to do over again, I'd take a lot more risks a lot earlier. It took too long for me to realize how good I am," she laughs. Jo gives the credit for her enlightenment to a supportive boss. For that reason, and others, the company has been right for her.

"I had helped many fast-track male managers move up the corporate ladder. When my boss asked me how I'd feel about helping a woman move up over me, I reacted by deciding that it was time to put myself 'out there'. Suddenly everything was different. I realized how competitive I am. The company wasn't keeping me back, I was keeping myself back," she said. After that conversation with her manager, she went after an upper management career.

Jo encourages self-scrutiny, especially for women on the way up. She thinks women should understand how much time it takes to become an effective manager.

"I spend an enormous amount of time for my company — dinners, meetings, conferences. It suits me, but it may not be worth all the effort for some. You need to continually ask yourself some searching questions," she observed. (Her love of the team, the chance to shine within the large structure, means that she willingly makes the necessary compromises. The solo and partner types are less inclined to do this.)

The "searching" questions that Jo alluded to were these:

1. How much time do I want to devote to my job?
2. How will I feel when important personal plans conflict with business obligations?
3. Is this job one I *really* want to keep doing?
4. Do the benefits outweigh the liabilities?
5. Do I belong in this company?
6. Do I like this product or service?
7. Am I doing all I could do, using all my potential?

Much of Jo's work involves the establishment of work environments that meet employee needs for on-the-job training. That challenge is highly rewarding, she says. Since one of the basic purposes of her company is to foster human communication, the corporate values are in harmony with her own. There are abundant opportunities for advancement and recognition, which are major needs for Jo.

"Each of us has the opportunity to make change happen if we're willing and able to begin the change within ourselves. Once I realized that I was standing aside for men, I found plenty of opportunity to advance. There are always problems to solve," she said.

Jo likes to encourage women to take more risks, to learn how to be powerful and forthright. "Most of all, women in business need to know that it's okay to laugh. I sometimes think today's career woman takes life too seriously. If you can't laugh at yourself, as well as at events, the trip won't be worth the fare," she commented.

Jo is beginning to think about her future alternatives. When her corporate role ends, she says she might have to try her hand at her own business. "I'd make a heck of an entrepreneur. It would be fun to take those kinds of risks."

Most people want the chance to make a contribution to their organization, but sometimes they have simply picked the wrong type of organization in which to achieve recognition.

Your niche might be a "where" problem, not a "what" problem. Jo says that when you are fed up with your job, have the courage to leave and find something else. She says the security of the telephone company keeps many people there who would be better off in another job. For her, the first choice, over thirty years ago, was the right one.

Change is scary. There is tremendous internal and external pressure to maintain the status quo. But security and certainty are no match for the rewards that come with doing what you really want to do. You will have all the security you want when you use your talent in the right career.

THE PUBLIC SECTOR?

For many people, work in the nonprofit or government fields is a fulfilling niche. Unlike the private sector, where businesses generate their own income from sales, the public sector relies on donations or taxes (private or government funds) for income. The amount of income delegated to any project depends on political judgments about the *social* value of the programs and the competition for available funds.

The fields are vast — health care, the arts, libraries, law enforcement, and all government at the city, county, state, and federal levels. Good, solid, beneficial, and satisfying careers are available to those who wish to be part of a public organization. There are numerous opportunities even in a small city for public service.

ADRIAN'S STORY

One city manager told me that her job was like being an orchestra leader. She did not have to know how to play all the instruments but she had to know how to get them to play together. This function fascinated her. She had been active in politics since she was a teenager and had studied political science in college. Her passion was consistent with her work.

During her senior year in college, Adrian interned with city managers and fell in love with the dynamic interplay that occurs among competing interest groups. She particularly liked the city council and city manager relationship because it kept her in touch with local concerns. Another factor that appealed to her was the public relations work — talking to the members of the press and other media representatives. Since the job was close to the roots of local government, she was able to maintain a close circle of contacts in her community.

Additionally, Adrian found out that the real function of a city manager is to act as an advisor. This position was a perfect personality fit for her. A student of human nature, she was challenged by the daily problems that related to the political decision-making process.

"We're all just human beings trying to gain what we see to be our fair share of resources. Tax money is limited. I perform a balancing act to oversee the fair distribution of those resources. It boils down to the question, What's fair?

"Government service can be extremely rewarding. Recently I helped persuade city residents and the city council about the benefits of constructing low-income units for older adults. This project is close to my heart because of what I've seen the cost of housing do to those on fixed incomes. We need to do what we can locally to help seniors. Communities must take the initiative and assume the responsibility for solving their own problems," she insisted.

As you can see, Adrian, a "team" type, is in harmony with her values, social relevance, and altruism. She can use the vehicle of political action to create results that are important to her. Her long-range goals include more in-depth work with the aged.

"I feel that one of our greatest resources, the wisdom of the older person, is being ignored. I want to help educate the community to the worth of the years after sixty-five," she said.

The resources of our vigorous older population are too great to be wasted. They also are passionate — and are already taking the initiative in researching how they can be useful in society. Many older adults are active in the community now — doing both volunteer and paid work.

Government and agency work require a special kind of leadership. The opportunities are there for those who have a clear vision and the *patience* to work through the maze of committees and appointed officials — otherwise known as the bureaucracy. Yet the rewards are well worth it, as Adrian will attest.

JAMES' STORY

"It's worth it if you can keep your eye on the results. They may not be exactly what you had in mind, but change does occur, although slowly," commented James, who is a director of finance in a health systems agency, with a Ph.D. in Public Administration. Like Adrian, James was drawn to government work through his studies in college. His field of interest was budget management, and he finds he enjoys organizing, forecasting, and distributing government funding. James' work is at the county level and his job brings him into contact with state and federal agencies, funding sources, and hospital administrators.

"Health care is a growing field and I like being involved in helping the providers (hospitals and nursing homes) achieve their objectives. The problems revolve around cost containment, so I use my strengths in budgeting, providing financial information that is vital to any program's success. I also teach public administration courses at the masters' level to health care specialists. In this way, I stay informed about the latest developments. I love teaching, and the health care field is full of opportunities. New blood, pardon the pun, is always needed," he laughed.

According to James, the practice of medicine will be more entrepreneurial in the future. This is because insurance companies and government sources of funds will seek the most competitive price for medical services of all kinds. Alternatives to expensive hospital treatment are already occurring. Small outpatient clinics are replacing hospital stays, for example, and the tremendous advances being made in medical technology are cutting costs and eliminating personnel.

James advises those who pursue health care as a passion to research the industry thoroughly before investing years of training into what may become obsolete in the future practice of the healing arts. "Talk to hospital administrators, physicians, technologists, nurses, and other health practitioners in your area. There will be opportunities, but only for those who are able to adjust to the idea of health care as a business. Actually, though the changes are disruptive now, the consumer will benefit economically from a more efficient, less wasteful system in the future," he said.

Both Adrian and James agree that the best way to determine whether government work is for you is to meet with public service professionals first, in an "advice call" approach.

"People in public service are very approachable, perhaps more so than the private sector," said Adrian. "I met with many city managers, mayors, city council members, and city employees before I decided that this field was right for me. I began as a staff member, did more than I was asked to do *(a key to success)*, met the editor of the local newspaper, and asked questions about the city. All were pleased that I was so interested in their interests. Mutuality of interest is the key."

"Government jobs are filled in a different way than the private sector, through eligibility lists and tests. However, you still need to inform yourself and know 'who's who' so you can enter at the level you want. Attend city, state, and other government meetings, write letters, and meet *good* people," James advised. "We all have the same objectives, whether or not we are elected. Our job is to respond to the public interest."

The public sector may be your best niche if you like the service aspect that such jobs provide. Get familiar with the people and activities and see if your enthusiasm and interest are piqued. Remember, you will know it is your niche if you are "in love," if you are fascinated, if it is your *passion*. Connect your passion with your work. Then you will do what powerful people do — you will know how to pick your niche.

SUMMARY

Passion Secret #5:
Powerful people know how to find their niche.
They follow their passion.

1. *Relationships* are the foundation of business.
2. What relationship type are you most like: *partner, team, solo?*
3. The key to productivity is to do what you love to do.
4. *Stay* in the niche you love.
5. What size company do you feel comfortable in? Small (less than twenty employees)? Medium (twenty to 500 employees)? Large (500 or more)?
6. Spend thirty minutes a day reading about various niches, jobs, or companies in which people have fun. You can learn from newspapers, magazines, books, and newsletters.
7. See the world of work for what it is: abundant with problems to solve — people problems, data problems, and object problems.
8. Spend a few minutes a day reflecting on your past choices. Did you think about your personality fit before you took your

current job?

9. Are you drawn toward entrepreneurism? If so, study it, learn about it. Are you blessed with intellectual honesty? Can you see things (people, places, events) as they *are* — not as you want them to be?
10. What about the public sector? Do you like politics?
11. Frequently readjust your plan as you learn more. Keep daily tabs on your feelings. Self-scrutiny is like fine-tuning a precision instrument — you!
12. Do you feel confident with your decisions? Do you like making decisions? Are you happy with your past decisions? What would you change?
13. What could you do to solve problems right where you are?
14. Do you think because you are a woman that you must make way for men? Do you think because you are a working woman that you have to be serious? Do you laugh frequently — with good, open humor?
15. Do you think because you are a man that you have to be serious? Do *you* laugh frequently — with good, open humor?

THE GREAT VALUE OF RESEARCH

Step Six to finding your passion is learning how to do research on the organizations and people you want to know more about. To find accurate information, you must know where to look. In this chapter you will use easily available information to glean enough knowledge to approach the individuals you are going to meet. The purpose of your research is to acquaint you with the current developments in the fields of work you would enjoy learning about. You will be locating specific organizations and people within those organizations from your top six categories of work (completed in Chapter Four).

Passion Secret #6:
Powerful people enjoy the process of research; then they act and move ahead on the information they have.

Their tolerance for uncertainty and their ability to move forward on the basis of incomplete information set them apart from more cautious people. Successful people earn respect from others because they do not seek perfect certainty before they act. They listen to their *feelings* about data, then act on those feelings.

You may remember times when you got caught up in the process of looking and never took any action. A Saturday's shopping trip to a large mall can be like that. There is so much merchandise — so many brands, styles, colors, so many things to choose from. After two hours of shopping, your senses are so overloaded that your only goal is a quick departure.

For powerful people, the process of looking is intriguing in and of itself. They have a great desire to know and they remain open to information. They learn to quickly sort out what is not useful. They pace their acquisition of information, remaining conscious of details and how those details fit into the larger picture.

Let us look at another definition of power. *Power is the knowledge that your decisions are based on your free choices.* There is a big difference between being power-motivated and having personal power. Power-motivated people rarely keep whatever power they do achieve. They lose this power because others who helped them "get there" take away their support. Remember the concept of mutuality? (Two or more people with similar interests.) When you violate that concept enough times, when you take more than you give, a boomerang effect begins. It may take weeks, months, or years, but it will come around. And the mighty (and power-motivated) fall.

If power is the ability to take action, doing effective research gives you the confidence to take action. When you know what is really going on in any situation, you make fewer mistakes of judgment. That is your goal — to get it right this time; accurate information, rather than a blind leap, ensures that you will do the work you love, have associates that are fun to be around, and make all the money you and your family need. When you take your time to do your homework, you are free of the stress that comes from the frustration of not doing a thorough job.

In Chapter Four, you read about Jane, who wanted to find a job as a negotiator. I touched briefly on how she implemented her plan (which led her to her passion — a career in shipping and maritime law). Let us review these four preliminary steps:

1. Identify your marketable strengths.
2. Identify your relationship type.
3. Do your research on the organization.
4. Call the companies for information.

STEP 1: IDENTIFY YOUR MARKETABLE STRENGTHS

Jane identified her marketable strengths, and then reviewed and memorized those strengths until she knew them as well as her own telephone number. She also knew her values; she knew her requirements for a work setting, and she decided what kind of people she wanted to associate with. Knowing the kind of people you want to work with is extremely important!

You discovered your strengths when you wrote about your pleasures in life (Chapter Two). Remember, you use your personal strengths automatically when you are intensely interested in what you are doing. Similarly, you will know your values (as Jane did) if you filled in the blanks in Chapter Two where you narrowed your choices to five values.

STEP 2: IDENTIFY YOUR RELATIONSHIP TYPE

Jane discovered that she liked being a partner and a team player, using her skill with people to create happy compromises. Working in harmonious surroundings gave her pleasure and increased her performance. Ironically, you spend more time with the people you work with than with the person you marry. Yet most people take a job based on just two or three interviews. It is like the girl who looks and looks for "her man" and finally just accepts one without giving it any serious thought. It is a crazy way to pick a partner. And work is essentially a partnership involving relationships — between yourself and others who choose to do similar work. We rarely think that we have that much choice in a career. But you do, you can, and you will have that much choice, once you see how the personality fit plays an integral role in your work choice.

STEP 3: DO YOUR RESEARCH

Take the time to do your research on the organizations you want to know more about. When you know the answers to the questions — who, what, where, when, how, and why — you are ready to consider an offer. Until then, do not walk down the aisle.

Who: Find the names of the people who lead the field. What types are they? Partner, team, solo?

What: What is the actual business activity that generates the income? What is the organizational structure?

Where: Where are the geographic locations of the enterprise?

When: When was the business started? Is it a seasonal one?

How: How is the marketing of the product or the service done? How do they advertise their existence? How are the products created? How are the services performed?

Why: This is the most important question of all! Why does this organization exist? What market need does it serve — social, economic, philosophical, pleasurable, practical, aesthetic, intellectual? A combination of these?

Take out your completed Categories of Work assignment covered in Chapter Four and look at the areas that sparked your interest.

Look at the final cut — the top six categories that interested you. Take category one and think of all the facets of that one category. Let us say your top category is finance. How many different facets are there to finance? Literally dozens. Finance means many things, including the circulation of money, the granting of credit, the making of investments, and the provision of banking facilities.

You can see from this simple definition process the many avenues opening up for career possibilities in any field. Now that you have seen how finance was defined, do this with your top six categories. With a clear picture of the ways money is involved in the finance category, begin training your mind to create images and pictures. If finance is one of your top categories, how do you see yourself working with money? Are you exchanging it, circulating it, granting credit, making investments? Are you working in a bank? Are you a stockbroker?

One of my clients wrote an extensive analysis of all the jobs involving the production, marketing, and influence of a single book. I insert it here to illustrate the innumerable opportunities in the world of work, and to stimulate your imagination as you continue your research.

The Jobs Behind a Book

Begin with the tree: forester, plant geneticist, lumber workers in various categories, support systems for lumber workers (real estate sales, construction, civil engineers, heavy construction equipment — drivers, superintendents, sales, manufacturing, etc.). Industrial engineers, trucking (drivers, managers, sales, manufacturing thereof), entrepreneurs, financiers, banks, and credit institutions. Furnishers of food and housing for all these types. Legal services for all these types. Local, county, and state or federal government agencies.

The tree is on its way to the mill: buyer, paper engineer (paper chemist, civil engineer, industrial engineer), plant designer, various mill workers (skilled and unskilled), marketing specialist, clerical support services; financial, legal, and political support and/or regulatory in-house and outside systems; product designers working with customers and engineers to produce new and improved products, to maintain quality in current products, and to develop new production systems. Sales organizations, in-house and outside advertising agencies (artists, account executives, copywriters, management, and support services).

Meanwhile, back at the typewriter or word processor or computer or whatever, we have the stimulus for all this activity — the writer(s). Researchers, librarians, typists, literary agents, stationery and office supply stores (and all the buying and selling that involves), magazines, books on writing (and all the support systems that produce them — other writers, editors, publishers, sales forces, subscription services, artists, printers, type designers, etc.). Graphic support (artists, designers, typographers); support in necessary computer hardware and software; editors, publishers, sales and promotional support, TV and radio programming. Financial, legal, and clerical support systems for all this. Public relations and marketing specialists, trade publishers and publications, salespeople for the publisher, bookstore, library and book club buyers (decision makers), book reviewers.

Customers — lots of them with money in hand, an avid interest in the subject, and an abiding interest in telling other people to buy the book.

And, alas, we have the entrepreneurs who buy and sell or destroy publishers' remainders; the destroyed ones go back to pulp and into the cycle again.

If the book makes money enough for people involved along the way, we add travel agents, investment counselors and brokers, CPAs and tax specialists, real estate brokers, interior decorators, and all their support systems. And legal — the legal people are always with you, win or lose (contracts, copyrights, lawsuits, etc.; even until the end of the world, when they probably are in charge of arrangements with St. Peter).

Locate Companies in Your Interest Category

We are so bombarded with words that their precise meanings sometimes become obscured with time. Use your dictionary to look up the definition of each category you have chosen. Sharpen your mind by pretending that you have never seen the word before. You bring no preconceived ideas and are therefore open to a new appreciation of the word.

Next, apply your category of interest to specific companies or entities. You can use the index section in the Yellow Pages of your telephone directory, which is updated every six months.

Turn to the pages where your categories are listed, and select one of the six categories you have chosen. Now choose six companies or entities that are actively engaged in that activity. (You will eventually select six companies in each of the six categories so that you begin with what is called a "marketing sample" of thirty-six organizations — small, medium, and large. For now, however, I want you to concentrate on one of your categories.) At this point you will not know very much about most of the companies. Just pick any six at random.

Let us use finance as our example again. The six companies could include banks, investment organizations, stock brokerages, or financial positions within an organization, e.g., treasurer, controller, accountant. Make sure you vary your selections choosing small, medium, and large organizations.

This is an excellent time to call any friends and associates you may have and ask if they have any ideas or information about the organizations or people in your categories of interest. Ask them if any name (a person or a company) comes to mind for a good advice call candidate. Stress that your purpose is to arrange a conversational meeting, *not* a job interview.

STEP 4: CALL THE COMPANIES FOR INFORMATION

The next step is to call the companies and ask for whatever information is available to the public. This can be in the form of brochures, annual reports, or advertising material. A good part of any company's budget is spent on advertising. You can freely reap the benefit of these advertising dollars.

When you call a company for this purpose, ask for the person who is in charge of mailing annual reports or other information to the public. Sometimes you will be connected to the marketing department, other times to the treasurer's office or communications or public relations department. Introduce yourself by saying something similar to: "Hello, my name is ___________, and I'd like to have copies of your brochure, catalog, annual report or other advertising materials mailed to me."

If the company is *publicly* held — that is, if its stock is traded on one of the public exchanges — an annual report is available. If it is *privately* owned, financial information is not available. In any case, some kind of data is always available on a company. If you are asked why you want the material or what company you are with, just answer, "I'm doing some private research and am interested in learning more about your organization."

Be sure to ask for the name of the person you are connected to and make a note of it beside the company's name. Your purpose is to establish new contacts (relationships). Now you will know the name of at least one person who works for the company — a person who can help you. Be polite and interested in him or her. If your inquiries are met with hostility or suspicion, watch out! This reaction is a red flag signaling that this organization is not right for you.

When you receive the reports and other data in the mail, sit down and read each one carefully. You should be checking on the organization's sales volume, expenses, philosophy, presentation of product — all clues as to whether this company is right for you. Sometimes just reading the annual report indicates that this is not a good company to contact. Use a marker pen to underline things of interest, and make notes. Imagine yourself working for this company. Would you be pleased with their image? Does it match yours?

After receiving between five and ten responses, you will be ready to approach a representative of a selected company that interests you.

The most valuable information comes from talking to experts in all areas of work. Many highly successful careers are built in small organizations as well as big ones. It is not always true that bigger is better. The best opportunities for personal and professional growth come from exposing yourself to the right kind of mentality and philosophy for you. Many innovative and dynamic teachers and mentors can be found in small to medium-sized organizations. Generally, the people in smaller companies like to wear many hats and are acquainted with all aspects of the business. They tend to be generalists, not specialists. Perhaps you like to specialize. You do not have to choose associates at this point. At this stage of your self-marketing process, you are looking for where to put your talent, not whom to get to pay for it.

ESTABLISHING NEW CONTACTS

Let us continue with our example of finance and review the entire process involved in researching one interest category, which is done primarily through establishing new contacts. It can be broken down into eight steps:

1. Identify six banks, investment houses, or other financial institutions.
2. Read your research data; there's much more available in the library. Use the resources list at the end of this chapter. Your librarian will help you.
3. Select a person to contact. Ask your friends, co-workers, and others for the names of appropriate people.

4. Write the person a carefully composed letter designed to arrange a meeting between you. (See Chapter Seven for guidance in this area.)
5. Follow up with a telephone call no more than four days after sending the letter.
6. Schedule an appointment (an advice call) with the person. The advice call is covered in detail in Chapter Eight.
7. Go to the appointment, which is designed to accomplish these three objectives: to make a self-presentation, to gather information, and to ask for referrals.
8. Write a thank-you letter to the person no later than the day following your meeting.

SELECTING A PERSON TO CONTACT

The next part of this chapter covers Step Three above: selecting a person to contact. But before examining the procedure, I would like to ask you to look at your list of affirmations, your "ten most wanted" list in Chapter Three. One of those affirmations should include a "want" that describes your future career. Did you describe in detail the kind of person or persons you want to work with? Now that you know what relationship type you are (from your work in Chapter Five), perhaps you had better write your affirmation again so that you are even better prepared to find your target. You can use the following blanks as a guideline to describe *your ideal* work environment.

My new associate(s) is/are perfectly compatible with the type that I am—_______________ (partner, team, solo). We recognize each other's special abilities and encourage, inspire, and support personal and organization growth. I use my _______________, _______________, _______________, _______________, and ____________ (top five strengths) and fulfill my _______________, _______________, _______________, _______________, and _____________ (top five values).

I discover my associate(s) with ease. It is fun to look, learn, and complete the process of research. My associate(s) is/are ______________, ______________, ______________, ______________, and ____________. (Enter the desired characteristics of the people you work with.)

It is useful to read this affirmation aloud every day, changing it to suit your needs. After the picture is clear, you will be ready to take some steps to locate the people you will want to meet in your area of interest.

This part of the process makes most people apprehensive because it brings up images of the future meeting, and you may not be sure yet what you are going to say, even though you will be well prepared for your encounters. The only attitude that works here is simply to go ahead and let yourself be scared. You will get over your apprehension after you have completed a few well-conducted meetings (or advice calls). Then you will be more confident in your approach. Remember, at this point I am just "walking" you through the process — relax and let me guide you.

Whatever work category you have selected, the chances are good that you already know someone in that area, or that you at least know someone who knows someone. Remember the concept of relationships? That is what contacts are. It is very helpful to *practice* the advice call technique with people you already have a connection with. If you were researching the finance area, you already undoubtedly have several contacts, such as your banker or your local branch bank manager. He or she knows the community very well, and probably belongs to clubs or organizations that increase his or her value as a resource. Remember to ask your friends for ideas.

How do you select a person to write to when you do not know anyone in the company? First, decide on the department or area of interest. Do not write to the president of a large company. Focus on the *section* of the company that interests you and identify the person who is most knowledgeable about that section. Let us continue with our finance example. Call the company and ask for the name of the person who knows the most about, for example, commercial lending. The receptionists, secretaries, and other assistants are usually helpful if you keep the right tone in your voice (self-confident, warm, and polite). Always ask for the assistant's name. Next, ask for the name and correct title of the person you want to meet. If the assistant asks you why you want to know, say that you are writing a letter and want to verify the correct name and title.

Once a client of mine called a company for the name of a person in her area of interest, and had a stimulating conversation with the receptionist. The receptionist invited her to come by any time and indicated that she would be glad to talk to her! My client not only got the name of the right person to send her approach letter to, but in the process also established a good relationship with the receptionist.

In another instance, the phone call went right through to the person the client wanted to meet! Though she was unprepared for this, she kept her head and explained the reason for her call. Her "contact" agreed to meet with her, and asked when she would like to come in. Naturally, she did not have to write an approach letter, since she had already approached him by phone. Be flexible — use the process in your own way and to your own advantage.

Sometimes your attempts to locate the right person will not go well. Your attitude under these circumstances is crucial. Do not take rejection personally. Remember, the person who is giving you a hard time does not even know you, so it cannot be personal. When you are treated poorly by representatives of a company, it usually means the company is in trouble and the employees are reflecting that situation. On the other hand, repeated failure to establish contact may be a signal that, on an unconscious level, you may not really want the contact to occur. This is a good time to look at your pleasure assignment (Chapter Two) and see if you have really pinpointed your passion. If it is right, the pathway will almost always clear for you. If it does not, you may have gone after what seemed to be an obvious choice, and missed a better (though perhaps more subtle) choice.

If the first person you talk to is not the right one, remember that eventually you will be referred to the person who can help you. Stay relaxed — if you find yourself getting nervous, irritated, or tense, take a break. Come back to the process another day or even another week. It has been said that genius is perseverance in disguise.

The Approach Letter

Now let us discuss Step Four in our list: writing a letter to the person you want to meet. The letter itself is based on your knowledge of the person and company you want to know more about. In the next chapter, I go into much more detail about this letter. The title of the person you write to will vary, depending upon your focus of interest. Usually the president or owner of a small firm is most knowledgeable about the overall picture of the company. In larger companies, select the manager in the area of your particular interest.

I encourage clients to use advice calls internally — within their own company — before going outside. Sometimes the opportunities are right in front of you. A client who came to me thinking he needed to change companies found that his real opportunity was under the same roof; all that was necessary was a shift in his direction. We will call him Philip.

PHILIP'S STORY

Philip's story will show you how his approach letter led him back to where he was, and out again.

Philip felt he was the token minority in the company; he felt he was unappreciated, underpaid, and overworked. He had had his own business before he started to work for a large forest products company. His work was good, but his attitude troubled not only himself, but also his supervisors. He was creating an uncomfortable work environment because of what he *believed* about that environment. (Of course, many times the work situation is decidedly unsatisfactory. An objective look will help you decide what action to take.)

Philip went through the eight steps I just outlined and began meeting people in other companies. He found out that he was extremely marketable. His confidence rose. As his self-esteem grew, he noticed that "things" got better where he was. He was starting to have different beliefs about his environment.

"Everyone seems to be more cooperative than I've ever seen them," he said. "My supervisor spent a great deal of time with me the other day explaining her situation and the pressures she was facing. I didn't know the company was contemplating so many major changes. She even said she'd noticed a shift in my attitude and expressed appreciation at how cooperative I'd become!" he laughed.

This situation is not uncommon. The end of Philip's story proved to be a new beginning. As his self-esteem grew, he was receptive to other opportunities. His company offered him a $10,000 raise and a new title. He accepted the promotion, and sent each of the people he had met with in other companies a brief letter thanking them and letting them know the outcome of his search. In this way he maintained mutuality of interest and kept the relationships intact.

Few people realize the importance of doing this kind of research, not only to manage our careers properly, but to manage our lives properly. In Philip's case, he needed to increase his self-esteem, and in his job interviews he had the opportunity to see himself through others' eyes. Accurate information on how we are doing is very valuable, but unfortunately very rare. There is a form of mental and verbal blockage at work in our culture that encourages parents, spouses, supervisors, friends, and even lovers to withhold vital information from us. In case you doubt this, ask yourself how recently someone told you what a good job you are doing — in specifics you could accept. It seems that we are more inclined to offer criticism rather than praise.

This habit of withholding praise from each other may have its roots in our heritage — a belief that praise inflates the recipient in some way and is detrimental to the development of character. However, I find that human beings become miracle workers when they receive kind, generous encouragement. I have yet to see genuine praise create an egotist. It is the *lack* of enough praise and love that creates egotism.

Most powerful people have usually created a situation in which they receive plenty of praise for what they do well. At some significant stage in their growth and development, they received encouragement from others about themselves that inspired and uplifted them. If your life is devoid of praise and encouragement, you can become bitter, like Philip. Once he realized that others perceived his value and strengths, he became a more optimistic person.

Philip's story continued long after the first big raise. He devised such a good accounting system that the parent company became aware of his talent and asked him to consider a move back East. He came in to discuss the promotion with me, not sure if he should leave a stabilized position. He was apprehensive about what the attendant changes and move would mean to his family and home life. I asked him what he *felt* like doing.

"Inside, I really want to take it on," he said. "In two years I could come back, in line for a controller's job. There may be drawbacks in the new position, though. I'd be overseeing many people and I haven't done that before."

"Are you comfortable with the adjustment your family will have to make?" I asked, knowing his wife had an excellent job with a major retailer.

"They're very flexible and have no qualms," he said.

"Then what is the problem? I hope it's not your old negative self-image giving you trouble!"

Philip smiled and said he had carefully considered all his fears, and one kept popping up. "I guess I haven't conquered my fear of criticism yet, Nancy. I'm afraid if I don't do a good job, I'll disappoint everyone," he said.

"If you don't take the job, who do you think you'll disappoint?" I asked.

He thought for a few seconds and then took a deep breath. "Me," he said.

"And who's most capable of assessing your worth and evaluating the situation?"

"Me!" He laughed this time.

After we spent another twenty minutes or so developing the strategy to negotiate for his compensation, he made up his mind to take the position. He had taken another giant step. A year and a half later, he stopped by to tell me he had secured an even better position than that of controller. We had a fine reunion. Six months after that he came in, excited and smiling, with a plan for his own business.

"You've come full circle, Philip," I said.

He agreed and added that this time he knew exactly what he wanted; and what was even better, he understood what the experience of his last two years had meant for him.

"I finally realized that I was blaming everyone for the problem inside me. I kept trying to change everyone else to be what I needed to become, appreciative of myself. You can't be successful in business or life with that attitude, Nancy. The good Lord just took me on a journey to teach me that I needed to grow up, if I were to have my own business again. I was too arrogant and angry before, too. Now I see how wonderful people are."

"Including yourself, Philip," I said.

If you, like Philip, are contemplating a change, do not quit what you have until you have spent time looking outside and making comparisons. You may find that your present job can be changed more to your liking. People get bored with repetition and want new challenges to confront. Those challenges can be created in many ways. Keep your mind as open and as receptive as possible. Get your ego under control.

ASSESS YOUR ENVIRONMENT

Take a good look at your present environment. Write a short paragraph about all the people surrounding you in your daily life. Who inspires you? Who needs your praise and inspiration? Who uplifts you, informs you, and makes you think? If you are unable to think of anyone, you can see why your life is stale and joyless. It is time to find some inspiration. The word inspiration literally means to breathe in — do it! Breathe in the information, the stimulation, you need. All powerful people do.

SUMMARY

Passion Secret #6:
Powerful people enjoy the process of research; then they act and move ahead on the information they have.

1. It is very important to remain open to information.
2. Remember that powerful people are not the same as power-motivated people.
3. Learning to do effective research encourages you to take action.
4. Know your strengths and values as well as you know your address.
5. Learn how to discover information about organizations you are considering — who, what, where, when, how, and why.
6. Learn everything you can about your top six categories of interest.
7. Use research materials well. All are available in the business section of any library.
8. Talk to experts — people who do their work well.
9. Keep in mind that this process is a process.

10. Call companies for names of possible contacts. Read your local newspaper, journals, etc. to determine the names of those you would like to meet. Ask your personal associates for ideas and names.
11. Genius is perseverance in disguise. Take it easy. Time is relative; you always have *enough* time. The complete process will normally take a number of months.
12. Gather data to write your approach letter (covered in Chapter Seven).
13. Look inside your company. How would you improve it, what costs could you cut, what increases in sales could you help make? How could you increase efficiency?
14. Stay with your present job, in commitment and attitude, while you consider other opportunities. On the other hand, do not be afraid to voice your discontent.
15. Inspiration comes more quickly to you if you are inspiring to others first. We all need to give to others. Do it! Have a generous heart.
16. You are the best resource you have. Ask yourself who in your life makes you think, who inspires you to take action in your life? Where are your sources of strength and encouragement? For whom are you that source? Invest in self-development courses, seminars, speakers, books — whatever you find intriguing, whatever will assist you in developing your personal resources and talents.

Note: Ideas can come from the most unexpected sources. You may be casually reading an article in a magazine or newspaper that gives you the information you need, or the name of a valuable prospective contact. If you get excited during your reading or during a conversation with someone, pay attention! The excitement lets you know you are on the right track.

7

THE APPROACH LETTER

The writing of an approach letter is the seventh step on the path to your passion. As I said earlier, this letter allows you to approach and meet with all those people who share your interests — your passions! It is extremely powerful when done with care and enthusiasm.

When you are worried about how the recipient of your letter will react to you, expressing yourself clearly and naturally is difficult. You must keep reminding yourself that *you can write effectively if you write from your heart.* Writing is a craft that takes time to develop. If you did the autobiography assignment in Chapter One, you have gained confidence in your ability to write. This is another important reason for beginning your passion journey with a written autobiography — it is used as a tool by English and creative writing teachers to help students find their own unique means of expression. Writers have a Niagara of long-stored personal feelings about events in their lives that must be released. After the initial flood comes the still, reflective writing that is focused and clear.

The approach letter is designed to put you in contact with the people who will help you decide where you are going. An effective letter will put you in touch with effective people. So do not take any shortcuts — the penalty for taking shortcuts is mediocrity. Excellence requires extra effort — and the reward is fulfillment of your heart's desire.

Earlier, I talked about the concept of mutuality as connecting links of shared power. Mutually powerful people know how to make the connecting links from one point to another; they understand and implement the ideas I am describing to you in this book. Frequently these people are described as having "magnetic" or "electric" personalities. They indeed magnetize and draw people, ideas, and information to them.

THOUGHTS ARE ELECTRICAL

Electrical power is a good metaphor for the phenomenon of mutuality in an exchange of personal energy between two people. It takes the combination of positive and negative energy to turn on your lamp. Electrical wiring shorts out when too much strain is put on either the positive or negative energy. Personal relationships function in the same way because there are two electrical beings involved, transmitting feelings and thoughts.

A master electrician is a troubleshooter with any problem involving electrical wiring. One young and highly intuitive electrician told me that when she is called on to solve a wiring problem, she always starts at the meter and works her way back. I told her that her business was just like mine. I, too, start at my client's "meter" with a written autobiography; in this way, I begin at the beginning to uncover the source of problems (what you believe and how you think). You have started at your "meter" in the preceding chapters and have taken your "electrical" problem (your belief system) apart. You have learned about your strengths, abilities, desires. You are now ready to learn the secret of creating and maintaining relationships that last.

Begin to notice the electrical nature of your thoughts — how they transmit, how they actually create physical circumstances. Your daily thinking, consciously analyzed, will show you what thoughts and feelings fill your mind. Most of us hold in our feelings because we think we should not be feeling what we feel — boredom, anger, hatred, or envy, for example. But as soon as we judge our feelings, we stop the source of valuable information. In order to be truly passionate and focused, you must be honest emotionally, with yourself and others. As you prepare to write the approach letters that will lead you to the meetings with your contacts, pay attention to your thoughts and feelings. Are you excited, curious, scared, or indifferent? These thoughts transmit themselves to others. Allow your feelings to direct you. Identify any fear inside you, and deal with it constructively. It is the only thing standing between you and mastery of the next passion secret.

THE KEY TO SUCCESS

Passion Secret #7:
Powerful people know how to make and keep lasting relationships (contacts).

Most people fail to do the simple things in life — give a word of praise, write a thank-you letter, make a phone call, or invite someone to lunch or dinner. In contrast, successful men and women have an ongoing appreciation of those who helped them get where they are, and they always have time to foster their important relationships with others. And they know which relationships to end, as well.

Copy the behavior of focused people to get you where you want to go. Yes, it takes effort. But knowing how to connect with people will save you years of trial and error. One method for developing these new contacts is to write a letter to a man or woman you would like to meet. The approach letter is a good marketing tool. Based on genuine interest, you will learn to write the kind of letter that will get you in to see most of the people you wish to meet, but only if they share values similar to yours.

The letter is based on mutuality. Once you have mastered this concept, your self-confidence will soar. You will meet so many interesting people that you will wonder why you never explored this simple avenue to success before.

Remember, when you focus on your passion, your thoughts reach others who are also similarly inclined. Best-selling author Napoleon Hill calls this phenomenon the "master mind concept." Minds in harmony, with similar objectives, create a master mind, which is far greater than the sum of its parts. These letters and the follow-up meetings connect you with those who share your thoughts and passions.

By now you have lists of people and companies you would like to know more about. You have read annual reports and articles and now need a face-to-face verification of interest. Is this your niche? Is it a good fit? Your choice of a person to write to will depend on where you are in the process. Send your first three letters to people you already know. Even if you could pick up the phone and easily arrange to have lunch with them, try writing an approach letter instead. If you can practice this writing technique without much stress at first, you will be more relaxed.

Pick out three people you know. You could select your banker, a teacher, a lawyer, a businessperson. Think about each one. What do they do? What do they like? Sketch out a paragraph on them and their work, their successes, accomplishments, or hobbies. This exercise will encourage you to focus on the other person, rather than on yourself. *Their* interests are the key to creating the mutuality between you.

PETER'S APPROACH LETTER

One of my clients had a friend he frequently went sailing with, a man who worked for a major bank in the leasing department. I advised Peter to write his first approach letter to his friend John, as he was well respected in his field and easy to work with. Peter asked me how to approach his friend, since they were so well acquainted that a letter might seem odd.

"True, except that you want his advice on your career change and that's a conversation better handled in a more formal setting rather than on your boat," I replied. "You are interested in finance. That was one of your top six categories, so you'll be going to him to learn more specifically about what he does. His office is the right place for that."

Peter was a top salesman for a pharmaceutical firm selling medical testing services to physicians, and he did very well in his position until the company was acquired by a larger conglomerate. The home office had shifted from the West to the East Coast, and because there was now considerable delay in getting the medical results back to the doctors, the fine relationships Peter had built with physicians in his territory were endangered.

"I'm going crazy; all those years right down the drain!" he moaned.

Peter was conscientious enough to keep the communication channels open, to inform the doctors of the changes, but he realized that he no longer wanted to be a scapegoat for company decisions he could not control. The time was right to change his course. We worked on the first letter to his friend, concentrating on the bank, its future, and his friend's function.

"What has he accomplished there that he's *excited* about?" I asked. *(Passion clue!)*

"He told me that his big success was in competing with a much larger bank. His competitor uses the Chinese army technique. They have so many assets that they flood out the competition. My friend has developed personal contacts who want him to handle their accounts. His bank's standing is almost secondary in consideration to them. Several customers told him that even though the bigger banks were stronger financially, they lacked John's personal touch," he said.

"That's just what you've done, Peter, in your own situation. Remember how you told me the doctors selected you over bigger competitors because they knew and trusted you," I said. (Both Peter and his friend understand the importance of creating good business relationships.)

"Sure, we have a lot in common," he said.

"Let's put that in the first paragraph." Here is the opening we came up with:

> Dear John:
>
> You may wonder why I'm writing a letter to you, since I've known you for years and we have so much in common. I've always admired your ability in your work — the bank is more profitable because of you, just as I am better off just knowing you. You know how to listen, analyze, and come up with sound advice, both for me and your customers. No wonder your customers choose you: they see what I see.

That is the first paragraph — very personal and full of genuine appreciation. You cannot "fake" this approach. It is individual and focused. Read it aloud to see if it sounds like you are talking in a friendly and casual manner. (In a letter to a friend, it is acceptable to use the pronoun "I" as much as Peter did.)

In the next paragraph, Peter talked about himself. A few brief sentences described his background and what he has accomplished. Even though John knew Peter, he would need a phrase or two to get the gist of Peter's approach. I asked Peter what his top strengths were.

"I'm an excellent salesman, I know how to listen, and I get along with high echelon professionals as well as with most other people," he answered.

"Okay, what else?" I asked.

Peter paused and said he could put his skills into five phrases — he is a hard worker, a quick learner, attentive to detail, good at communication, and has good organizational skills.

"Because you understand marketing you know that John's job is basically the same as yours. You sell medical services and he sells money, true?"

"Exactly. So I should say that I know how to do what he does. Isn't that presumptuous?" he asked.

"Only if you say it wrong. Try this second paragraph."

> As you know, I've been considering a shift in my career. I've spent the last few months thinking about what I do best. I've had considerable success in selling — both myself and my products. I've been effective in varied situations, from leading my platoon in the war to convincing doctors I could solve their testing problems. I'm organized, communicate well, learn quickly, and pay attention to detail. Like you, John, I enjoy helping my company make a profit. Because I respect you and your field, I'd like to talk to you to ask some questions about how you market your financial product.

That is an example of a quick and easy way to communicate. It is honest, simple, and not presumptuous. Presumption is manipulative. That is why most business letters miss the mark. The writer expects a return. You must have no expectations, but rather create an ambience that *invites* results.

While you must be without expectations, you can still have an abundance of expectancy. There is a subtle difference between expectations and expectancy. With the former you expect a certain outcome. You make a contact, but because you are already holding predetermined results in your mind, the person you are meeting with often picks up those expectations and mentally backs away. You have not created the climate to encourage the results you wanted. All relationships founder on the rocks of expectations. Expectancy, on the other hand, is an open mental attitude — a knowledge that the outcome of any situation depends upon creating the proper environment in which the desired results are encouraged to come about.

Now that you have a stronger sense of your personal power, you are ready to create some results. You are well prepared and ready to go. But if you expect to be perfect in your first meeting, you will have trouble being satisfied with anything less. If you operate from "abundant expectancy," you know that you are going to do well whether or not you please others. That is the right attitude — with this frame of mind you can just be you. What is important is that you set up the experience that lets you know how you are doing. Remember Passion Secret number three: Getting there is all the fun. You are relaxed, yet prepared for whatever comes.

A well-written approach letter prepares you to hold a successful advice call. The advice call is covered in detail in the next chapter. For now, keep in mind that the letter prepares for the meeting in which you will learn about your potential passion. Although it is the face-to-face contact that creates an electrical exchange, the approach letter is the initial conduit of your energy to the recipient.

When Peter finished his letter, the last paragraph contained these words:

> I'll call shortly to arrange a meeting. I realize you are busy, so I'll take no more than thirty minutes of your time. I'm looking forward to seeing you.

With this last statement you maintain the initiative. You will call and arrange the meeting. Most people mail a letter to someone that says, "If you're interested, call me." And "they" never call.

The correct weight and color of personal stationery is important, an impression of quality and care. You are more likely to invite a favorable response when your letter is aesthetically pleasing. If your handwriting is good, handwrite the letter in business style — date, inside address, body of the letter, and signature. Put your return address on the outside. This style applies whether you are writing to a friend or someone new. This is what Peter's entire letter looked like:

34 Main Street
Your City, Anywhere
Date

Mr. John Smith
Manager, Leasing Department
Fortune Bank
123 Pine Street
Your City, Anywhere

Dear John,

You may wonder why I'm writing a letter to you, since I've known you for years and we have so much in common. I've always admired your ability in your work — the bank is more profitable because of you, just as I am better off just knowing you. You know how to listen, analyze, and come up with sound advice, both for me and your customers. No wonder your customers choose you: they see what I see.

As you know, I've been considering a shift in my career. I've spent the last few months thinking about what I do best. I've had considerable success in selling — both myself and my products. I've been effective in varied situations, from leading my platoon in the war to convincing doctors I could solve their testing problems. I'm organized, communicate well, learn quickly, and pay attention to detail. Like you, John, I enjoy helping my company make a profit. Because I respect you and your field, I'd like to talk to you to ask some questions about how you market your financial product.

I'll call shortly to arrange a meeting. I realize you're busy, so I'll take no more than thirty minutes of your time. I'm looking forward to seeing you.

Sincerely,

Peter Johnson

Peter followed up with a phone call four days after he mailed the letter. His friend was delighted with the approach.

"I'd really like to talk to you. Thanks for the letter; I was surprised but pleased!" he said.

They had a very productive advice call in John's office. Peter asked all the right questions (I cover these in the next chapter), keeping his attention on John and his work. I had asked Peter to imagine himself as a business reporter whose task was to write an informative piece about bank leasing after his meeting. He surprised John with his knowledge of leasing. Peter had read all the leasing material from the large competitor bank as well as from other sources. He was interested, informed, and enthused — and his attitude of "abundant expectancy" paid off.

"Peter, I never knew you were so interested in financial packaging. What about considering our bank for your career change? I know you're a hell of a salesman and we need marketing experts. Few of our financial people understand sales like you do," he said.

"John, I know sales, but finance is new to me," Peter replied.

"I could teach you that. Believe me, you know more than you think. In exchange, you could work with our staff on improving sales. This is a highly competitive field. Banking is not what it used to be, when your customers used to walk in to give you their business," he explained. "Now they carefully evaluate a bank before deciding to be a customer."

Peter held advice calls with three or four other people in the bank. He also met with representatives of John's competitor bank. We had worked on that letter very carefully.

HOW TO WRITE AN APPROACH LETTER TO SOMEONE NEW TO YOU

When writing an approach letter to someone with whom you have had no prior contact, you must be friendly, but you cannot display the intimacy that prior personal contact allows. In the first paragraph — as you write about your contact, his or her company, and the field — be a bit more distant than Peter was with John, but still be sure to choose words which convey enthusiasm. As you compose your letter try not to use the personal pronoun "I" in the first paragraph. Sometimes you must, but with a little practice you should be able to manage four or five sentences without an "I." Most letters that companies receive either try to sell something or are in the form of a job application. You do not want to be categorized either way, so do not use the language of either approach.

An effective approach letter will read smoothly. As I mentioned, it usually takes about three attempts before you get it just right. Your own style will begin to emerge. Do not be afraid of informality. (We are all just people.)

Peter's letter to the head of a bank leasing department (whom he had never met) began with an acknowledgement of the bank's fine reputation. Bankers are sensitive to their image. Here's the first part of that letter:

Dear Mr. Jones:

Your bank's reputation for excellence is well known and your leasing activities in agribusiness in this state are a model

> for others to follow. You provide a service for your farming customers that works well for both small and large enterprises. You must feel considerable satisfaction.

The approach is complimentary and knowledgeable. The recipient is intrigued and is ready to read more. He knows Peter knows his business. You can use similar wording for almost any enterprise, whether it is agribusiness, airplanes, or art. If you are following your passion, the right words to use will come to you. If the language feels forced after several tries, you may be off track. Rethink your objective. You cannot fake passion.

The second paragraph should begin with a brief description of yourself and why you are writing the letter. Peter said:

> I am a marketing professional with a background in all facets of sales. For some time I have been interested in the kinds of activities your company pursues *(notice, you focus in on the recipient)*. I would like to learn more, particularly about agribusiness leasing and the corresponding developments in related industries. I'm excited about the future of leasing and your observations would be helpful to me. I would like to meet you in person and ask some questions. At this point, my visit is for information, not a job.

In paragraph two you express who you are and slowly bring the reader to a realization that you would like to meet with him. He is usually flattered and pleased that someone out there is aware of his existence. So rarely do we receive recognition for our achievements that a complimentary letter makes us pleased — as it did for Peter's friend, John.

The third paragraph simply said:

> I will call in a few days to arrange a meeting. I appreciate

the value of your time, so be assured that I will take no more than thirty minutes.

The entire letter Peter wrote looked like this:

34 Main Street
Your City, Anywhere
Date

Mr. Jim Jones
Manager, Leasing Department
Competitor Bank
456 Main Street
Your City, Anywhere

Dear Mr. Jones:

Your bank's reputation for excellence is well known and your leasing activities in agribusiness in this state are a model for others to follow. You provide a service for your farming customers that works well for both small and large enterprises. You must feel considerable satisfaction.

I am a marketing professional with a background in all facets of sales. For some time I have been interested in the kinds of activities your company pursues. I would like to learn more, particularly about agribusiness leasing and the corresponding developments in related industries. I'm excited about the future of leasing and your observations would be helpful to me. I would like to meet you in person and ask some questions. At this point, my visit is for information, not a job.

I will call in a few days to arrange a meeting. I appreciate the value of your time, so be assured that I will take no more than thirty minutes.

Sincerely,

Peter Johnson

Variations occur, of course. The more individualized you can make your letter, the better. *If your letter sounds as natural as you talk*, it is well written. There are more samples of approach letters at the end of the chapter. You can write these letters to any person in any field. They work well for artists, musicians, or other people in nontraditional work settings, too — do not think this approach is only for the corporate world. If you are a singer and you want to appear in a nightclub, write the letter, and hold an advice call with the owner before asking for a singing spot. Adapt this approach to fit your passion! (You will find a sample letter targeted for creative artists at the end of the chapter.)

Many times, we become stiff and formal when we write, and the letter sounds like it was written by formula or rote. There is no *feeling* in such a letter. When you finish your first draft, read it out loud. You will hear the tone better. Rewrite it until it sounds like you when you are speaking informally. Ask yourself how you would feel if you received your letter. "Is this me? Do I talk like that when I'm enthused about something?"

When you write to a busy person to request a meeting, he or she naturally will want to know the purpose. People do not enjoy having pressure put on them, feeling that someone is after a job or something else that they will feel uncomfortable about. Your letter, on the other hand, requests only the person's perspective, advice, and knowledge — none of which is threatening in any way, none of which will require him or her to do anything for you.

Because you have approached your contact in this manner, without causing the person any stress, he or she will more than likely share his or her knowledge with you, listen to you, and refer you to those who can further your search. Thus, you have tapped into the circle where you can hear about your contact's needs, problems, and desire to solve those problems. You have come to the place where problems are being dealt with and decisions are being made. You and the person you are approaching may decide that you are the perfect "problem-solver!"

RESEARCH FIRST, APPROACH LATER

This method of researching first and approaching later works precisely because you take the initiative, familiarize yourself with aspects of the field you are interested in, and approach a potential employer from a stance of knowledge which increases your self-confidence and earns the respect of others. That is why you have an advantage over other job-seekers. The better your research and the stronger your persistence, the greater the likelihood of making the system work for you. Once you have mastered the techniques of self-marketing, you are in charge of your career for life. You are able to *take action* — the definition of power.

MAIL LETTERS IN VOLUME

It is a good idea to send out at least ten letters at a time. If you send only one or two letters, the chances are that the recipient might not be available to meet you, for one reason or another. Then you may doubt the effectiveness of what you are doing. (There are exceptions to every rule. One of my clients fell in love with one company, wrote just one letter, and had several subsequent meetings that cemented the match!)

The ten letters should be sent after the initial three to friends or acquaintances. You should also wait to send the ten letters until after you have held three *practice* advice calls. You will be more aware then of what you are doing and why. It also helps to enlist the aid of a friend or counselor during this process. We are social creatures and we need praise and encouragement as we grow and learn.

THE FOLLOW-UP PHONE CALL

After you have written the approach letter, the next step is the follow-up phone call. Make a list of the names and companies you will be calling. Allow a space for the secretary's or assistant's name. Make your first call fairly early in the morning, at the beginning of the working day. Be reminded of these basic facts regarding human nature:

1. People are always interested in themselves and like to feel important.
2. In a work setting, the person's mind is on the company and the work he or she is doing.
3. You are third on the list of priority of the person in your target work setting.

Assume that you will get the consent of the person you are contacting. The best people in sales are sure of themselves and their product. They assume that enough customers will buy. You are only one person and you need only one career position out of all the thousands that exist. You have taken the time to be thorough in your research and in your approach. If you run into trouble getting through, do not be discouraged. Be persistent. (Continued problems at this step are sometimes connected to personal fear — yours and theirs. Or you may want to reassess if this is what you really want — it may not be your passion.)

If the firm has a switchboard, ask for the person you wish to speak with. If the operator gives you a direct number, make a note of it on your list. Once you reach the secretary or assistant, your conversation will go something like this:

"Hello, my name is __________, and I'd like to speak with __________."

The assistant may give one of three answers:

"He/she is not in," "He/she is busy," or "One moment, please."

If he/she is not in, you say, "Fine, I'd like to leave my number." If busy, you say, "Fine, I'll call back. What is a good time?"

Always ask for the assistant's name. He or she is a person, too! When you call again, use the assistant's name — you have now started another relationship.

Phone work is a way to test your communicative skills. Nowadays people are more relaxed about business; it has become more human. By telephoning, you will learn how to establish rapport. You will need the assistant's cooperation. Some examples of my clients' experiences may help.

If the assistant asks: "What is this concerning?" Your response should be truthful and concise. "Mr./Ms. ______________ is expecting my call." And, that is true. Remember the last paragraph of your letter?

The assistant may say, "Let me put you through to the Personnel Department." You respond, "That won't be necessary since I'm not calling to apply for a job." And you are not. You are *investigating*, not applying. Not yet. (You have not even "dated" yet.)

The Personnel Department is involved in the necessary paperwork for the company and is designed to screen out unqualified applicants. Many of my clients are in the personnel field and love their work, but they did not get their jobs talking to the Personnel Department! They established relationships with the people who had the *power to take action*. You must keep in mind that an interview with Personnel may be discouraging when you are still in the advice call stage.

Request that you would like to speak to Mr./Ms. ______________ . If the individual is in a meeting, either leave your number or ask the assistant for a convenient time to call back.

ELAINE'S STORY

Elaine had visited four or five companies and talked to a dozen career and recruiting experts (her interest category) before she decided on her target contact. She had called him five times, and he was always in a meeting or out of the office. She and his assistant had talked enough so that Elaine felt comfortable enough to jokingly ask, "Betty, what *is* a good time to reach him?" Betty laughed and said, "Call him at 8:30 A.M. sharp. He'll pick up the phone. That's about the only time someone is not in his office."

She called him the next morning and Elaine explained briefly who she was. He was not sure what she had in mind even though he had read her letter, but he was willing to meet her.

"Do you prefer the first part of the week or the last?" she asked, giving him a choice.

"Tuesday is fine for me," he said.

"Morning or afternoon?" Elaine asked.

"How's 10:00 A.M. for you?" he asked.

"Perfect. I'll be there at 10:00 sharp," she replied.

A self-directed person is irresistible to a decision-maker.

Elaine designed a proposal for the man she would be meeting, which combined career development and recruiting. His company was a small but growing group of home improvement retail stores. (The areas of design, decorating, and fabric selection were included on her list of priority *interests*. Her *skills* were in selecting, training, and motivating employees.) She identified the problems she wanted to solve, and when she located a person who had those kinds of problems, she persisted through five phone calls, finally enlisting his assistant's help in making the contact. Her approach to him was well thought out, personal, and focused. His reaction was open and receptive, and she got the job!

Elaine wanted to select good employees and motivate them so that they stayed happy on the job. She knew *the world of business needs problem-solvers*, individuals who focus on turning unworkable situations into profitable ones.

You can be a problem-solver in your work, because no one else has the exact combination of your passion, abilities, and skills, as Peter's friend knew about Peter.

Peter's story ended with a job offer, from his friend's bank. Today he is a leader in the bank-leasing industry, specializing in agribusiness. He continues to advance his career by applying the principles of mutuality. He compared his new position with his old one at the pharmaceutical firm.

"The difference is that now I wade through fields of produce rather than doctor's offices to make my sales. I love it! My customers are so proud of their businesses, farms, and vineyards. I often stay for dinner after we conclude business," he said.

Peter and Elaine built relationships based on the concept of mutuality. They will continue to succeed as long as mutual interest prevails.

SAMPLE LETTERS

This section gives you a few more sample letters. They are not meant to become your actual letter, but just to open your mind to some creative and constructive methods for getting that first contact with the person and company you are interested in.

The first letter was written on the recommendation of a respected employee in the Personnel Department. In this situation, the personnel department was informative. The letter is another referral from the same company employee. Insiders can be very helpful in putting you in touch with the right contact. The writer spent quite a bit of time making each letter to the individuals within the same company a little different. This extra effort engages your creativity and is well worth the extra time.

552 Small Avenue
Largetown, CA 94000
Date

Mr. Bob Lane
Marketing Manager
Data Processing Equipment
Computers Inc.
Digital Road
Middletown, CA 95000

Dear Mr. Lane:

I heard about Computers Inc.'s reputation for quality products and decentralized management from Jay Jones, in your training division. He said you were the person with the most up-to-date information about your marketing program.

For the past four and a half years I've worked in scientific application of programming. I'm making a transition to software sales and technical sales support. Your perspective will help me take the right steps and avoid the wrong ones! Please understand I am not coming to you to apply for a job.

I'll call in a few days to arrange a day and time to meet.

Sincerely,

Clark Jones

552 Small Avenue
Largetown, CA 94000
Date

Mr. John Smith

Marketing Personnel Manager
Computers Inc. Corporate Headquarters
Silicon Road
Largetown, CA 94000

Dear Mr. Smith:

Jay Jones, in your training division, said you were the person with the right information when it comes to matching individual talent with your company's needs. He said you would be available for an information meeting to discuss marketing and sales positions in your company. Please understand the purpose of the meeting is not for a job, but for information.

I've been in scientific application of programming for the past four and a half years. I'd like to use my technical experience in software sales and sales support. Your perspective would be valuable to me. I know you're busy, so I'll call in a few days to arrange a brief meeting.

Sincerely,

Clark Jones

When Clark and I first started working together, incidentally, he was so stiff in his communication I finally suggested that he enroll in an acting class. He did, and he discovered a new "act," honesty. The classes gave him an unusual methodology for telling the truth, and he found he enjoyed them a great deal.

The woman who wrote the following letter first met her contact while taking a class from him. Many university extension courses are taught by capable business and professional people who are passionate about their work. They are excellent advice call candidates.

452 Middle Avenue
Largetown, OH 44000
Date

Mr. Steven Lee
Vice-President, Executive Financial Counseling
Bank of The North
Money Way
Largetown, OH 44000

Dear Mr. Lee:

As chairman of the Certificate Program in Personal Financial Planning at the University Extension, as well as in your position at the Bank of The North, you set the direction for future financial planners. You also understand the qualities that are needed for successful counseling. I took a course from you recently and found it to be very useful.

I am interested in my own personal financial planning, but more importantly, I want to help others with investments. I am currently employed as a systems analyst on a project to develop an accounting and reporting system for the Supply and Distribution Department of a large oil company. My master's degree emphasized finance and quantitative analysis, while my undergraduate degree prepared me for a career in clothing and textiles retailing. I am currently considering a career shift that is more in alignment with my natural interests, and I believe that the future looks bright in the financial planning profession!

I would like to meet with you to verify if this choice is a good fit for me. At this point I am gathering information and am not coming to you for a job.

I will call shortly to arrange a meeting at your convenience. Because I appreciate the value of your time, our meeting will take no more than thirty minutes.

Sincerely,

Jenny Webster

In the following letter, Jenny uses the resources in her own firm — the Women's Forum — to find individuals who share her interests.

452 Middle Avenue
Largetown, OH 44000
Date

Ms. Charlotte Jones
Account Executive
C. B. Sutton Investments
Lowell Avenue
Largetown, OH 44000

Dear Ms. Jones:

Although it was well over a year ago, your presentation at a dinner meeting of my company's Women's Forum made a distinct impression on me. Your humor lightened and gave perspective to your topic of finding a financial advisor. You mentioned that a large firm, presumably such as C. B. Sutton, offers the advantages of a good reputation and recourse for any unsatisfied clients. As a financial planner in a large firm, and with your involvement in teaching financial planning, you have a unique perspective of the profession.

I am interested in my own personal financial planning,

but more importantly, I want to find out more about the financial planning profession. I am currently employed as a systems analyst on a project to develop an accounting and reporting system for the Supply and Distribution Department of a large oil company. My master's degree emphasized finance and quantitative analysis, while my undergraduate degree prepared me for a career in clothing and textiles retailing. I am currently considering a career shift that is more in alignment with my natural interests, and I believe that the future looks bright in the financial planning profession.

I would appreciate your perspective on that future, and would like to meet with you to ask a few questions before I commit myself to a decision. At this point I am gathering information, and am not coming to you for a job.

I will call shortly to arrange a meeting. I appreciate the value of your time, so please be assured that our meeting will take no more than thirty minutes.

Sincerely,

Jenny Webster

In the following letter, Jenny picked up an idea for a contact from her reading. In this particular case, the woman she wrote to was too busy for a meeting but she arranged for her assistant to see Jenny. The meeting went even better than she had expected, since they were more like equals! Jenny's tone in this letter is less reserved than her previous one, because the article in *Money* magazine clearly showed her prospective contact to have a humorous and unpretentious personality.

452 Middle Avenue
Largetown, OH 44000
Date

Ms. Jane Jones
Investment Corp. Inc.
123 Main Street
Middletown, OH 43000

Dear Ms. Jones:

You were quoted in the April issue of *Money* magazine as saying that "sensitivity to people's needs is as important as putting numbers together." Your approach combines intuition, empathy, and financial savvy — an unbeatable combination!

I am interested in my own personal financial planning, but more importantly, I've developed a fascination with the financial planning profession, especially because of experts such as yourself. I am currently employed as a systems analyst on a project to develop an accounting and reporting system for the Supply and Distribution Department of a large oil company. My master's degree emphasized finance and quantitative analysis, while my undergraduate degree prepared me for a career in clothing and textiles retailing. I am currently considering a career shift that emphasizes my natural interests, and I believe that the future looks bright in the financial planning profession. I like the way you think, and know that your perspective on the field would help me understand the skills your job as an investment counselor requires. I would like to meet with you in person to ask a few questions before I make a definite decision about a career change.

I would like to call shortly to arrange a meeting. I appreciate the value of your time, so please be assured that our meeting will take no more than thirty minutes.

Sincerely,

Jenny Webster

In the next letter, a client sets up a meeting, and in his second letter we see a good example of a follow-up letter he wrote after the meeting.

649 Pine Avenue
Largetown, NY 10000
Date

Ms. Joan L. Edwards
Vice-President, Finance
Clothing Unlimited
Main Street
Largetown, NY 10000

Dear Ms. Edwards:

The retail clothing industry is undergoing significant change due to competition, market restructuring, and cost pressures. Clothing Unlimited is mounting major responses to these challenges. As head of your company's key financial planning, you're contributing to development of new product lines and services, and searching for more profitable product/service mixes and cost-effective distribution methods. In addition, your efforts at expanding and strengthening Clothing Unlimited's position in international markets place you in the forefront of providing effective solutions to difficult problems.

I am a financial and corporate planning professional with a background in international economic evaluation. The expanding role of Clothing Unlimited into financial and other nonclothing product/service lines is of keen interest to me. I would like to learn more of your approach in developing these new areas, and I'm especially fascinated with your efforts to expand into world markets.

I have chosen to write to you, Ms. Edwards, because I like the exciting challenges I see coming up in the industry. Based on your knowledge of the industry's direction, I would appreciate your perspective on future prospects, and would like to meet you in person to ask you a few questions.

At this point, my purpose is not to look for a job, but to gain more information, so that I can make my future career decision more knowledgeably. I will call shortly to arrange a meeting. I appreciate the value of your time, so please be assured that our meeting will take no more than thirty minutes.

Sincerely,

Phil Steele

In the above letter, Phil combined his natural interest in this company's products with his fascination for strategic planning and expansion. He is a long-range thinker, and likes projects that take time to accomplish. He set up a meeting with his contact. The next sample letter is a follow-up after his advice call was held.

649 Pine Avenue
Largetown, NY 10000
Date

Ms. Joan L. Edwards
Vice-President, Finance
Clothing Unlimited
Main Street
Largetown, NY 10000

Dear Joan:

Your explanation, in our meeting yesterday, of Clothing Unlimited's organization, planning approach, and areas of business interest was most informative for me. Your concepts for incorporating nonclothing product lines into existing operations are being pursued in an imaginative and vigorous fashion.

Your expanding activities in international trade are timely from a strategic standpoint. It is obvious that you are spending much time in planning a long-range structure that will allow Clothing Unlimited to expand its business, especially in the nonclothing product line. This strategic planning is an exciting project for you.

I enjoyed meeting you and truly appreciate the quality of our discussion. You have been most helpful to me in gaining an understanding of the nature of your company and its innovative ideas. Since our conversation, I've had some ideas on Clothing Unlimited's business expansion. When I draft a brief strategic plan, I'll give you a call and see if you are interested in seeing it. And if you believe there is anyone else with whom I can explore these topics further, I'd be grateful for your referrals.

Sincerely,

Phil Steele

Notice how in the follow-up letter he summarizes what was covered in the meeting, and requests the names of others he can talk to about his areas of interest. In addition, because Phil got *excited* about the company's proposed expansion, he intends to draft a strategic plan and present it at a later date to Edwards. He could include this plan as part of a "proposal resume," discussed later in Chapter Eight. Phil is laying the groundwork for further contact with this company.

APPROACH LETTERS FOR CREATIVE ARTISTS

Approach letters are just as effective for creative and performing artists as they are for businesspeople. The media, show business, the arts — all are receptive to the advice call approach. "Right livelihood" for the artist includes years of supporting oneself while mastering one's art form. After all, Renoir did not hesitate to paint porcelain in a factory while studying and growing. He and Monet ate beans for weeks on end, and yet Renoir looked back on that time as being full of happiness and excitement.[1]

The artist, like the entrepreneur, is primarily a solo type. Their values are generally not those of the majority of the population. While material possessions, status, and security are enjoyed, they are not as important as creation, friendships, and freedom. It is crucial that creativity be seen for what it actually is: a vivid imagination linked up with the desire to express something. Creativity, after all, *creates* something, makes it happen, produces a tangible result. It follows that the creative artist and entrepreneurs must have energy and a capacity for hard work. Most of all, creativity requires a disciplined imagination — not controlled or held back, but channeled.

We have already discussed how important friendships are to us all. They are vital for most artists and entrepreneurs, for the cross-fertilization of each other's creativity. The word "friend" is used in its true meaning, not carelessly, as we do when we call acquaintances our friends. The only mind that can understand a creative mind is one that is also creative! Think how many teachers and other authority figures you had who stifled unusual behavior, who did not have the sense or appreciation of spontaneity. Were you married to or "friends" with those who thought you were too strange, too imaginative, etc.?

The creative person is usually "too" something — yes, you are more passionate!

Your approach letter can help you develop artistic and entrepreneurial friendships. It follows the same format as all the other approach letters. Focus on the recipient. Do not overestimate people in the arts or media or small business. Radio and television especially tend to present inflated images of people. Remember that creative people are just people, doing their jobs — but they work with passion.

Do not write your approach letters until you have done your homework. For example, if you want to talk to a television producer, watch the show. Study it. Make notes. Compare it to other shows. Go to classes in television production — a good way to meet the right person. *Work*. Nothing impresses other creative people like your willingness to work. Then write your letter. You will have no trouble figuring out what to say!

Bear in mind that television (and other media) is most interested in presenting what is *already* successful. Think how a hit show usually generates a succession of similar ones — most of them unsuccessful! Radio is a more experimental and intimate medium than television, generally, and is experiencing a renaissance that will continue for years.

Artists and other creative people often teach classes at your local community college or university. Call the campus and ask for the catalog — you will be amazed at the resources available to you. By taking a class from these people, you will quickly discover if you have the talent and desire to succeed. If you want a personal critique from experts, you may have to pay a fee, but the money spent can save you years of struggle.

If you are well along in your art or craft and want to offer something to the media, the approach letter will still follow the same outline: the first paragraph focuses on the recipient, the second paragraph on you, the last paragraph suggests a plan of action. In this case, enclose materials that substantiate your qualifications, such as brochures or tapes — some evidence that shows why you would make a good guest on their show.

The following is an approach letter I wrote to meet a local television producer. The host of the show, Nancy Fleming, talked to me and gave me her producer's name. Letters to people in the media should always be typed. Because they get so much handwritten fan mail, you will want to look businesslike and direct, by contrast.

Ms. Shirley Davalos
KGO TV
Channel 7
277 Golden Gate Avenue
San Francisco, CA 94102

Dear Shirley:

Nancy Fleming suggested that I send background information to you since you are in charge of booking her guests on the show. You must feel pleased to be the producer of such a fine show. Nancy thought the area my business covers would be of interest to her viewers.

I've been a career consultant in San Francisco for over six years. I work with individuals and companies who retain me as their advisor to solve all kinds of career problems. My clients run the gamut, from first-time job seekers, re-entry men and women, to those who are employed and want more: satisfaction, money, and personal growth.

Nancy said that the focus for the show could be on two topics, college graduates and re-entry job seekers. I'm happy to talk about both. I've enclosed a brief bio, some pieces I've had published, and an outline of the service our company provides. I'm looking forward to meeting both of you.

Sincerely,

Nancy Anderson

NA:cc
cc: Nancy Fleming

I had listened very carefully to Nancy Fleming while we talked. As it turned out, the audience response was so strong that I was invited back several more times. The experience gave me what I needed, exposure to the world of television.

My editors suggested that I include here the approach letter that accompanied my submission to them of the first chapter of this book. They contacted me right after they received it and said they were very interested in seeing the entire manuscript.

Mr. Marc Allen
New World Library
58 Paul Drive
San Rafael, CA 94903

Dear Marc:

The first law of money is: do what you *love*, the money will follow.

Most Americans are not in the right work and haven't the tools to discover their passion and how to make money at it. For over seven years I've worked as a career consultant in my own business in San Francisco helping individuals find the work they love. Before this business I was a journalist, interviewing and writing about subjects from hard news to features. I've combined my two passions, counseling on careers and writing, to inspire others to achieve what I have. The result is my book, titled *Work with Passion: How to Do What You*

Love for a Living. The book fills an ever-present need — happy, productive work. The audience is all who earn their living and who want the satisfaction of a career they like so much they'd do it for nothing, but don't. They get paid, and well.

I've enclosed an outline, preface, and first chapter for your perusal. The book is finished.

I've selected you because of the work you've done with Gawain's *Creative Visualization* and Ross' *Prospering Woman*. The layout, editing, and design are exactly what I want. I think my book is a next logical step for you, from visualizing, to prosperity consciousness, to working with passion. Thank you for considering my book.

Regards,

Nancy Anderson

P.S. I've enclosed a tape of a recent KGO Radio guest spot to give you an idea of how I come across. Promotion of the book is very important to me. I want very much to be involved in marketing the product I believe in so strongly.

The letter was obviously effective. You are holding the results in your hand.

SUMMARY

Passion Secret #7:
Powerful people know how to make and keep lasting relationships (contacts).

1. Your thoughts are things, literal entities that connect with other entities. Similar minds working together create a "mind

trust" and in effect create a greater mind. Similar minds working together are more powerful than one mind working independently.

2. A well-written approach letter is an objectification of mental energy. Directed to a like mind, it is a powerful communication tool.
3. Your first three letters should be directed to people you already know. Mutuality already exists and you can observe how the exchange works.
4. You cannot "fake" relationships. You must be in harmony with your genuine passion.
5. Your strengths can solve big problems.
6. *Expectations* demand certain specific results, and often lead to disappointments. *Expectancy,* however, is creative and open, and the results are always good.
7. Your approach letter assumes consent and is written on carefully chosen stationery. Write or type it flawlessly. Send ten letters at a time.
8. Make your follow-up phone calls four days after you mail your letter.
9. Be natural with the secretary or assistant. Always ask his or her name, and be friendly and polite. Be sure your letter has been received. If it has not, say you will call back in a few days, and thank them.
10. If you are referred to someone else in the firm you contact, get the person's name and write an approach letter first, even if your original letter was passed on to them. Personalize each contact. Many of my clients have had good referral meetings because their original choice was absent, too busy, or not interested. Turn obstacles into opportunities. One client learned that the person she wished to meet was scheduled to leave on a flight that afternoon, and she volunteered to drive

him to the airport. He accepted. Later she got a job offer from him. Be flexible. Suggest breakfast, lunch, dinner, coffee, wine, etc. Also, express your willingness to meet a week or two in the future.

11. Do not be surprised by success. When agreement to meet comes, do not hesitate. Make firm plans and keep your appointments. Watch that fear does not suddenly sabotage you with sickness.
12. Every man or woman with business problems is hoping a solution will walk in the door. They have no idea you exist. So *walk in* — and enjoy building a new relationship!
13. While you are making these appointments, be aware of people and events that may "accidentally" present themselves — old contacts, a friend's suggestion, a phone call. Do not think of the process in terms of a rigid plan. You never know how the process will work — but it always does, sometimes disguised as a chance happening. The results you want do not have to happen in your advice calls.

had to the airport. He accepted. Later he got a job offer from [illegible] He [illegible] [illegible] [illegible]

[illegible]

[illegible] will wait at the door. They have no idea you exist so [illegible] and move? [illegible] relationship [illegible]

While you [illegible] appointments, be aware of their [illegible] that they [illegible] [illegible] a [illegible] Do not think of the [illegible] [illegible] the next [illegible] how the [illegible] will [illegible] and it always [illegible] [illegible] have happened to you [illegible]

ADVICE CALLS

Passion Secret #8:
Powerful people trust their instincts.

You are ready now for Step Eight on your path to your passion: how to hold the advice call. There is nothing mysterious about an advice call; you have them all the time, but you have not labeled them advice calls, or informational interviews, as they are called in Richard Bolles' book, *What Color Is Your Parachute?*[1] This chapter is second in importance to Chapter One, in which you learned how to analyze the forces that shape your beliefs about money, work, sex (this includes gender beliefs), and religion. Both chapters hold the keys to power: how to relate to yourself, and how to relate to others. This chapter focuses on how to establish a relationship with the person you interview. Your preparation will keep you from wasting his or her time.

When I say that you have advice calls all the time, I refer to those seemingly casual conversations that occur when you are gathering information about a person or subject that interests you. These conversations can occur in a relatively simple situation, such as shopping for a television set, or some other service or product. You ask questions, listen carefully, and when you have gathered enough information, you make a decision. Or these conversations can happen at more important times when you meet someone you like, or whose work is intriguing. The difference between your "casual" advice calls and those that we will be discussing in this chapter is one of focus: now you will be focusing on your career. Let me show you how it works with the following illustration.

BRIAN'S STORY

Brian was a thirty-year-old Hispanic man, striving aggressively to become an attorney. He had received his undergraduate and graduate degrees from good schools and then set out to pass the bar examination, meanwhile taking a job as a contracts administrator in a government agency. He took and failed the bar exam six times! I met him after the sixth round, while I was a consultant with city government. Brian had pushed himself to his limits as he had done his whole life. He came from a family where few members had high school degrees, much less the Juris Doctor. He was proud of his achievements in school, in sports, and his role as an up-and-coming leader among his people. He was recognized by his peers as a man to watch. Yet he could not pass the bar exam.

The day we met, I knew from his answers to my questions about life and work that his quest for the law degree reflected a need for status, not a passion or an urge to *practice* law. It took several meetings before his entire story emerged.

"I've never failed at anything I set out to do in my life. I am determined to be a lawyer. I know the law, yet I can't pass the bar," he said, the wounded pride quite obvious in his face.

"While you're waiting for the results of your last attempt, why not take a look at other alternatives?" I asked. He agreed.

During our meetings, I observed that he was a conceptual person, intense and serious. He had a form of mental "tunnel vision," focusing on only one way to do something. I felt he had the capacity to pass the bar exam from the work he had done on his assignments. I also felt that at a deep level *he did not want to practice law* — and that explained his failure to pass the bar. The source of his problem obviously was in a conflict of values — something not presently apparent to him. He was a fighter in a battle he had set up to lose. In subtle ways, we usually get what we really want. Yet sometimes it is the opposite of our *conscious* desires and plans. Remember that a goal has to be authentic for you to accomplish it (Chapter Three).

Brian used the advice call technique and executed it almost flawlessly. He mailed twenty-three letters and had twenty-one meetings! In the process he discovered why he had failed the bar exam. His early attempts at approach letters, as well as the follow-up thank-you letters, were stiff, legalistic, and boring. In trying to sound like an educated man, Brian did not make sense. No wonder he could not pass the bar exam! He used pompous words and phrases and bureaucratic jargon. Brian had to learn that in order to change his old habits and venture into new territory, he had to say what he really thought and felt. When he spoke from his heart, he became articulate again.

He simplified his writing, and his speech became more precise, displaying a quieter, more assured quality. Brian learned that he could be himself, and that success came to him most easily when he could tap *all* his natural resources, including his ethnic background. He also discovered in his advice calls that the higher up in the hierarchy he went, the more tolerant the people became. He left the biased and prejudiced contacts at the foot of the ladder, and never saw them again. Brian's words explain the methodology and purpose of an advice call, for himself and for you.

"Nancy, an advice call is like a racquetball game. You have to play the ball as it comes to you. You're a challenger, developing your job search differently than others, beating the system by using these improved methods. You have meetings with people you choose, playing a spontaneous match where you have to learn to trust your natural reflexes, your instincts. It's the most challenging set of matches I've ever played.

"I finally realized that I would never have been happy practicing law. I thought being a lawyer would give me status as a minority person. I now know I wanted the legal information and mental discipline of a law study program, and automatically assumed my next step was passing the bar. Not true — not for me. The job offers I've received in my two areas of interest, finance and merchandising, require the use of all my strengths, those I already have. I thought I could never get what I wanted unless I was an attorney," he said.

How did twenty-one meetings with individuals in his areas of interest teach Brian in six months what he did not learn sitting in the classroom for seven years? Brian shared his insight into this experience.

"When you're in college your focus is on the next set of exams and papers, on getting good grades, on taking in and analyzing information. The most important thing — how your training fits into your life as a whole, and into your passion — gets lost in the scramble to finish school and start your career. On campus you're isolated from the world in order to think and study. Formal education is not an integration process, at least it wasn't for me. I was so caught up in proving myself that I never took the time to reflect, to ask myself, Why am I doing this? I just did it!" he laughed, not the overly serious Brian of old.

Actually, the most important lesson for Brian was discovering that his passion had nothing to do with his race. He had a natural desire to excel. He had imitated what he mistakenly thought was the "Anglo" path to success, an education focusing on the intellect. Along the way he had minimized the importance and richness of his culture, its quiet, intuitive strength, not realizing that power in our American culture comes from drawing strength from the blending of one's own culture into the larger society. Coupling one's origin, whatever it may be, with the surrounding culture is the route to power and influence. And the mastery of the language of the larger society is the key to one's position in society, reflecting status more surely than a bank account or title! Look at the movers and powerful people in business, the arts, and politics. They are articulate, and nourish their powerful roots, whatever their heritage may be.

Brian was forced to become articulate, concise, and clear in his use of language. Law school had emphasized formality in language. He learned to drop the legalistic jargon, the affectations. There are many ways to master the language: read only *good* writing, take speech training, join theater groups — there are many widely varying routes to the same destination.

Brian has moved up in his career. His aggressive, competitive nature is well rewarded in his new job, a position in sales. He now spends most of his time talking to corporate treasurers and individuals with large sums of cash, convincing them to purchase his company's certificates of deposit for large sums of money ($100,000 and up). His mental and verbal skills got him the job and led to a remarkably fast start in his new company. He says:

"I love the environment, the competition (notice the *team* personality in his language). Our company is the challenger in the investment field — an upstart, a maverick. We're hitting our competition hard with a quality product. There's a scoreboard in the office with everyone's name on it and the weekly results of our production written for all to see. It's inspirational when someone scores!"

The following is a summary that Brian wrote about his recent career experience (and his work in the ten-step program outlined in this book).

"Getting to where you want to be in a career while feeling defensive is extremely difficult. While on the defense, one is influenced by the expectations of society, colleagues, family, and friends. Does the system dictate that I be a teacher, lawyer, computer programmer. . . ? If I do not achieve what I perceive others to covet, am I a failure?

"Nancy's program brought me to the realization that my life is in my own hands. It is not what society dictates or covets that makes the difference between success or failure. It is what is generated from within each one of us that allows us to move forward — and we all do it differently, in our own way.

"The ultimate challenge, in moving through this program, is to have the courage to look consistently within yourself and visualize those attributes that make you a winner. Courage brings confidence, which in turn generates passion.

"Like any source of energy, passion needs to be stoked and nurtured because you never remain the same. When you've completed the program, the glow from within will have only begun."

Brian has now come full circle. He is in the right work relationship and his teammates and leader inspire him; his company is, like him, the "underdog." He now sees his minority background as an asset, and is proud of it. He recalls what he learned from his father: "My father is an unusual man. I now realize that I learned about love of work by watching him. He is proud of what he can do with his hands. Nobody tells him who to be; he is his own man."

RIGHT LIVELIHOOD

You also will find and experience integration of the self, just as Brian did. But do not assume that you need a lifetime of "hard knocks" to come to self-understanding. The self is a continuously unfolding flower with infinite petals. The self expressed through "right livelihood" is love personified, as Kahlil Gibran writes:

. . . and all knowledge is vain save when there is work,
And all work is empty save when there is love;
And when you work with love, you bind yourself to yourself,
  and to one another, and to God.
And what is it to work with love?
It is to weave the cloth with threads drawn from your heart,
  even as if your beloved were to wear that cloth.
It is to build a house with affection, even as if your beloved
  were to dwell in that house.
It is to sow seeds with tenderness and reap the harvest with
  joy, even as if your beloved were to eat the fruit. . . .
Work is love made visible.[2]

Before I begin the explanation of what an effective advice call is and exactly what to do once you are in front of the person you have written to, let me rephrase the most powerful secret in the book, Passion Secret number five: *Powerful people know how to pick their niche. They follow their passion.* Simply put, they love their work. Money, status, recognition — all those values you looked at so closely in previous chapters — are a reflection of doing the work that is right for you. By work, I mean any activity that brings you the income *you want* — not someone else's standard of income.

The most difficult part of the work I do as a career consultant is getting people to believe in Passion Secret #5. Even when personal experience has verified the concept in their lives, most people will not believe that "money comes to you" when your work is in harmony with your passion. I believe that the logical mind, the left side of the brain, rejects the mystical relationship between *right livelihood* and success. After all, we spend all those years and all that time and money educating ourselves to fit into the "job market," as Brian did. How discomforting then when we hear stories of a woman making thousands every month selling her patchwork kitchen aprons to eager gourmet cooks, or an attorney who developed much-in-demand (and high-priced) seminars for labor negotiators because he loves teaching as much if not more than practicing law. Over and over we hear about those who have "made it" and wonder what we are doing wrong. We keep hitting our heads on the low bridge of frustration.

In his book, *The Seven Laws of Money*, Michael Phillips, a former banker and president of POINT, the *Whole Earth Catalog* money-giving group, stresses the importance of a balanced approach in the dispersing of money:

> Right livelihood is a concept that places money secondary to what you are doing. It's something like a steam engine, where the engine, fire, and water working together create steam for forward motion. Money is like steam; it comes from the interaction of fire (passion) and water (persistence) brought together in the right circumstances, the engine.[3]

Phillips suggests two questions to ask yourself to see if you are integrating your most desired activities with your livelihood. Powerful people (remember the definition of power — the ability to take action) achieve right livelihood.

> First of all, do you think you can undertake your work for a long time? Right livelihood could be spending your whole life as a carpenter, for example. One of the qualities of right livelihood is that within it, within the practice of it, is the perfection of skills and qualities that will give you a view of the universe. Constant perfection or practice of a right livelihood will give you a view of the whole world, in a sense similar to Hemingway's story of the old man's life as a fisherman gives him a connection with the entire world, and a "whole world of experience." What are the rewards? Right livelihood has within itself its own rewards: it deepens the person who practices it. When he is twenty years old he is a little different

from the person he will be at thirty, and he will be even more different when he's forty, and fifty. Aging works for you in the right livelihood. It's like a good pipe or a fine violin, the more you use it the deeper its finish.

Another thing you can ask yourself about right livelihood is whether the good intrinsic in your livelihood is also good in terms of the greater community. This is a hard question to answer when you are asking it about yourself. It's hard to establish criteria, but a carpenter can certainly be doing good for the community in a very powerful sense. All of this is by way of saying that you shouldn't separate the idea of doing good from whatever your livelihood is; they can be integrated. With a right livelihood you would not be doing what you are doing and at the same time saying, "I'd rather be a nurse, I would rather be head of the Red Cross." The dichotomy would not be necessary. What you would be doing, in your eyes, would be as beneficial to the community as any other function.

The stories of the people in this book are examples of the concept of right livelihood. My clients envisioned their prospective job or business and worked hard; they gave their plan the necessary time to come to fruition. Successful people take about eight to ten years of dedication to their right livelihood before full achievement, full recompense. If you are to succeed, you, like them, must be patient: you maintain clarity of vision; accept yourself as you are; see the journey as fun; implement your plan; pick the right niche; continually gather information; enjoy the research; make and keep lasting relationships; have self-discipline and finally, always trust your instincts.

The eight passion secrets discussed thus far in this book are reflected in the concept of Phillip's First Law of Money: *Do it! Money will come when you are doing the right thing.* The advice call is the crucial step that brings you nearer to your goal.

THE ADVICE CALL

As you prepare for your first advice call, keep in mind that many people you meet will not be in their right niche. Some people you meet will be threatened by you, and give you discouraging information. You will know that you have had a good advice call if you feel good about yourself and the other person after you leave — regardless of the meeting's outcome.

If you feel discouraged, do not always assume there is something wrong with *you*. The other person may have been threatened by your presence. When someone loves what they do, they always encourage you. Conversely, when the person is insecure, he or she may use you to show off, brag, play "see how well I'm doing," or give you unwise advice (for example, "sounds like the book you want to write is the same idea I've already heard three times this year"). If this happens, know that you must be powerful or you would not be provoking such a strong negative reaction.

An occasional destructive advice call can leave you feeling wounded. If so, you may need a counselor, friend, or support group at this point to help sort out the truth about what happened. It is rare that you will experience what I have just described. On the whole, you will meet good people. So ignore those few who are not supportive of you.

My clients have interviewed hundreds of men and women in all kinds of jobs and businesses. Like Brian, they come in after several calls and say, "Wow, there are so many unhappily employed people out there! I feel lucky to be taking the time to get it right. One person I met with said he envied me — he wished he had done what I'm doing."

You too are giving yourself the opportunity to "get it right" — or you would not be reading this book. Statistics abound on job dissatisfaction, and you know from your own experience that most people are not doing what they love. This knowledge will remove any fear that the people you want to meet are in any way superior to you. They are not. Most people will be happy to talk to you — friendly, interested listeners, who are thoughtful in their approach to life and work.

The advice call is a relaxed meeting between you and a person who is in a line of work that interests you. This meeting is designed to put both of you at ease so that conversation occurs and information is exchanged. You need to get information, to research various possibilities. The other person needs to know you and your interests. Mutual concern about a particular niche in work sets the tone for two people to help each other achieve their individual aims. The approach works whether you are gathering information for a job or for your own business.

Once you hold at least three advice calls, you will discover an ability you did not know you had: *you can meet and interview anyone!* As your awareness grows, you move up on a learning curve that otherwise would take years. The method is quick and easy — and powerful.

YOUR FIRST ADVICE CALL

Your appointment is set. You are a little nervous because you have never done this before. You can reduce your anxiety by rehearsing with a friend or trusted adviser. My clients rehearse with me before their meetings. I assume the identity of the contact. My client introduces him- or herself and begins the interview. Our rehearsal is quite informal. We laugh together over the "mistakes." Many of my clients have found that admitting their nervousness to their contact helps break the ice and makes both of them feel much more comfortable!

As with any performance, stage jitters are normal but tremendously motivating. Your instincts are forced to take over and *your instincts are your best guide*. Even clients who have been in sales or in the theater get nervous about their first few advice calls. That is because it is so personal. The opportunity to test yourself soon becomes enjoyable, however. Many clients have told me they enjoyed the advice calls so much they were sorry to end the process and go to work! It is like Brian's analogy to a racquetball game: if you like to play, you want to get on the court.

However, you can continue the advice call technique even after you are on your new job. Advice calls keep you fresh and informed. They are an excellent business development tool.

The advice call "script" begins with a greeting to the secretary or receptionist. Notice him or her and the surroundings. Is the office organized or confused, calm or excited? Use all of your senses, your instincts. Can you see yourself working here? Are you comfortable? If yes, why? If no, why not?

In a few moments your new relationship (contact) greets you. Shake hands warmly and firmly. Look in their eyes and smile. Eye contact is best done if you remember how you look at someone you are intrigued with. It is not a staring gaze, but rather a considering one. Tell yourself (silently, of course) that this person is going to enjoy this meeting. They will, too. For you are paying attention to them and want to hear what they have to say. Think about it. Who do they have to talk to about their work, their successes, their concerns? Their boss? Their friends? Their wife or lover? All those people have a vested interest and are not objective. *You are!* What a gift you have given this person just by showing up.

Take a few minutes to refresh his or her memory and to set the tone. "John, or Mr./Ms. ____________ (whichever is appropriate), I want to thank you for taking the time to meet with me. I realize the value of your time. As I said in my letter, I'm looking seriously at your field and want to know more about the way your business works and how your job fits into the whole picture. I've spent the last few months thinking about myself and the skills I want to use. I know now that I'm a good communicator. I speak, write, and listen well. I'm organized and thorough, and I enjoy all kinds of people and get along well with them. I analyze and solve problems. Of all my skills, I feel the key ones are my maturity, sense of humor, and balance. I don't take life or myself too seriously." (The introduction varies with your own combination of abilities, of course.)

In three to five minutes you have given the person a wealth of information, "handles" he or she can identify rapidly. Your approach is reflective and self-assured, not pushy or arrogant. You *have* thought about your skills. You do not always begin your meetings with all these words, but somewhere in the conversation you will express your strengths and values. Remember, all the self-knowledge from your work in preceding chapters is meaningless if you do not take action. Now you are ready to express yourself, hear yourself. How do you feel now? Do you like what you hear?

The advice call is as much for the other person as it is for you. As you speak, he will be making mental connections: thinking about his business, people he knows who are like you, places he could use you.

Next, you say, "I have been researching the kind of work that interests me. I read all available material (you can get specific here — what did you read?) and picked several people to talk to about what I've learned. And that's why I'm here now, John. You are one person I really wanted to meet, so I'll begin with some questions, and ask your opinions. At the end of the meeting, I'd like to know if you can refer me to other people who would be helpful in my search."

You have given him your agenda. He knows what to expect. He knows you do not have a "surprise" for him, such as, "Do you have any openings?" This last statement is the reason why many people dislike interviewing. A person comes in, resume in hand, and puts the pressure on. No one likes this approach even if there is an opening. Why? Because selecting people is painful. You have to make a personal judgment under stress. Far better that you get a chance to look at someone without having to hire them. Then you can really listen and observe.

How many times have you met someone on a casual basis and considered hiring him or her or thought about what a good co-worker he or she would make? Most good jobs are filled just this way. Someone *knows* someone, as a friend or former co-worker. The entire recruiting world operates on the age-old question, "Who do you know that . . . ?" Word-of-mouth, networking, call it what you will, but it is the way companies fill the majority of their needs — on personal recommendation.

The advice call approach works equally well whether you simply wish to change positions in your field or within your company, or whether you want to explore an entirely new option. If you are already familiar with the field, obviously you adapt what you say to the individual situation. In any case, the approach brings you face-to-face with people so that you hasten the word-of-mouth process. You are becoming known, in a way that is quicker and easier than waiting for an outside chance of recommendation. The best part about advice calls is that frequently you are talking to decision makers who are planning company changes and forming new objectives. They have yet to write a job description because they are still busy defining the problem.

ERIC'S STORY

One client, who picked transportation as his top interest, talked to five people in the trucking industry, his favorite area. He spoke with leaders in several areas — private business, labor, and government — so that he developed full understanding of the industry's problems. Deregulation, labor, competition — all these were crucial issues to those people that Eric interviewed.

"The labor leaders told me that the old tough-guy image was on the way out. They were now thinking about new personality requirements for the labor representatives who work with management. I asked them exactly what was needed to be a labor negotiator in the years ahead," Eric said.

Here you see the early stages of job definition. As it turned out, Eric was helpful to the man he was talking to. The question had provoked a thoughtful analysis of the *needs* of the labor leader. Eric was able to make intelligent observations because of the thoroughness of his research and his experience in previous meetings with other industry leaders. His quiet, unassuming but firm manner made a good impression on the labor leader, who stopped to pause and reflect.

"You've certainly been thorough in your approach. You said as you began our meeting that your top strengths included a down-to-earth ability to communicate and excellent organizational skills. Those are two of the qualifications that any negotiator must have. Have you decided yet about whether you want management or labor as your career?" he asked.

He had started thinking about Eric as a potential employee because of Eric's personality and background. "Labor needs professional, well-balanced, and dedicated people," he said to Eric, "not someone who's out to get the boss. Rather, the ideal is a commitment to strong representation of the working man's position. You seem to have an understanding of that position, Eric."

Eric had gained some of that knowledge by driving a truck before he attended college. He was now close to completing his bachelor's degree in Industrial Relations. With graduation pending, Eric needed to find the right job and that is when he came to me for help in locating the right niche for his talents.

Before Eric made his first advice call, he had to know what questions to ask. Asking the right questions can be the difference between accomplishment and frustration, success and failure — as I am sure you have discovered in your own career.

Use the Research Interview Data Sheet at the end of this chapter as an outline to keep track of your interviews as Eric did. Fill out the page as soon as possible after the meeting. Otherwise, you will forget important points. Writing while the information is fresh is best. In addition, you will find that the Factor Evaluation Work Sheet at the end of this chapter is a useful tool for weighing the alternatives that will lead you to choose one position over another. You may have other job characteristics to add in order to measure your own requirements when selecting a company to work for.

CREATE YOUR AGENDA

You determine the agenda in an advice call, not the person to whom you are speaking. You have three objectives:

1. Presenting yourself — your strengths, values, and what you have defined so far as your objective.
2. Gaining information — ask questions, probe for problems you would like to solve.
3. Asking for referrals — "Who do you know that would be informative for me to meet?"

Your interview will stay on the right track if you imagine a list of questions — some that probe for problems, some that evoke positive responses. They will fall into three categories: personal, industry, and company. You might give the terms *plus* and *minus* to these questions. The "plus" questions are designed to draw the person out, as well as to elicit information. The "minus" questions probe for problems. You must begin your questioning in a way that encourages the individual to share his or her knowledge. That accessibility usually occurs first with industry "plus" questions. For example, a "minus" question — such as "How does competition in your field affect recruiting good people?" — can start the meeting on a negative note. So wait until later to get to the bothersome parts of the business. (However, sometimes your sympathetic ear will encourage surprisingly frank discussions of problems early on in the meeting. Again, there are no unbendable rules. It all depends on the individual situation.)

Examples of "safe" industry questions are: "What do you see to be the trends in your field for the next few years? What changes in the market have occurred that may have set or altered these trends?" Since one cannot speak in generalities forever, your interviewee will begin to connect industry answers with his or her own circumstances. For example, she may reply: "The trend in the cosmetic industry is toward total personal care. More Americans are taking better care of their bodies by eating properly and exercising frequently. That's why we've introduced a vitamin supplement packet to go with our basic skin care products." Now you will ask some company "plus" questions. When she has exhausted that information for you or appears reluctant to go further, move to another safe "plus" question, in either the personal or industry categories.

The following are examples of plus and minus questions to ask during your interview. You will not have time to ask all the questions, of course. However, several will be crucial in getting the information you need. Let us begin with a list of plus questions. These are generalized questions that will (1) give you some ideas about the scope of your questioning, and (2) establish the proper tone and approach. Your own questions will be more focused and refined, appropriate for the individual situation.

Plus Personal Questions

1. What is the most significant contribution you have made to your firm in the last year? The last five years?
2. What person (or persons) have you recruited who has gone on to fulfill the potential you recognized in him or her?
3. What attributes are necessary for success for a person in your position?
4. How have you changed the nature of your job?
5. What are your short-range objectives? Your long-range objectives?
6. What professional in the field do you admire most and why?

Plus Industry Questions

1. How are profits maximized — improved cost cutting, marketing, strategy, superior product or service?

2. What is responsible for the positive or innovative trends in the industry? Are they social, political, or individual trends?
3. What factors are responsible for the growth of the industry?
4. What specific research has the industry found useful in terms of profits or growth?
5. How has the development of the industry come about and what new strategy is being used to continue or diversify that development?
6. What are the overall earning potentials of your industry?

Plus Company Questions

1. What is the overall philosophy of management here in your organization? How is that specifically implemented? How can you personally measure that philosophy?
2. How accurately are new developments and markets perceived, and what is the management style? Open, vertical, horizontal?
3. What are the long-range goals of the company? The short-range goals?
4. What has been the major achievement of the company in the marketplace?
5. What makes your company better than others in the same field?
6. What combination of aggression and analysis has been used to capture the market share?

Minus Personal Questions

1. If you could do whatever you wish professionally, what would that be? What would it mean for your organization? What prevents you from doing it?
2. What feature of this position that you are presently holding would you change or eliminate?
3. What development has occurred in your field that you did not envision in your career plans? What did this development

mean for your future and the future of others in the field?

4. What does increased government activity mean to your profession?
5. If you had to do it all over, would you join the same field and the same organization? If yes, why? If no, why not?
6. What is the opinion of professionals you respect about the growth potential in your field in the next five years?

Minus Industry Questions

1. What about government regulation in the industry — is it a plus or a minus? Local, state, federal?
2. Are you affected by environmental restraints? Are you affected by any interest groups?
3. Is your growth fast or slow? Is it typical of the field?
4. How about supplies or suppliers and personnel? What material supply problems are there? Are you able to attract and keep good people?
5. What specific trends affect you? (Markets drying up, hostility toward the industry, cost factors, etc.)
6. Do you have too much competition, too little? Why is the competition better or worse?

Minus Company Questions

1. How does your firm respond to government regulation? What costs have been incurred as a result?
2. Who is responsible for responding to government regulations? What other political factors are at work in the industry that affect your organization?
3. How are you attracting people to keep up with your growth? (If growth is unusually fast.) What markets will you lose if you cannot attract people? What particular skills and abilities do you look for to help you increase your share of profits and earnings?

4. How is quality control maintained? By whom?
5. What influence do inflationary trends have on your business?
6. What are you doing to capture and keep your share of the market?

As rapport develops between you, move to the minus questions about industry, then personal matters, then company affairs. Move back and forth, being sensitive to individual reactions. Your skill as an exploratory questioner will increase with each interview. The entire process is designed to develop your self-confidence, instruct you in accurate knowledge of the marketplace, and aid you in the correct placement of your talents. The process will lead you to your goal.

The following blank interview grid is included here to help you create your own questions for each individual advice call. You are going to focus on the lower righthand section — the minus questions about the company, the problems. Your ultimate purpose during the advice call is to identify the problems, to see if you want to be the problem-solver! The examples of plus and minus questions will aid you in creating your own. Picture this grid in your mind as you work through the interview.

INTERVIEW GRID

Plus questions Personal 1. 2. 3. 4. 5. 6.	Plus questions Personal 1. 2. 3. 4. 5. 6.	Plus questions Personal 1. 2. 3. 4. 5. 6
Minus questions Personal 1. 2. 3. 4. 5. 6.	Minus questions Personal 1. 2. 3. 4. 5. 6.	Minus questions Personal 1 2. 3. 4. 5. 6.

Your interest in the individuals you speak with will be genuine since you have been thorough in your research and have developed intelligent questions to ask. If you make the individuals feel important by focusing on their areas of expertise, they will enjoy your visit and be inclined to help you as much as possible.

Remember to rely on your natural instincts. They will guide you when you are in doubt. Preparation is important. Read, practice, think, inform yourself. Then in the face-to-face meeting, be flexible and receptive: "Play the ball as it comes to you."

Once a client went in to meet with a manager of a training department and stayed all day! The manager had arranged to include several employees at the meeting with my client, who was surprised but delighted. Naturally, his agenda changed accordingly. He had five advice calls in one day!

THE THANK-YOU LETTER

After my client left the meeting he sat down and wrote a brief summary of each of the five people, including details on his or her background and position. Then he took an extremely important step: *he wrote each a personal, handwritten thank-you letter.* His natural instinct told him to follow up and acknowledge a favor that is granted.

The First Paragraph

Write a thank-you letter to the person you meet no later than a day after your meeting. This letter should be as carefully written as your approach letter. It also has three paragraphs. The first paragraph goes something like this:

> "Thank you very much for the time you gave to me in our meeting on (date). I know how many demands there are on your time so your courtesy, attention, and advice are especially appreciated. You obviously like what you do, and your enthusiasm is a tribute to that commitment."

Keep it simple and in *your own speaking style.* Do not be afraid of friendliness or of an unusual way of turning a phrase. If you have the skill to write in an upbeat fashion, as long as you are sincere and respectful, your thank-you letter can be even more powerful. One client wrote:

"You're the most inspirational marketing pro I've ever met. When I left your office my head was full of ideas and my step several degrees lighter! Now I know why your products are so successful in this town. With people like you, your company has the market cornered. Your encouragement of me made my day. No, it made my week! I thank you."

Mailed promptly, your letter will arrive in time to recall your presence in a positive way. It is almost like a second meeting. Think about how you feel when you receive a positive, personal letter. You feel special. Powerful people know how to do the things that make people feel special. They follow their instincts; the golden rule works. Treat everyone you meet as you would like to be treated, and suddenly doors open for you.

Once you are in your new job, send *everyone* you interviewed a note telling him or her how your search ended. Also tell each person how he or she helped you in that search. One client told me that piece of advice was worth my entire fee!

"Three people called to thank me and invite me to lunch to celebrate, and one of them offered me a great job with him if I became dissatisfied with my new employer," he said.

The Second Paragraph

Now, let us work on your second paragraph of the thank-you letter. Concentrate on the subject matter covered in your advice call. Refer to your Research Interview Data Sheet, a sample of which is at the end of this chapter. Make up one of these for each meeting you have, even including those "accidental" advice calls (the talk with someone you met on the bus, the casual encounter — any time you gain more knowledge about your passion). It is like coming to class on Wednesday after your professor's lecture on Monday. He asks, "What did I say on Monday, class?"

You raise your hand and say, "You said the influences that affected the development of the laissez-faire economic system were social, political, and religious." Then you give examples of developments in those three categories.

In your interview, you covered — *by subject headings* — the outline of your "professor's" (contact's) presentation. Do the same in your thank-you letter. Like this:

> "In our recent meeting, you said the communication industry faces many challenges in the future: technological,

> social, political, and personal. The industry is changing so fast that today's invention is obsolete almost as soon as it is invented. I was fascinated to hear about the high demand for trained personnel in the cable television industry — and that VCRs have led to an unending need for good software. I'll follow up on your suggestions to talk to the people you mentioned. From what you told me, my skills will be needed in the exciting future ahead."

The writer paid the recipient of the letter the highest compliment: the writer listened and *heeded* what was said. Nothing makes a teacher feel better than when a student takes action on his or her hard-learned knowledge. The faster the action, the brighter the student.

One part of your second paragraph should focus on a time in the meeting when you were both enthused. Think of eyes, body language, voice tone — at one point you were both on the same wavelength. Repeat that moment in the letter. Re-create your mutual enthusiasm by mentioning the pace of change in the industry. That concept was an exciting one for both of you in that particular meeting.

The Last Paragraph

The last paragraph of your thank-you letter is a statement of your future intentions. For example:

> "I appreciate the suggestions you gave me to call Mr./Ms. _______________ (or to check with you later if I need more information, or do more research, or any or all of the above). I will keep you informed of my progress. Thanks again for your warmth and kindness."

By including a statement of your intentions, you keep the relationship alive. After you have had more meetings, you may find it useful to go back to an earlier contact. In many cases, you will meet a particularly nice person who takes an interest in what you are doing — one you will want to meet more than once.

JOB OFFERS

Trust that *your enthusiasm* is the key to career and life success. Enthusiasm sells ideas and products. You cannot be enthused unless you know what inspires you, what makes your energy level rise. For some it is trucks, for others it is art, for others it is computers or satellites. Whatever it is for you — and only you know the answer — trust your instincts and write a letter to someone who shares your enthusiasm. Learn how you can help that person become even more successful. Add your power to other power sources and multiply your light.

Job offers will come to you in the process of holding advice calls. Usually, it takes between fifteen and twenty-five meetings to focus on what you really want. When you have a clear picture of your objective — and not before — the right job offer will appear. Some of your early advice calls will seem fuzzy, hard to remember, possibly unsatisfying in some respects. After the initial meetings with an individual in a company, you will frequently be introduced to others within the organization.

At your second or third meeting you will be more informed, knowing better what specific questions to ask. Do not "sell yourself" at any point. Instead, listen carefully, and when the time is right, move to a more assertive exchange. When you know what you want, ask for it. Some of my clients have gotten right to the "close" and then they stop, waiting to be asked. A typical closing conversation occurs like this:

"Well, John, you've met with several people here in our firm. What do you think about our company?"

The questioner wants to hear your level of interest. Do not play a cat-and-mouse game that drags on endlessly after you have decided you have the interest and the ability to help a company solve its problems. Present the *solution*. The solution has *you* written into it. You can even write a rough draft of the problems and take it with you into your third or fourth meeting. This is how most consultants get their business. They do what is called a "needs assessment" before they propose a solution (which includes their consulting time) to the employer. If the solutions are sound — time, cost, manpower — they are hired. You are doing the same thing.

Like the consultant, you are a problem-solver. Problems will involve people, data, or objects. Brian, our would-be attorney, combined his data skills (analysis of financial reports) with his people skills (ability to get along with all kinds of people and involve them in cooperating for mutual benefit).

Brian had seven meetings with bank representatives before a job offer was extended. Both he and the representatives of the bank gave the relationship time (two months) to develop into a good match. If you are given an offer after only one or two meetings, that is a yellow flag. Someone is too anxious. Do not expect quick closes; they rarely stick. Respect the employer's need to determine that you are indeed the solution to his or her problem. Hiring mistakes are costly, in terms of morale and money. Be patient. You may be told, "We need to think it over and get back to you." If so, say something like this: "That's understandable. When can I expect your call, or would you prefer that I call you?"

Be sure to keep all avenues open until you make your final decision. You may think an offer is one-hundred percent certain, but you should still continue with your other meetings. Things change. Disruption may occur which has nothing to do with you. If you are discouraged or simply tired out, take a break. Go fishing or backpacking, or do anything that refreshes you.

You will work harder creating the job or business than you will after you are in the position. Do not think something is wrong with you if you wish the process would hurry along. This adventure you have initiated is hard work; think how few people are doing what you are doing. Why? Because it takes a rare combination of tenacity and commitment to complete such a task. However, the rewards are endless. They just keep coming: money, satisfaction, and the personal knowledge that you are a powerful creator of what you want. All of these rewards will validate your hard work.

THE NEGOTIATING PROCESS

In real estate transactions, counter-offers are an accepted practice. With job offers, few of us think we can come back with a counter-offer. Usually, we are so glad to finally get an offer that we accept quickly, and then we think about what else we could have negotiated for after we return home. Talk to any respected recruiter and he or she will tell you that negotiation is the rule, not the exception. In fact, one of your advice calls should be with a person who recruits in your field of interest. You should ask about his or her job and the strategy that works to make good matches.

Do not talk about money until you get an offer. You must know what your responsibilities are before a figure can be determined. When asked about your expectations, be truthful. But, at the same time, say that the final figure depends on the job itself. In many cases, as you talk with decision-makers, you will uncover other areas where your skills can be helpful. Just because you are pleased by the offer, there is no reason to lose sight of your overall objectives.

Elaine (in Chapter Seven) showed the employer how she could recruit and lead in-house career development training. She set up her own schedule and got his approval. He had no way of knowing her energy level and desire until she told him what she could do for him.

Only you know your capacity, your passion, your level of interest.

Three Questions to Ask Yourself

Let us say, for example, you are offered a base salary of $40,000 with benefits that total $5,000 (medical, vacations, profit sharing, etc.). Do not accept on the spot unless you are absolutely sure. Take twenty-four hours or the weekend to think about it. Ask yourself three questions:

1. Does this match my earlier goals? Do not forget the figure you wrote in your affirmation exercise in Chapter Three! How flexible do you want to be?
2. Is this position a match for my current abilities? My values?
3. Most important, will this package prepare me and provide continuing growth for my long-range goals?

If your answer is "yes" to all three questions, accept the offer. If you say "no" to any one of the three, *design a counteroffer* that gives you what is missing. If the money is not sufficient, ask for fifteen or twenty percent more. You can ask for additional sheltered fringes, such as a car, a parking space, travel, or entertainment expenses rather than money. The tax bracket you are in will make the difference here. Check the tax tables to see what you would actually take home. What matters is your net figure, not your gross figure. Most job offers have a range of from three to six thousand a year, depending on the individual's skills and background. In a very small firm, under ten people, ask about the chance for eventual equity in the company — the key to independence!

Simply say to the person who extended the offer that you would very much like to work for them and require $____________ a year. You are in a good position to counter once the decision has been made to hire you. *Do it.* What can you lose? At the very worst, all they can say is no. Then it is up to you to ask in turn for an early salary review or some written commitment that ties your performance to the salary you want. *Try to structure a compromise in which everyone wins.* It is a matter of maturity and realism on both sides.

The second question you will ask yourself refers to your job function. Ask your employer for the duties you would like. Show him or her why these are important to you. As in all negotiation, this is best done face-to-face. Your sincerity and accurate self-knowledge are very persuasive. Do not force or sell. Present your requests calmly and confidently. It is in this negotiating stage that you will most appreciate all the experience you have gained by following the process that leads to your passion. You already know about other alternatives and you do not limit your thinking, believing that you must settle for less than you really want. You know you can find your niche.

The answer to the third question, whether this offer will assist you in your total development, comes after you have reviewed all of the work you have done (the autobiography, the exercises, and the results of all your meetings). Add up the pluses and minuses. Be realistic. Listen to your instincts. Then, write down your assessment of your unmet needs and how the job can be expanded to meet those needs. Perhaps the job can be designed to include those areas after you have proven yourself. Take a copy of your draft with you when you meet with your prospective employer so you can quickly come to an agreement that satisfies you both.

VARIATIONS ON THE ADVICE CALL

So far, this chapter has covered the steps to take using the advice call approach. But there are numerous ways your niche may become apparent to you. You may see an advertised opening that fits your goal. Feel free to respond to the opening. If you are interviewed, be sure *you interview them*, just as you would on an advice call.

Friends or acquaintances may tell you of openings. Follow up by first determining who is the decision-maker, and then write an approach letter, or call if you are more comfortable with direct contact. As you progress in your "campaign," you will develop your own style. Your increase in self-confidence will give you a corresponding increase in spontaneity. Some contacts will be personal enough to telephone without writing first.

Occasionally, you can get the information you need over the

telephone. For example, you may follow up one of your letters and the recipient wants to handle matters over the phone. "Why don't we just discuss this right now. How can I help you?"

First, refer to your letter. "As I said in my letter, I'm investigating an area of work that appeals to me. Before I make a decision, I need to know the answers to several questions. I'd enjoy having the chance to meet you in person. Conversations like this are best done in person, I've found. If your schedule is full this week, how about a day next week?"

Usually, he or she will agree to meet if you sound like a person who is self-assured and interesting. If the person insists on a phone interview, go ahead — ask your questions. A good one to begin with is: "Tell me how you happened to choose this field and your company?" As he or she expands on the answer, the exchange will become friendlier and the possibility of meeting personally will increase. Ask again for a later meeting, perhaps after you have talked to more people and have more information and questions. Thank the person for whatever help you received. Be gracious — it works.

Some clients of mine have such superb telephone personalities that a letter to everyone was unnecessary. Their tone, self-confidence, and approach was enough to establish a rapport and the appointments were made. They always wrote thank-you letters, however. You may have an unusual ability to communicate verbally. Use it when your instincts guide you.

RESUMES

Your resume is a necessary tool when you are looking for a job in the same field, but it can get in the way when you are changing careers, positions, products, or services. You need to meet people in person to discover how your skills and background transfer into the new work. Sometimes you may need to take course work to come up to speed, sometimes you may even need to get a graduate degree. But if the work is what you want to do, no sacrifice is too great. Continue to work at what you know how to do while you learn and grow.

Sometimes what you are already doing is transferable — fund raising is very much like sales, for example, and marketing is the same process regardless of the product or service. The important question is do you connect emotionally with the product or service? When you make this connection you have identified your passion. Until then, hold off writing a resume.

There is a wrong and a right time and place to use a resume, and they are listed below.

The Wrong Time and Place

1. Mailing it before an advice call.
2. Handing it to someone as you begin a meeting. The paper gets in the way if used prematurely.
3. Answering an anonymous want ad. The organization you want is honest and direct — no subterfuge.
4. Circulating it to friends and companies (mass marketing of you does not work).

The Right Time and Place

1. After you have defined your objective.
2. When it is written for the *specific* place and person you want to work with.
3. Following several meetings with individuals whose interest matches yours.
4. When you *know* it is right. (Follow your instincts.)

A resume will show the recipient that you are qualified to solve specific problems in a work setting. By looking at one or two pieces of paper, the recipient will be convinced that you can fill his or her needs. But unless you know those needs, a generalized resume is ineffective. Many of my clients have found their niche without ever using a resume.

The right time and place for your resume is usually after the fact — after you have determined that the person you have just met needs a written confirmation of your qualifications to help make his or her enterprise a success.

THE PROBLEM-SOLVING PROPOSAL

A proposal defines the problem and presents a solution (you) in detail. Describe your background and the situations in which you solved similar problems. With this approach you display your knowledge, with the language peculiar to the field — "buzz words," if you will. The following proposal format sample is Eric's (the client discussed earlier in this chapter who was interested in the trucking industry). You will recall that Eric had met several times with individuals in both labor and management and had uncovered the need for pleasant, down-to-earth, communicative problem-solvers with an understanding of the entire industry. Eric's personality, education, and experience as a trucker appealed to top management because they knew the "macho" style of middle management in the trucking industry was fast becoming out-of-date.

Eric Jones
Street Address
City, State, Zip
Telephone

Objective

My short-term objective is to obtain a supervisory position in the trucking industry. My intermediate goal — within a year — is to be an operations manager. In the long run, I envision myself as the chief operations officer of a company like Delta Industries. This decision has not been taken lightly. I have worked in the trucking business as a truck driver, tester, trainer, and foreman. I am completing my degree in Industrial Relations at the University of San Francisco. For the past few months, I have met with senior executives in the transportation industry and have become reasonably familiar with current transportation problems: deregulation, labor, recruitment, and competition. On the basis of my experience, education, and discussions, I have decided that I wish to pursue a career in the trucking industry, primarily in operations. In this field I would use my talents to schedule and organize routes and supervise drivers in order to solve the traffic flow problems. The results would be greater profits and more satisfied drivers.

What I Have to Offer

1. Communication. I am an honest and friendly person who communicates well with all levels of people. I've specialized in industrial relations and I know about workers' problems and can communicate effectively with them. My wide range of experience with different groups of working-class people has taught me to be patient, understanding, and adaptable. Additionally, I am a good listener and learn from each person I meet. Because I know how to listen, I can get close enough to people so that they feel free to open up. Then we're in a better position to exchange ideas. Patience with people is a key to effective communication. I have patience.
2. Organization. Organization of others begins with organization of self. I've taken the time to think through my goals and objectives. I've put my priorities in order and considered my options. The foundation of good management is the ability to critically analyze information: financial and technical data on

operations, market research studies, proposals for new investments. Organizing the affairs of a company, then, begins with personal objectivity and an understanding of problem-solving.

3. Creativity. Creativity is involved in everything — from deciding on how to decorate an office to reorganizing a work schedule, to calming down an angry driver. I organized and led a creative volunteer project at an elementary school in San Francisco when I was a student at San Francisco State University, and learned that creative ideas like the ones I have are always available for future use in yet unforeseen circumstances. Once I drove home a disabled truck by using a coat hanger I found on the side of the road. Creativity is merely a matter of looking at a problem in a different (and sometimes unconventional) way.
4. Leadership. Leadership results from early and varied experience with independence. I was raised to be independent. Rather than blindly following someone, I choose colleagues I can learn from. l choose those I follow based on what I want to accomplish. By selecting my mentors wisely, I have strengthened my own leadership qualities.

This resume proved to be irresistible to the people he wrote it for. Because Eric did his groundwork, he got the job he wanted.

When to Use the Proposal Resume

The proposal format is suitable for those situations in which the position you are seeking is still to be defined. The employer or potential business partner is still in the thinking stages about his or her needs.

It is a myth that company owners and managers always know what they need to solve their problems — as any management consultant can tell you. Many times they are not even aware they have a problem. An objective outsider (you) can often see a problem and its solution very quickly. You can use this fact of human nature to your advantage when you find a position, a "niche" that you would like to fill.

THE FUNCTIONAL RESUME

Another kind of resume is functional, focusing on your top four or five skills. This resume is best for you if your old job titles — including your present one — do not sound like the title of the new job you are after. In this type of resume you translate what you did, showing that the skills you have are the same ones that are required for the position you are interested in. The skills you list should convince the employer that you are qualified for the position.

In the following functional resume, Susan (the psychologist we met in Chapter Four who wanted a position in executive recruiting) stressed the ease with which she gets acquainted with the people in power, the decision-makers. That she owned her own private practice displayed her entrepreneurial abilities.

If you have ever had a paper route or a "cottage" business — making or selling a product or service out of your home — or even if you have ever been a waitress, *you are an entrepreneur*. Be proud of that. Put it on your resume. The courage it takes to be a waitress, for example, is often underestimated. Some of my clients who are waiters and waitresses changed their minds about restaurant work after we talked.

"Waitressing is so demeaning," one young client named Joan said to me.

"Do you realize that the restaurant sets you up in your own business every night?" I asked.

"What do you mean, *my* business? They own the restaurant."

"I know, but you have access to five or six tables that are cash flow sources. You are like an independent contractor; the restaurant picks up the overhead, and you and your effort produce income. Your tables and what happens on your shift are your business," I said.

Joan's eyes brightened. "I never thought of it like that — but it's true! My attitude determines my tips. Of course the kitchen has to run smoothly, too. But overall, the cash I generate from my tables depends totally on my performance."

A week later, she told me she had had her best week ever. "I run a great little business," she bragged.

She was able to see how she had always been an entrepreneur. In New Zealand, her home, her parents had owned their own little convenience markets. We used a functional resume format for Joan, like Susan's. It is best if you keep your resume to no more than two pages.

Susan Smith
Street Address
City, State, Zip
Telephone

Objective:

Executive recruitment position with responsibility for development, organization, and follow-up of sales effort.

Desire position where strong communication skills can be used with senior management and decision-makers.

Summary of Qualifications:

Effective communicator with the desire, organization, and drive to accomplish set objectives. Diverse experience as a problem-solver in the following areas: motivation, supervision, and evaluation of all levels of staff, as well as that of work and communications flow, planning, and coordination.

Education:

Ph.D. work, Transactional Analysis, Psychodrama, Union Graduate School-West, San Francisco, 1978.

Ph.D. work, Counseling and Human Systems, Florida

State University, 1975.

M.S., Vocational Rehabilitation Counseling, Florida State University, 1972.

Advanced training, Vocational Evaluation, Florida State University, 1971.

B.A., Psychology, Jacksonville, Florida, 1969.

Planning, Organizing, Coordinating:

Planned and coordinated from scratch various programs, for example, the Isis House program, treatment center for abused adolescents. Represented group in the civic and professional community. Planned and developed a program for treatment of alcohol abuse and trained staff to operate the program. Developed work evaluation facility for Goodwill Industries, including culture-free psychological test battery, instructed staff and counselors in its use, measurement, and interpretation. Developed and taught courses at the university level.

Training Supervision:

Hired, trained, and supervised wide variety of employees, professional and nonprofessional. Instructed, directed, and taught concepts relating to policies and procedures for overall implementation of organizational goals and objectives.

Written and Verbal Communications:

Wrote grant proposals, job descriptions, and case analyses. Made written and oral reports on client progress, psychological evaluations for court proceedings and vocational planning. Served as member of speaker's bureau, addressed numerous civic and professional groups, represented commission in appearances on radio and television. Successfully led and directed many group and individual seminars/meetings.

Professional Experience:

Consultant/Vocational Counselor, 1978–Present — Psychotherapy, Psychodrama Institute of San Francisco.

Consultant, 1978 — C.U.R.A. Inc., Program development, staff training.

Clinical Director, 1977–1978 — Isis House, Program and staff development.

Private Practice, 1973–1975 — Group, individual, and family therapy.

Honors:

Psi Chi, National Honor Society, Psychology. University Honor Society. Department Honors and Trophy. Kappa Delta Pi, National Honor Society, Education.

Personal:

Single, excellent health.
References: Available upon request.

THE CHRONOLOGICAL RESUME

The chronological resume, a linear outline of your past, is used when the job or business you are after has more or less the same title as your previous positions. Highlight your background so that your resume is no more than two pages. If the job you want is different from what you have done before, the summary and objective is written to show that your experience has prepared you to do what you say you want to do, as Brian did for the financial institution that hired him, *after* he held several preliminary meetings.

Brian Martinez
Street Address
City, State, Zip
Telephone

Objective:

Financial sales position with responsibilities for market research, budget analysis, planning, and representation of financial products to clients. Particularly desire position where my skill with people can be used.

Summary:

Mature, balanced, and perceptive with a natural ability to communicate with groups and individuals — whether labor, business, or government, regarding financial information. I take time to listen to all views and enjoy organizing and creating workable solutions. I speak and write clearly and effectively and am comfortable with supervision of people and budgets.

Education:

J.D., Hastings College of the Law, University of California, 1975.

B.A., Political Science, Stanford University, 1972.

A.A., Diablo Valley College, 1970.

University de Guadalajara through the University of San Francisco, Guadalajara, Jalisco, Mexico, summer session, 1969.

Experience:

Contracts Specialist/Program Officer, 1977–Present, Alameda County Training & Employment Board. Write government contract packages and instructions. Negotiate contracts with funded programs, cities, and school districts. Supervise $2.5 million budget.

Union Shop Steward, August 1977-March 1978, Service Employees International Union Local 535-ACTEB/ACAP Chapter.

Technical Assistant to Local Government, August 1976-June 1977. Consultant in human service capacity to local governments in Alameda County service area.

Law Clerk/Organizer, June 1975-August 1975, Migrant legal services and the United Farmworkers Union, Santa Maria, California.

Student Professional Worker, June 1974-August 1974, Mayor's Summer Employment Program, City of Los Angeles.

Industrial Relations Specialist, June 1972-August 1972, United States Department of Labor, Labor Management Services Administration, D.C.

Youth Developer, February 1972-June 1972, Stanford University Youth Opportunity Program. In cooperation with Stanford faculty and administration, created jobs on Stanford campus for high school youth. Interviewed and placed youths in relevant jobs.

Awards:

Stanford University: Mexican-American Legal Defense and Education Fund, Law School Scholarship; Stipend from Stanford Internship Program in Washington, D.C.

Diablo Valley College: Scholarships: Academic Senate; Walnut Creek Women's Cooperative.

Interests:

Jogging, racquetball, and philosophy.

References:

Available upon request.

THE YOUNG PERSON'S CHRONOLOGICAL RESUME

The chronological resume is the most effective type of resume to use when you are young and inexperienced. The key to the effectiveness of the resume is in stating your objective and summarizing your qualifications.

The following resume is a good example of how a young person without extensive job experience presented himself in an effective way. The California Conservation Corps requires that each Corps member prepare a resume when their tour of duty is over. While he was in the Corps, this young man had uncovered a passion — yet I wanted him to summarize all the skills he had learned.

First James did a rough draft, then he and I redesigned his resume. Note how directly and boldly he states who he is and what he wants. He is the partner type, so he knows he must find the right supervisor — and he states it right on the resume.

If you have never had any kind of job at all, perhaps you have hobbies or have done volunteer activities that have helped you develop some skills. For example, if you have learned to play the piano, you have developed tactile strength, and a good sense of touch. You might enjoy working in a nursery where you would plant and touch flowers, or any kind of environment where touch is important, such as ceramics, fabrics, or clothing.

James Smith
Street Address
City, State, Zip
Telephone

Objective:

Line cook position with quality restaurant specializing in fine cuisine.

Summary of Qualifications:

Mature, reliable, determined individual with natural

curiosity about food and its preparation. Experienced at getting along with wide variety of people. Work well with fair, informative supervisor.

Experience:

Cook Specialist, 1982-Present, California Conservation Corps, Monterey Satellite Center.

Solely responsible for operating a cafeteria-type kitchen. Plan monthly menus, purchase and budget food items. Prepare all three daily meals. Maintain health and safety codes; supervise kitchen personnel. Teach and train personnel, set policies/rules for operating efficient kitchen.

In addition to the above duties, I fulfill all the duties of a Corps member: Trail construction, landscaping, minor carpentry, erosion control, fire fighting, emergency response, power tool operation, wet land restoration, minor masonry, flood control.

Summer Experience:

Janitor, July-Nov. 1980, Apple Valley School District, Apple Valley, CA. Assisted in summer cleaning of school rooms, floors, painting, landscaping.

Kitchen Helper, 1979, Howard Johnson's Mill Valley, CA. Prep cook — salad bar, helped cook during rush hours. Dishwasher, cleaning machines, busboy, table setup.

Personal:

Age 20, physically fit.

References:

Available upon request.

The chef at the "quality restaurant" who hired James said he knew James was the employee for him after he met with him and read his resume. Six months later, James was employee of the month, six months later, employee of the year!

THE ONE-PAGE BIOGRAPHY

The one-page biography is an alternative to the resume. It is an excellent way to present yourself if you feel a brief introduction is necessary. It is especially effective following an advice call where there is sincere interest. You can tailor it for the specific situation and highlight your strengths, education, accomplishments, and expertise, as well as summarize your present job.

Keep your biography to two paragraphs. Brevity is not only the soul of wit, it is also heartening to the reader if you shorten your life to the highpoints. The reader will see a pattern without having to wade through a two- or three-page resume.

The following is a sample bio of a bookkeeper who had a successful advice call with a publisher. She loves to work with figures and also has a passion for books:

> As a free-lance bookkeeper with six years' experience working for various small companies, I've come to realize that my most satisfying jobs have been with organizations involved in the arts or in communications. Before I moved to California from New York in 1983, I put myself through college by keeping the books for a local radio station and a community newsletter. During this time I acquired the experience and knowledge to become a full-charge bookkeeper. And at the same time I learned a lot about radio broadcasting and publishing!
>
> I have always enjoyed working with figures, and have developed my organizational skills so that I am able to efficiently work for two or three clients at a time. I presently work for a small art gallery and a health spa, and want to

> expand my business to include one more client. Because I am an avid reader (I belong to a weekly book discussion group), my objective is to use my talents and expertise in a communications field, such as publishing.

The publisher hired her for a part-time position that led to full-time employment as Chief Financial Officer for his dynamic, growing company.

RESEARCH INTERVIEW DATA SHEET

As I mentioned earlier in the chapter, it is very helpful to write up a "research interview data sheet" for each advice call you make. Include the following information:

Date of Interview ____________

COMPANY ____

Main Product/Service ________________________________

NAME OF PERSON _____________________________________

TITLE ____

COMMENTS: Salient Points

1. What did you learn about this person? ____________________

____

2. What did you learn about the industry? ___________________

____

3. What did you learn about the company? ____________________

____

4. What referrals did you obtain within the company? Outside the company? ____

____

5. What problems seem to be of most concern to this person? _____

____

In the following Factor Evaluation Work Sheet, rank the companies you visit on a scale of one to ten, according to their effectiveness in providing the listed job characteristics. This is a good time to review your work on values in Chapter Two. What job characteristics were most important to you then? Have your values shifted at all?

FACTOR EVALUATION WORK SHEET

Position:

Job Characteristics	**Company I**	**Rank 1-10**	**Company II**	**Rank 1-10**	**(etc.)**
1. Aesthetics					
2 Achievement					
3. Advancement					
4. Affiliation					
5. Altruism					
6. Authority					
7. Climate					
8. Commute					
9. Compensation (initial)					
10. Compensation (in two years)					
11. Creativity					
12. Equity opp'ty					
13. Ethical harmony					
14. Harmony with Career Objective					
15. Independence					
16. Intellectual Stimulation					
17. Pressure, Stress					
18. Recognition					
19. Security					
20. Status, Title					
21. Variety					

UNCONVENTIONALITY WORKS

When all is said and done about job-search techniques, doing what one is not supposed to do is often the solution. Many years ago, for example, when I was interviewing for a job counseling contract, I stopped in the middle of my presentation to the woman who had the power to hire me.

"What are you doing in this place?" I asked, turning away from my flipchart.

She looked startled, and sat back in her chair.

"What do you mean, what am I doing here?" she asked.

"Well, you're obviously an entrepreneurial type — I can't see you being happy in government or corporate work."

She told me later that she decided if I had the guts to tell her what I thought with so much money at stake, that I was the person she wanted to work with her clients — street-smart, low-income people who had learned how to con most social workers.

"Well, it was so obvious, I had to say something," I laughed.

The contract gave me a steady income while I wrote *Work with Passion*, and also a revealing picture of the futility of most government programs. The woman who hired me later went on to become an executive recruiter, traveling all over the world to find the right people for her clients. In the next chapter, I discuss how you will know when you are ready to go out on your own. And I will give you some examples of clients whose independence took them on the narrow path to freedom.

SUMMARY

Passion Secret #8:
Powerful people trust their instincts.

1. Pay attention to conversations you have that excite or fascinate you (passion clue!). These may be advice calls in disguise.

2. An advice call is like a racquetball game: stay flexible and play the ball as it comes to you.
3. The self, expressed through "right livelihood," is love personified. Work is love made visible.
4. Right livelihood is a concept that places money secondary to work.
5. You are responsible for creating the agenda in an advice call Your three objectives are: (1) to present yourself and your strengths and goals, (2) to gain information, and (3) to ask for referrals.
6. Ask "plus" and "minus" questions in your advice call in the three areas of personal, company, and industry. Focus especially on the "minus" company questions, because here is where you find out where the problems are — and you could be the problem-solver!
7. Always write a thank-you letter to those you meet with.
8. Learn how to negotiate a job offer.
9. There is a right and a wrong time to use a resume.
10. Use the proposal resume when the job position is still in the stages of definition.
11. Use the functional resume when the job you want has a title or functions dissimilar to your present position or the ones you have held in the past.
12. Use the chronological resume when the job you want has more or less the same title as what you have been doing.
13. Use the chronological resume when you are young and inexperienced, emphasizing your objective and qualifications.
14. Use the one-page biography when a short presentation is indicated.
15. Write up a Research Interview Data Sheet on each advice call you make.

16. Write up a Factor Evaluation Work Sheet on each company you visit. Evaluate the companies on their ability to provide the job characteristics you value the most.
17. Do what you are not supposed to do. Boldness is disarming. If it is motivated by honesty, it is irresistible.

9

LIFE YOUR OWN WAY

Living life your own way requires that you master the basics before you innovate. Just as the Olympic athlete must conform to the highest standards before he or she can move on to professional status, you too must learn to play by the rules. Then you are free to expand, even break the rules.

Passion Secret #9:
Powerful people know that freedom is the result of self-discipline.

If you are willing to make the extra effort that good work requires, entrepreneurship offers rich rewards — emotional, spiritual, and financial. If you value independence, you outgrow the need for supervision and structure when your foundation is secure. How do you know when you have reached this point?

1. You are responsible. You avoid playing the roles of victim, rescuer, and persecutor.
2. You are organized and efficient.
3. You are intellectually honest. You see people and events as they are, not as you want them to be.
4. You are mature. You make molehills out of molehills, mountains out of mountains, the latter often the result of your own or others' dishonesty, which you are not afraid to confront.
5. When it comes to money, you pay. You know exactly where you are financially at all times.
6. You are quick to adapt to change; growth is more important than your ego.
7. You are wary of fast growth; your pace is slow.
8. You are balanced between your needs and the needs of others.
9. You trust yourself.

At this point, even though you may occasionally fail to live up to all of the above, you are ready to innovate, either in tandem with someone who does what interests you, or by studying with someone you pay to train you in the process. Does the thought terrify you? Good, you are close to doing life your own way. When my clients reach this juncture, there is often tension between them and bosses, supervisors, and co-workers, because the self is screaming for *room* to spread its wings. If my clients do not take the initiative, they are often fired, demoted, or set off to one side. It took a showdown out of a 1930s gangster movie to blast me out of a plush office I shared with a partner in a skyscraper in San Francisco and into a back-to-basics basement office, where I began to write *Work with Passion*. At times I was sure I would wind up a bag lady, but instead I got the contract I mentioned in the last chapter, and changed my entire life: I divorced, moved, moved again, and eventually worked out of my house — which turned out to be the ideal setting for me and my clients.

I would never have succeeded in my business had I not spent

hours, days, months, and years with individual clients, slogging through their fears (and mine). I had experience in the rhythm of my business, too, so I knew not to give up hope in slow cycles. My emotional strength surprised me, and surprised all those who watched me go through trauma that would have staggered many people. But I could not imagine getting a job; the freedom to experiment was enough to keep me going every day. I had a book to write, and the support of clients who thought I was great, even when I fell forty floors down and landed in the basement. Perhaps it was because I never treated my clients as though they were sick and I was well. And I was not afraid to call it like it was. They knew I did not want to sit around listening to problems that could be solved by taking big risks: get the divorce or the necessary counseling, sell the house, send the grownup kids out on their own, write the letter, talk directly to the person who was bothering them, whether family member or so-called friend. In other words, do as I do, otherwise, I do not want to hear it.

Make no mistake, I know how frightening it is to take action. One must be clear-headed. But I would rather risk the chance that I could be wrong than wait until I am one-hundred percent sure. I could be dead by then, life gone on without me. A good rule of thumb for me is that if I feel bored and restless, I had better take action, or I send out signals that draw change to me, sometimes in unpleasant ways.

The most frustrating times in our lives are when we do not know what to do. When I am confused, I try to concentrate on what I can control. I take care of business details, check more books out of the library, go for longer runs in the morning, focus on the everyday interactions I have with myself and others. Often I discover some unconscious information that needs to be assimilated, insight I could never have gained in busier times. In our society, we are so enthralled with information, we overload our minds. Like a computer, the mind must be downloaded periodically, emptied of useless thoughts and ideas. Once my mind is quiet and clear, I know what to do, or not do. Until then, I wait.

Begin with a small step. For example, one of my clients had the choice of early retirement or part-time employment. I suggested he stay on in the part-time position because he needed the income while he developed his business. On the other hand, if you have enough income saved and you are experienced at what it is you want to do, the wisest move is to leave, so that you can concentrate on the new work. One of my clients had two years' income saved when he plunged full time into his new business, writing newsletters and developing sales. Within ten months, he was making as much as he did in his old job; in eighteen months, he surpassed his old income.

A client who was the top salesperson in his small company felt as though the owner stifled him. I suggested he talk to the boss. To his surprise, the boss suggested he take up golf, for both business and pleasure.

"That will probably be your passion," I laughed.

Within a few months, he was able to keep up with his teacher, whom he asked what it took to go on tour.

"I know I can do this, Nancy," he said, his tall, athletic frame sprawled on my couch. "But how do I make money while I learn?"

"Why do you have to quit your job?" I asked. "You have the kind of schedule that would allow you to play golf in the early morning and make sales calls the rest of the day, don't you?"

"Yes, my time is pretty much my own."

"You'll know in a year if golf is right for you. I'd be surprised if you leave your business expertise behind. In the meantime, you'll have fun, make more sales, and learn about the game."

His pent-up energy and perfectionism were ideal for the game he loved.

"I see all those senior men on the golf tours and I think, gosh, I could do this the rest of my life."

His natural athletic ability was a theme in his autobiography; he had kinesthetic gifts that had to be applied, if he were not to self-destruct. But it took the passage of time to see how those gifts could be used. History had to catch up with him — only recently had senior golf tournaments become popular, which gave him the inspiration to begin the game in his thirties.

Many of my clients are swinging into new uses of their talents, into careers unheard of a few years earlier, thanks to the positive changes in society. A regular job, five days a week, locked in a skyscraper, is death to creative types, like the personal banker who came to see me about her career.

"You need more than the work you do in the bank," I said. "Why don't you write a book about how to manage money?"

"How can I write about what I don't do well myself?"

"Writing the book will force you to correct your behavior," I said. "That's what writing did for me. You were an English teacher, you know how powerful the process of writing can be."

She lived on her severance pay while she wrote, draft after draft. Her book changed over time, as did her values.

"Unemployment is a great leveler," she said, describing how she felt about the meetings she attended with other job-seekers. "They really liked my presentation on how to survive during unemployment."

"That can be one of the chapters in your book," I suggested.

"I realized how childish I was with my boss in my last job, too. She was my mother and I was rebelling."

She went back to work as a personal banker, in a better environment, and her wealthy clients were a source of pleasure and information.

"It's no accident you're back in that job," I said. "You can learn from your clients, then use what you learn in the book."

After a few months in her new job, however, the same old problems began again. She felt pressured by the constant demands on her, the interruptions, and the continual push for more customers. We discussed how to relieve her stress, when suddenly she said, "Well, I don't have to get everything done every day, do I?"

We laughed — her syndrome of constantly trying too hard to please was out in the open.

"Maybe it's not your job, but your attitude toward yourself that needs changing," I suggested, knowing how many times excessive striving caused me to lose my balance. "Isn't patience the key to success with money?"

"Of course. My wealthy clients didn't get there overnight. They worked hard for their money, or if they inherited it, they still manage it well."

Often we are placed in situations we would not choose consciously, but a higher wisdom than ours knows what is best for us — and often, frustration is our greatest teacher. As human beings, we are perverse in our belief that a quick and easy way exists to solve our problems. Rather than resenting her job, my client learned to adopt the attitude of her clients.

"I'm getting paid now for my speaking engagements," she said the next time we talked.

"Have you ever considered taping your talks?" I asked, knowing that she spoke more easily than she wrote.

"People are always asking me to repeat what I say so that they can write it down," she replied, "but I never thought of taping myself."

Here you have an example of an unconscious competence, a skill that came so naturally to her that she overlooked its importance. She is an extrovert, one whose creativity is stimulated by contact with people who share her values. In the process of talking and listening she is inspired by her intuition to come up with original insights. Once she stopped fighting what life brought to her, she used adversity as her ally rather than her foe.

The desire to control life is death to creativity, as one of my clients learned. He was fresh from early retirement, hoping to use his experience with a large computer firm to help small business owners who serviced the larger company. He was working with a partner I knew was dishonest; this partner reflected the part of himself he needed to confront.

"You need to work on your own — you're not a partner type, you're a solo," I said. This was clear from his autobiography. He learned early to adapt to his single, alcoholic mother, then to his wives and peers. He compromised his dreams and desires because of others.

"You must have been miserable all those years," I said. "No wonder you drank all the time."

He thought he led a "charmed life."

"Oh, you were under a spell all right," I laughed.

His old self wanted things, a long list of boats, houses, and other possessions — goals he set in a seminar he attended before we met.

"What do you want all that stuff for?" I asked. "I'd be worn out just thinking about it."

He was so upset by what I said in our meeting he took the wrong turn off the freeway on his way home.

"Well, that's symbolic, isn't it?" I asked, and we both laughed.

Another client was a certified public accountant who had too many distractions in his life to ever accomplish what he said he wanted to do, which was to develop a public speaking career.

"I'd suggest you get your own life in shape first," I said. "Make your clients pay you on time. Discipline your staff, and set better boundaries with your wife. If you want to teach others, be a good example."

People like my client are a magnet for abuse because of their inability to set limits — behavior usually rooted in a childhood bereft of affection. But that did not excuse his self-imposed martyrdom, or his refusal to master the basics before he climbed higher on the ladder of authority.

CHANGE FOR THE BETTER

Change for the better is stressful. We are so used to struggle that it is hard to adjust to a life that works. My client who got laid off from the bank wondered how she ever tolerated the life she led in more chaotic times. Meanwhile, a former co-worker of hers remained embroiled in recriminations against the bank. Depressed and burdened by a mortgage, she was forced to take a job she did not like. My client sold her house, sent her grown children out on their own, and eliminated the clutter from her life.

"She doesn't understand why I don't want to be around her anymore," said my client.

"She would if she took the action you took," I said.

Independence is a difficult path, but the irony is that the sacrifices we make are of possessions and relationships we do not need. You can meet independent people in entrepreneurial settings; your local chamber of commerce meetings are often a good place to begin. Or, they might be right around the corner from you, in a small office with a window that opens onto a pleasant view, or in a retail shop that sells quality products. Walk in and introduce yourself, and ask for some time to talk to them about their businesses. As the old saying goes, the diamonds are in our backyard.

One of my clients found it hard to believe that, after a career in computers, he could start a photography business. I encouraged him to use his considerable talent, a gift made clear in the picture he sent to me at Christmas. A successful mountain climber, his pictures brought rave reviews from many people, he said.

"Work as a systems contractor while your photography business grows," I said. "In five years you'll make all the money you need from your photography business. Meanwhile, you'll be learning how to do a business you can do for the rest of your life."

A dream he had shortly after we began work told him he was on the right track. He was among a group of people preparing for a play.

The director in the dream was a woman who said he had no part — he was late so she gave it to someone else. He walked over to the person who had his script and took it from him. As he thumbed through the pages, he thought the others in the cast needed to know the context of the play — the past — otherwise they could never understand it.

My interpretation of the dream was that my client needed to work through his autobiography before he took action.

"I lost what was mine through internal conflict," he said about the dream, "a part I reclaim with joy."

DO NOT GO BACKWARD

The need for security draws us back to the familiar when we feel overwhelmed by the unknown. The void is frightening, but our tolerance for not knowing is a direct measure of personal growth. One of my clients kept going back to the past, working for bosses who lied and overextended themselves, then blamed my client — a repeat of his interaction with his alcoholic father.

"You'll never be happy until you're on your own," I said.

"But then I'd have no one to blame, would I?" he laughed.

His was a case of someone who had mastered the basics, but the insecurity left from his interaction with his father kept him in a subservient position. He was constantly criticized by his father, a man who failed in his business. He finally realized his father was talking about himself when he called his son "stupid."

EXPAND ON WHAT YOU KNOW

Your ability grows as you master your craft. You see ways to improve; you invent new techniques. A drapery hanger who invents a pleating machine, a computer expert who develops new software, an author who writes a new book, a doctor who creates a new medical device — all are the result of expanding on what you know.

Normally, it takes eight to ten years to become good at what you do. At that point, one either innovates or plateaus. Notice what you do over and over again, see how you get better with experience, whether it is buying a good loaf of bread, or finding the best restaurant in town. I never thought I would be hired to edit someone's book, but that is what happened after I wrote my own book. Soon, I had another editing client, a project that gave me a chance to improve on my last editing job. Your experience is valuable; helping someone do what you have done is so simple it is hard to believe you will get paid for your expertise. As Krishnamurti says in his book, *The First and Last Freedom*,[1] quiet observation of any problem by someone who is interested in the problem reveals its solution.

TEACH WHAT YOU KNOW

Every city has organizations that appreciate a good speaker. If you have a skill you would enjoy teaching to others, offer to speak to groups who would be interested in hearing what you have to say. My client who is writing her book on money is often invited to speak about her topic, which gives her a chance to hone her ideas.

If you are shy about appearing in front of a group, join Toastmasters, or take speech classes to learn how to present yourself. If you are a skilled speaker, consider developing a brochure that markets what is close to your heart. Contact a speakers bureau and let them know you are available. Teach courses at the local community college, or at a university extension program — an excellent way to develop yourself and your business. You may have a seminar organization in your city; if so, contact the owner and let him or her know about your topic. Use the advice call approach in Chapter Eight; learn about others before you ask for the sale.

CHARGE FOR WHAT YOU KNOW

If you enjoy changing what needs to be changed, and if the work you do is effective, consider charging for your time. Begin with your friends — the tasks you have done for free may be worth money. You are not going to be a lawyer without training and certification, but many services begin as a hobby: making baskets, home remodeling, gardening, upholstering, counseling, a myriad of ways to serve others' needs. The how-to books on the market are excellent examples of charging for what you know. The author worked until he or she came up with an idea that would help others improve their lives. Visit any bookstore and walk down the how-to aisles — you will be amazed by the ingenuity and the variety.

One of my clients was a master teacher, but she was tired of the bureaucracy. I suggested she start her own tutoring business. She was so successful, so in demand, I suggested she write about her methods.

"That's even scarier than starting my own business," she laughed.

USE YOUR ENERGY WISELY

As you progress in life, you learn to use your energy wisely. You learn how to say no, because you value your time. If you are married or living with someone, you work within these limits, especially if you have children. Relationships take time, which means you do not scatter your energy among superficial contacts.

One of my clients was forced to confront her tendency to do too much. She began to limit her mother's telephone calls, and her friends' demands on her time, so that she could concentrate on helping her husband's business grow. She managed the financial problems out of her home office, allowing her time with the children, and the opportunity to acquire entrepreneurial skills. Another client worked a flexible plan with her corporation, doing much of her work at home. Both women gave their children a good example of the new way to work, balanced and productive.

PICK COMPATIBLE PARTNERS

The work you did on your values in Chapter Two helped you select a compatible working environment. Your top five values also define the best personal relationships for you. If you share these five values with your intimate partners, you will have few conflicts, and those that do arise will be resolved quickly.

Knowing how introverted or extroverted you are is important, too, since difference in temperament is the root of many battles. Time alone is vital to the introvert, not so to the extrovert, who gets energized by contact with others. If you are an introvert, and you choose an extroverted partner, make sure that both of you allow for the needs of each other. For example, if you said that you were a number 3 on a scale of 1 to 10 in the introvert/extrovert scale at the end of Chapter One, you will need to be alone about seventy percent of the time, at work and in relationships. Conversely, if you said you were a 7 on the same scale, you will need to be alone about thirty percent of the time, at work and in relationships. It is not too difficult to see what would happen if these two people married each other — or worked together in a partnership. One would be overwhelmed by the other's need to be together, and the other would feel lonely.

Many conflicts arise because we do not know our temperament — what we need to feel relaxed and comfortable. If you are an extrovert, you may wonder why the introverts are exhausted after thirty minutes of a meeting, when you are just getting started. Or, if you are an introvert, you cannot understand why the extrovert needs to talk so long and so often. The answer is that both of you process information very differently; the introvert looks within for balance, the extrovert needs the feedback from others to know what he or she thinks and feels.

It is obvious that all of us are a mixture of introversion and extroversion. What is important is that you know what that mixture is for you, and for those with whom you work and live. This knowledge leads to good boundaries and mutual respect, which are crucial to mental, emotional, and physical health — and to working with passion.

SUMMARY

Passion Secret #9: Powerful people know that freedom is the result of self-discipline.

1. Life your own way follows mastery of the basics: organization, honesty, adapting to change, balancing your needs and the needs of others, and trust.
2. Be brave enough to remove the dead wood in your life, the parts of yourself you no longer need
3. Be honest — when it is time to go, set up a plan of action.
4. Be open to the unknown. Allow time for integration of the past before you proceed to the future.
5. Know that age is on your side when you sell what you know.
6. Consider writing what you know about the field you are in. You may be surprised at what you know. Consider marketing that knowledge.
7. Attend entrepreneurial meetings. Arrange meetings with owners of businesses you find interesting. You may hear what you were not ready to hear the last time you met with an entrepreneur.
8. Do not go backward. You will only antagonize people when you work, live, marry, or otherwise associate with those who do not support your growth and your passion.

9. Use what you know to make money. Charge for your time, your craft, your talent. Keep the job you have while you grow in skill.
10. Be careful not to overextend yourself. The symptoms are irritability, fatigue, and pessimism.
11. Choose your partners wisely. Check to see if you are forcing yourself to be with others more than is comfortable for you. Or, if you need more companionship, do not isolate yourself from those who can be a source of great pleasure — and information. Knowing who we are and what we need is life's greatest achievement, but that knowledge is not transferable. Each of us must create the work that fits our unique personality and passion, no exceptions, no exclusions.

MOVE ON AND UP IN YOUR LIFE

Passion Secret #10:
Powerful people know when they "get there."

You followed my directions well and here you are, at the end of the journey — at least at the end of our journey together. Now you are ready for the tenth and final step to finding your passion — knowing that you have "made it." How do you know when you "get there"?

You See Every Part of Your Life As a Success

You will know that you have arrived when you look at every part of your life as a success. You will see how each development was necessary for your growth. You incorporate what went before, and continue to develop, to move on and up. As you analyze your mistakes, you go through the process of assimilating and integrating all your learning. You have to be patient with yourself during this process, forgiving yourself quickly for not seeing what may now seem to be obvious. There is a time frame for learning our lessons — we cannot rush that dynamic growth. As soon as a shift in our thinking occurs, additional information pours in to reinforce those new ways of thinking. You continue to weave the tapestry of your life, and you see it as a unified, successful whole.

Your World Is More Vivid

There are other *clues* to show that you have arrived, in addition to liking your life. You will sense your world as being more vivid, more intense. All hues sharpen, become more defined — as they did for the great English poet, John Keats, who felt all life on his pulses.[1] Keats embodies the principle of working with passion, integrating mind, body, and spirit. His short life (he died at the age of twenty-six) is a remarkable study of focused passion, and his poetry reflects that life — intellectual, sensuous, aspiring.

Like the new laser technology in television viewing, creating uncannily sharp and clear images, the images of great poetry startle us with their accuracy. Advanced thinking and feeling is the same. You see more, feel more. You are now the child who *has* to experience. If the sun shines, that is fine, and if it rains, that is fine too. If you are fired from a job, you look for the opportunity the firing gives you. You know that it means more growth is coming. It is painful, but in the long run you welcome the opportunity to be a more aware actor. You lose some of what you have so you can go on to *more*.

You Become Selective in Your Choice of Experiences

At the same time that you avidly court life's experiences, you become highly selective when you have "made it." (*Passion clue: discrimination marks the truly passionate.*)

In his autobiography, the Irish poet William Butler Yeats described gathering carefully chosen experiences ". . . as if for a collector's cabinet. . . . True unity of being, where all nature murmurs in response if but a single note be touched, is found emotionally, instinctively, by the rejection of experience that is not of the right quality, and by the limitation of its quantity."[2] Once you have "gotten there," you turn down unwanted experiences that will bring you and others pain, sorrow, or guilt. You do not force yourself to be with people you do not like — including family members — or do what you hate anymore. No one can "trap" you because you do not trap yourself with illusion and self-deception. You examine your motives with the clear light of honesty, the most beautiful word in the English language.

You Are Honest and Forgiving

Our lives sometimes go in directions that have traumatic results (unwise marriages, divorce, loss of life, money, love). You are quick to admit your mistakes to yourself, and you set about making things right in your life. You apologize and ask for forgiveness in all situations in which you have hurt others. You forgive yourself readily. You will build anew from adversity and not linger in recriminating yourself or others.

You Find Meaning in All Experience

For those of us who have experienced the magic of giving birth, there is an understanding of the driving force behind creative experience. The child decides the moment of birth, not the mother. "Why all the pain, why so much time?" you ask yourself. You finally understand that nature has its own rhythm and time cycle. Realizing that, you do not choose to suffer anymore. You accept all your experience and give it meaning. In Victor Frankl's work, *Man's Search for Meaning*,[3] he described the attributes of those who made it through the horrors of the concentration camps. Those who went on to productive lives after their release saw meaning even in their imprisonment. Carl Jung says that all experience is explainable to the conscious mind when it is given meaning.

On a lighter note, you give meaning to your experience in much the same way as the characters in the *Peanuts* comic strip do — Lucy, Charlie Brown, Linus, Schroeder, and Snoopy eventually make sense out of the conflicts in their lives, all the while making us laugh at them and ourselves. The same principle can be seen in the structure of music: tension and disharmony finally come together in chords of resolution, the artist's goal.

You Develop Mastery

Another clue to "making it" corresponds to the concept of mastery. Mastery is the accomplishment of a specific task for which you are given recognition. When you are "best" at something, you perform with the precision of a champion. People who do what they do best do not look like they are working, they look like they are playing. Olympic athletes look like they are playing when their event goes well, as do Academy Award-winning actors and actresses.

You will be relaxed and confident when you master the tasks you set for yourself, whatever they are: rearing children, showing dogs, doctoring the sick, starting businesses, serving customers in every way. A young woman who works for the automobile dealership from whom I bought my car is on her way to mastery. She calls after every service visit to see if I am satisfied. She is so sincere I doubt she realizes the effect she has on others — she just does what comes naturally. Our passion is just like that, so obvious to observant onlookers.

Good coaches are masters at perceiving such talent, and they know how to correct their athletes: they do not overcorrect, nor do they over-criticize. Their suggestions are often subtle. My tennis coach, for example, says to me gently: "Turn your wrist half an inch; lean your body forward, into the ball; keep your knees slightly flexed." You are like the good tennis player when you have "made it." You find good coaches, you continue to improve your game, correcting all the time. Continual slight adjustments in behavior lead to mastery.

Another example of this principle is illustrated by the use of navigational devices on aircraft. Whether it is for a commercial airliner or a space shuttle, the computerized equipment constantly shifts and adjusts course from takeoff to landing. Rarely is the aircraft exactly on course. Ask any pilot and he will tell you that being slightly off course is the norm. Your personal navigational equipment is highly accurate as well. Your unconscious (imaginative) and conscious (logical) minds work as a team. When you have "made it" you give both equal status, confident that you will reach your destination.

You Stay Alert

You are alert, paying attention to all clues in the environment. You are now well aware that there are no "accidents." Daily life is carefully noted, and the people who come into your life for any length of time are studied for what they can tell you about yourself. You observe the person or group you associate with and understand their significance. You are the gazing, interested movie camera that records all data for later recollection, keeping only what makes you grow.

You Are Healthy

When you have "made it," you are rarely ill. But when you are, you examine your illness to see what part of your *thinking* is off balance. Emotions are behind so many of our ailments. You do not dam up your feelings for years, months, or even days. You laugh frequently, a good measure of mental health! You exercise vigorously, you eat and drink moderately. You sleep when you need it. In other words, you use common sense.

You Listen to the Unusual

The most significant clue that lets you know when you have "arrived" is that you are open to new ideas. You listen before passing judgment, no matter how unusual the idea or concept. Prophets are sometimes found in unlikely places, like the woman you converse with at your bus stop, or they are young in years, like your child. Prophets are always idealists, but they make us think. Nearly every major advance in civilization was once a cockeyed scheme that most people ridiculed. If you are worried that civilization now seems to be headed in a self-destructive direction, realize that the best help you can be to our world is to *improve yourself and follow your passion.* Powerful and passionate people change the world.

You Use Growth Resources

You use resources that speed up the assimilation and integration of your experience. You may go to a therapist for objective listening when you hit a snag. For some people, group therapy may bring personal clarity. Workshops, seminars, and various courses can be excellent focusing tools. You always learn more about yourself from exposure to new ideas or new presentations of old ones. The rule of thumb is: Does it work? Powerful people know how to use the self-awareness tools that work for them. They are self-oriented in the most positive sense.

"Selfish" is a word that has a different meaning to powerful people than it does to power*less* people. Powerful people are aware that their individual lives and activities will influence others. That is why they understand that their career choices are crucial, not only as an example for others, but as vehicles for self-expression. An ongoing understanding and examination of the self is necessary for continued clarity in making decisions.

You Fall in Love with Yourself

Once you have "made it," you revel in your individuality. You love both personal freedom *and* being responsible. You notice that you like being alone for hours on end. You are fascinated with this self of yours, who keeps on expanding — you almost feel as though you take up more room in the universe! You become acquainted with that "larger self" through meditation and through quiet times alone with your thoughts. You look more to him or her for guidance. Your "larger self," you discover, is always faithful, humorous, and persevering.

The result of your absorption in yourself is not narcissistic. It frees you to love and serve others more fully. You let yourself bloom.

Your Spirituality Is Individualized

When you have "arrived," your definition of God is intensely personal. You are aware of a force, a higher power, that permeates your life. You resist the efforts of others to impose their beliefs on you. Tyranny of any kind is heavy and dark. Spirituality is light — powerful and illuminating — and you radiate this light. Shining the light on darkness is the way to "lighten" your life. When your spirituality is individualized, you live a truly free life: ". . . their souls shall be as a watered garden; and they shall not sorrow anymore." (Jeremiah 31:12)

The following client stories, beginning with Robert's, are about people who already appeared "successful" in the eyes of others. The stories illustrate how each one learned to make the subtle corrections that allowed them to develop true mastery in their personal and professional lives. They are examples of how people learn to focus and release their personal power. These five have "arrived," and continue to move on and up in their lives.

ROBERT'S STORY

Robert had two degrees, an MBA and a law degree. His company had hired me to discover a better place to use him. He was not getting along with his supervisor and was not performing well in his job as a financial analyst. His work was sloppy, his lunchtimes stretched out to two hours, and he was frequently late.

His autobiography showed a consistent pattern of early discontent and rebellion, starting with his relationship with his father (a pattern you are familiar with by now!) and continuing throughout his early school years. It was in high school that Robert finally found a constructive use for his outspoken energy and his need to challenge authority. He joined the debating team and consistently won honors in every competition. After he graduated from high school and went on to college, his highest achievements came when he made presentations. He was a natural leader whose ability to communicate earned him frequent praise. Robert believed that graduate school, in both law and business, was the road to success, and continued his education into his late twenties.

"It was one law school professor who told me that a person's writing ability was the key to passing the bar exam. He said that even if you knew the law, unless you could write it, you'd never pass. I made up my mind that my focus in law school would be written and verbal analysis. And I passed the bar," Robert said.

Robert's top strength was communication, the skill he had continually developed since his high school years. He loved the excitement of performing before an audience, and had finely honed his skills at a professional level. But his present position did not require the use of his most valuable abilities.

"Why did you get into financial analysis — a position which requires you to sit at a desk and move numbers around?" I asked. (Getting "off the track" is easy to do, when you attempt to fit an image of success that "society" rewards.)

"I came to the company as a tax lawyer. Because I found I didn't enjoy tax law, my company transferred me to cash management, thinking it would be more exciting for me. It wasn't. I'm bored, and I'm not doing a good job. Until I did the assignments you gave me, I was beginning to think of myself as a failure," he said. (Do you see how even those who from all appearances have "made it" can hit low periods? Robert was not in a position where he could lead, and that was his passion.)

I met with Robert's supervisor and heard her story.

"For a whole year I've tried everything. He just can't do the work. I'm behind on my deadlines and I must replace him soon," she said. Her patience was exhausted. I asked her what she had seen Robert do well in the year he had worked for her.

Her face brightened as she described a course he had taught to all the accountants on financial report analysis.

"He was superb. He worked for days on that course. He wrote a manual, a course outline, and when he was in front of the group, he had total control. I was surprised at his teaching skill. Robert's a natural leader. After the class, many people asked me who he was. They thought he was the best instructor they'd ever heard," she said.

"Yes, and annual reports are not exactly 'up' material," I said. "If such a dry subject can be taught so excitingly, then why not have Robert teach and train people in the company, rather than *do* the tasks?"

She paused to reflect for a moment.

"Of course!" she said. "He's so good at communicating, no wonder he's bored. He hates his present job because there's no chance to perform, to do what he really loves."

Like bored children, bored adults often create disruption so they have something to stimulate them — a negative way of creating challenges.

The next step was to move Robert to a job that he liked. It was found that the tax department had a need to teach salespeople about the tax benefits to customers buying the firm's expensive computer equipment. The task required someone who knew tax law and who could communicate well.

"It's exciting to think about what I can do with this opportunity, teaching dynamic marketing types about tax benefits. I get along well with salespeople," Robert said.

"You're a born salesperson yourself, that's why. You've been selling ideas and concepts all your life," I said. "As you expand your activities, your niche will be a rare one; you'll be in great demand. How many people can combine a knowledge of business, law, taxes, and cash management with the ability to be an outstanding communicator?" I asked.

Robert's renewed self-confidence showed in his face. His body movements had changed in just a few weeks. His chin was forward, his eyes sparkled, and he was leaning on the edge of the couch.

"I feel great. I've learned so much this last year. I was trying to be something I'm not, a financial analyst. I thought that particular position in the company would give me prestige and status. But a position in which I do well is the best one for me," he said. (And because he is so highly regarded, he also has the "prestige and status" he coveted!)

Robert has arrived. He has "made it." He will have other challenges and he will be aware of his responsibility to meet them, while remaining faithful to his passion.

You may be in the right company, too, like Robert. Before you change companies, do some research inside your organization to see if there are internal problems you can solve effortlessly, enjoyably. Business dislikes turnover. It is costly. It is also hard on morale. Because Robert found his niche, his company reaped the benefit of a motivated performer. He will solve more problems, increase sales, and reduce costs.

The key to change of any kind depends upon the acceptance by others of a new way to do things. The development of your creative ideas hinges upon a "personality fit" with a decision-maker in your company. Resistance to change is quite real in business. If you have great ideas but cannot convince your supervisor or another decision-maker to try them, then consider looking outside your company to find personalities that will respond to you. Check to see if your personality is a partner, team, or solo type, using the exercise in Chapter Five.

Before Robert had done research within his company, he had considered other job offers, thinking that the only solution to his discontent was to move elsewhere. But once he saw how he could contribute within his company, he changed his attitude. "The next step in my career will be international. I'll travel and train personnel in all the subsidiaries — a dream job," he said.

Robert spends much of his time now thinking about how he will teach what he knows. He realized how all events can eventually work out for the best. The opportunity to travel, to see other countries, to experience the development of his company's products, and his own personal development — these issues occupy a mind that was formerly lost in a maze of negative events. The experience has enriched all of his life, including his family life. Remember that your mind is like the earth: what you sow, you will reap.

JAN'S STORY

One of my clients was an idealist, always carrying a banner. She had been through Zionism, Kibbutz life, Silva Mind Control — all designed to change the world. She eventually ended up working as a systems analyst.

Jan had always focused her power on outside organizations, blending her own goals into those of the group. Jan had a dynamic personality, usually leading whatever group she joined. Now, however, she had decided to look within herself for solutions. *Individuation*, Carl Jung's term for accepting our separateness, was taking place and it scared Jan. Her break from her causes had left a void. "I know what I don't want. I don't know what I do want," she said.

People who experienced the upheavals of the 1960s know about extremes; the clash of opposites has conditioned their thinking. They experienced the crumbling of social ideals which came under attack through demonstrations, riots, and the Vietnam War. The net result for many in Jan's age group is a desire to integrate personal and social values. The experience of a turbulent era created in many of us a willingness to consider alternatives. The 1960s were a symbol of the passages in emotional growth we all experience. As with death, divorce, or the loss of a job or a love, our whole world changes. For Jan, the turmoil of the past and the disenchantment of lost beliefs had created a malaise of her spirit. The present seemed flat, the future impossible to imagine.

Because Jan was always at the top of whatever organization she had joined, she seemed successful to others. Her present state of mind disturbed her, something she had never experienced. *(Passion clue:* You choose experiences that *scare* you just enough to force your growth.)

"Ask yourself why you designed a flat period in your life," I said. "Why do you suppose you have this time available to be thinking, analyzing, and considering all the possible alternatives you have?"

I asked Jan to keep a daily journal, and to write down at least a few sentences each day. This technique would assist her in staying alert to clues in her environment.

"It doesn't matter what you write. Nor does it matter what time of day you choose to write. Record whatever is on your mind — comments about what's happening in the world, at home, at work. Just make a note of your reactions," I said.

After a month of journal entries Jan began to understand what she was learning, and why she had taken a new path. One journal entry in particular became the key to a long-locked door.

"I started writing in my journal one day after seeing children on their way to school one morning. *(See the clue she picked up in the environment?)* I remember how terrified I was when I came to this country as a child. I couldn't understand or speak English and for weeks I didn't say a word. Remembering that time let loose a flood of memories — how important it was for me to find a new family! Could the reason for joining all those groups be based on a need to belong to a new family?" she asked.

"Your desire to blend in, to identify with a movement, could very well have started then. Seven years old is a tender age to be uprooted and find yourself in a strange country," I replied.

As Jan thought more about herself, she began to see her past as good preparation for work of a more independent nature. She had come full circle, to the point where she felt she could never work for anyone.

"I have to be on my own. And my work as a systems analyst is too oriented to 'things' and 'data'. I like people. I come home after a day of work and have trouble talking to my husband. His work is so people-oriented that it's disturbing to adjust to his conversation at the end of the day," she said.

We had come a long way in a few months. It appeared that Jan was ready to design her own business. We reviewed her passions, skills, and values. Jan's collage was extremely revealing. (Remember the collage assignment at the end of Chapter Three?) A collage is a self-image exercise that features the placement of pictures and words from magazines on a posterboard. Jan's had many scenes of food, dinners, picnics, and other gatherings where food and drink brought people together.

"I love food preparation. I always took charge of the food arrangements in all the organizations I joined. I've put on dinners for five hundred people. Every time we have company for dinner, my guests want my recipes. I just have a good sense with food," she said.

I suggested that she make several advice calls on caterers of various kinds. She called me one day after several meetings to tell me about a young woman she had met.

"We're like twins! She has a similar background, and she worked with computers until she couldn't stand it anymore. She loved to cook, and took cooking classes and started trying out her new skills on guests. One friend asked her to prepare the food for her wedding, and several wedding guests asked her to cater for them. After six months she had so much business that she quit her job, and now caters full time. She's so busy that she asked me if I'd like to help her with her next big job!" Jan was excited and enthused.

You can guess the story's ending. Jan is now a partner with the other woman, learning the business with no financial risk. She is happy, works hard, and sees limitless opportunities.

"Our next venture will be to teach cooking classes, and we're collaborating on our first cookbook," she said in a recent conversation.

Jan had "made it"; she just had to take time to sift through her thoughts before taking action. Powerful people know what to do when they get stuck. They go back to the past, regroup, and then proceed. They do not stop growing. Success is a motivation in and of itself. Successful people want to see *what else* they can do. They love a fresh challenge.

DAVID'S STORY

Another example of subtle correction occurred when a very successful salesperson came to me for help in his career. He was trying to break into international trade in the Middle East. His attempts to reach multinational corporations had been fruitless. With every letter and every phone call, he ran into the proverbial brick wall. David's skill as a salesperson was apparently ineffective in his new career search.

The number one salesperson in his company, David continually worked on improving himself, and had many of the qualities necessary for success. But what he needed at this time was a new method which would *open his mind to a different way of operating*.

At first David resisted my suggestions that he follow a definite program to achieve his objectives. He thought that all he needed was to improve his phone technique. He did not want to spend the time to write an autobiography and implement the ten-step process. He wanted a quick answer that would solve his problems.

"You can't beat your way into a company with a resume and slick phone techniques," I told him. "There's some pattern you're repeating that is holding you back, and I have to find out what it is. Your obstinate and stubborn desire to do things your own way stands between you and the dream position you say you want. When did that pattern start?" I asked.

David's autobiography revealed a fascinating story, unusual and rich with variety, showing an early exposure to religious, social, and political conflict. The Middle East environment in which he grew up, with its turmoil, secrecy, and suspicion, was the crucible that produced a fighter. I have reproduced excerpts from his story, which was originally thirty pages long, so that you can see an actual autobiography, and notice its revealing patterns. My comments are in parentheses to show you what to look for in your own story.

> Some of the earliest memories I have go back to my first year in kindergarten at the Armenian School in Jerusalem. All the children there wore red dresses with white lace collars. I remember sitting in class, hands clasped behind my back, reciting excerpts from the Bible. A very uncomfortable position to be in, reciting meaningless — to me — verses in the company of strangers. (David's earliest memory is feeling uncomfortable with his peers. He felt constricted. Your earliest memory sets the theme of your story.)
>
> Mother had the maid deliver fresh juices to me every day during recess and I hated juices. All the kids used to gather around me and ask me to share the drink, a request to which I gladly obliged. By local standards, we were well-off, though my mother always complained about money. She came from a traditional upper-middle-class family and married a middle-class man. She never got over that, especially since class distinctions are so important in that traditional culture. (This relationship with the mother and her class consciousness is a big red flag. Our mothers' beliefs affect us for years unless we examine them for accuracy, rejecting what does not apply to our lives. In your autobiography it is important to record the beliefs and values of both parents. Since David's father is in an "inferior" position to his mother, will David repeat this dynamic with the women he chooses? Will he always feel — like his father — that he is not good enough?)
>
> Most of the people around us were poor, especially since the Arab-Israeli War of 1948 was only four to five years before. Occasionally there were skirmishes on the border and

life was not very safe. (Even though he was young, his mind would absorb the fear around him). Many people had lost loved ones and property. My family lost their home and business and my father had to start all over again. We fled Jerusalem in 1948. I was a few months old when we lived with the Bedouins in the desert. I don't remember anything of my experience there. I was about three when we returned to the now divided city of Jerusalem. The house we lived in was a huge thirteenth- or fourteenth-century house of Arabian architecture with thick walls and big domes.

Rapid Change

After I spent two years at the Armenian School, my parents enrolled me in a German school for one year, and then a French private school for boys. I stayed there until graduation in 1967. This French school was nothing more than a stalag with "Brothers" running the show. Discipline and conformity were of primary importance. (Frequent change and then a repressive environment fostered his rebellious attitude.) Classes would start at 7:20 A.M. and end at 4:30 P.M. with two fifteen-minute recesses and one hour for lunch. I hated school until perhaps my sophomore year. My grades until that year were average or below average.

I used to feel very envious of those who excelled. I also considered them "sissys." They were the teacher's favorites. (A conflict. David wants to be the favorite, to get the attention.) I distinctly remember an episode during Catechism class where the Brother asked the model student and myself to come forward. Johnny was an A student, blond, blue-eyed, clean clothes and fingernails. I was dark, had dishevelled hair, and was meager looking. He asked us both to kneel and proceeded to outline the differences between devils and angels. Johnny was the example of the angel. I was so angry that I hit the

Brother, who later punished me with ten lashes and a detention. That was quite a venturesome act on my part, since at that time one did not dare even look in the eyes of a teacher when talking to him. (This is wonderful spirit — I laughed out loud as I read this story. David *can* be a devil when he wants to.)

Early Self-Image

I was an ornery brat. I spent most of my time climbing trees, and exploring caves and holes. I collected and lynched lizards despite the pleas and advice of my mother and aunt. I explored old castles or churches with some neighborhood kids.

I used to collect bottles, make some funny perfumes out of spices and liquid color, and sell them to the Bedouins who came to town on Fridays. I also hired neighborhood kids to run tiny concession stands at busy street corners. Later I found that those kids cheated me blind. I started buying squabs and chickens and other domestic animals and raised them for family consumption and for sale. (The early signs of the solo personality, the entrepreneur.) I knew a lot about animals at the age of ten or twelve. I also loved handcrafts. I built things like doghouses, carved model ship hulls out of pine bark, and won prizes at several Boy Scout and craft fairs. Carpentry was my best hobby.

I hated books. I never had time to study or do my homework. That enraged my mother. Since she was well educated by local standards, especially for a woman, she wanted me to stick to my books. I hated school and did not make good grades. Corporal punishment was common. I had a few lickings, but it was hard to pin me down since I fought back. As I grew up, I was so surprised to know that some teachers did like me. I was made prefect to ensure that all the other kids complied with the stupid rules. I "played the game." (Adapting to the system, making other kids comply with "stupid rules." David looks out for David. He's getting shrewd.) At fourteen or fifteen I spent most of my time in sports.

Exposure to an Audience

Then I became interested in music and I got in a band — the first such band in the Hashemite Kingdom of Jordan. I was popular. The band gained nationwide popularity. We performed mostly on stage. We argued and fought a lot amongst ourselves, especially myself and the lead singer, who was the best musician of the four of us. I felt he monopolized the group. Today this person is my best friend. Funny how jealousy has matured into such close friendship.

My Home Life

Our house was the gathering place for all our friends. Women dropped by — very unusual in those days. Mother could not stand the gatherings. She had migraines. Mother has always been ailing. (Mother is probably an introvert, forcing herself to conform and her body is rebelling!) I had my first sexual experience at fifteen with a beautiful married woman of twenty-two or so. Scared the hell out of me!

Dad encouraged our music and was really proud to see me perform as a musician and as an athlete. What an easy-going man. (Too easy going?) He rarely got angry and I can't remember him ever hitting me. He was my friend. Mother did the disciplining.(The mother took over the father's responsibility, which made her the bad guy.) She really worked hard, even with the help of a maid. The house was always in immaculate condition. Dad had many important dignitaries and business associates visit us. I was so proud when the Governor of Jerusalem used to visit with military escort.

I was very Westernized then. Blue jeans and T-shirts, singing *West Side Story* with my pals. We acted tough and got into many fights. America was an inspiration. When J. F. Kennedy was assassinated, we were very sad. It is interesting to see that those who felt that way then are now very anti-American and PLO supporters. America has got to play a more even-handed role in the Middle East. I enjoyed the outdoors a lot then, as I do now. I used to backpack in the Judean wilderness and visit Greek monks in remote monasteries. What a simple life it was. (I wonder if he will come back to this at the end of his life?)

College Days

I won a scholarship to Drew University. It came right on time, after the Six Day War in 1967. That was the worst time I spent in Jerusalem. Neighbors were shot, shops were looted. It was never reported in the American press. Israel certainly did not exercise its democracy with the Arabs. Every time I go there I get interrogated. I feel I am in an alien land. After coming to the United States, I got a deeper appreciation of politics, propaganda, and the American political process. Drew was an ivory tower. I loved it. I enjoyed my teachers and the academic atmosphere. My grades were very good and I enjoyed books for the first time in my life. I made a lot of friends there.

I got involved in the civil rights movement and the anti-Vietnam War movement. I was also involved in many extracurricular activities. I started and headed the International Club, joined the varsity soccer team, and went to the Nationals in soccer. I became president of my class. I also dated a lot. I enjoyed my education. Finally majored in psychology, met a wonderful girl whom I later married, and moved to Boston to attend school there and work. We were so anti-establishment at that time that I refused to work for a corporation. I took a mechanic's job, then later temporarily worked as a foreman in a factory. Those two years in Boston were a lot of fun.

My wife Dianne was the first girl I emotionally got involved with. I had really never had a steady girlfriend. We had the same aspirations and interests. (Not much experience before marriage.)

Kentucky

The back-to-the-land movement was a dominant factor in our move to Kentucky. We wanted to live on a farm and after two years in Kentucky, we bought one. Little did we realize how difficult it was to live on one, and the investment it took to start and run it.

Kentucky was the heart of America to me. I became involved in social work. I still did not want to work for profit. What naivete. I was very proud of the fact that I was working for humanitarian and constructive reasons. Slowly I started realizing how tied up and interrelated the social structure is. I enjoyed work tremendously. The director and two people on the staff and I became very close friends.

Then politics came into the social agency and our director was axed for trying to reform the system. I got involved in lobbying at the state legislature to pass a new bill which would create a separate services department and which would insure that the appropriate federal funds were spent intelligently. Politics and the democratic process definitely was one of the most interesting experiences of my life. I started realizing what power and connections meant. At the same time, I started losing interest in my work since I was not being rewarded enough materially or even spiritually. I stayed on to fight for what I believed in, for more than one year. We finally won, not only through justice, not only because we had proof, but because we essentially had accumulated political power. My friend and former director was reinstated to his post. It was time for me to leave.

I started looking around for alternative careers. I did not want any more schooling. After taking special classes in work evaluation at a couple of graduate schools, I felt that formal education was not what I wanted to pursue.

Betrayal Number One

In the meantime, I was very much involved with Common Cause, the Sierra Club Issues Committee, and my farm. I was also building a large addition to our house. I got involved with cars, photography, and other hobbies. My wife was not a part of my world. She did not have the interest and I was not sensitive enough at that time to notice us drifting apart. To my shock and dismay, she fell out of love with me and in love with a very dear friend.

To this day, it amazes me how well I took it and how accepting of them I was to the point where I helped them out on several occasions. Up to that point, my relationship with my in-laws was very good. I respected and admired the character and industry of my father-in law. My mother-in-law was lethargic, extravagant, disorganized, and very insecure. She was also very loving. (How can she be "loving" — David needs to define what he means by the word "loving"), but there was a resentment in me for her unfavorable qualities. (I doubt he ever expressed these feelings.) There are very few women whom I have ever admired, especially among the older generation. Perhaps society never gave them the chance to excel. (Here he is really talking about his own mother. I pointed this out to him. I suggested that women in earlier generations used all kinds of covert behavior to get what they wanted. David's generalizations about women reflected his repression of his own feelings — toward his mother, the former wife, his "best friend," and his in-laws.) So, after my separation with Dianne, I started feeling a certain coldness from both of my in-laws. Kentucky was not a place to stay anymore. I wanted to move on. The urge to move into a cosmopolitan atmosphere was dominant. I felt I needed to uncover my buried drives and interests.

Off to California

Dianne by then had broken up with her lover. We were still friends. She got a transfer to California and asked me to join her as a pal until I found a way out. We sold our house, bought one in California, and moved. We had a platonic relationship. (David never ended his connection with Dianne. He is getting ready for more hurt. Why?) She quickly found a boyfriend in California and moved in with him. I started a company on my own selling bath chairs and related accessories for the handicapped. I enjoyed it but did not make enough money. After about six months, I joined a pharmaceutical company and moved out of the house. Dianne and her boyfriend moved in. We had a verbal agreement on the settlement of the property. I got about eighty percent of the joint ownership in cash. We got an uncontested divorce with the promise that she would pay me the rest when she had the chance to save the money.

Betrayal Number Two

To my utmost disappointment, she later reneged, claiming that I got more than my fair share. (David would have seen this coming if he had seen Dianne as she was.) That was the worst thing she could have ever done. It really hurt. It sure does surprise me to this day that I still feel a certain loyalty to her and that I'll help her out when I can. (This does not make sense. Where is his anger? David, the fighter, rolls over and plays victim.) My in-laws added more salt to the wound by severing their relationship with me. (Which is what David needed to do with them!) They don't call even when they're in town, although they are very nice when I call. (David does not listen to his feelings about them, otherwise he would say how he really feels to these people. He is afraid to terminate contact; he lets them take the responsibility to *end* what is hurtful to him, no doubt copying his father's behavior.)

I hated my current job at the outset. I took rejection personally. I did not know my customers, the territory, the products. After about a year things began improving, to the point where I looked forward to starting a new day. Every day is a learning experience, leading me to where I want to go. I enjoy the company of most of my business associates. I don't feel I am selling, but giving a service. It has surprised me to see my sales results. If I am so good now, just imagine how much better I will be with more experience.

Conclusion

Reading what I have just written, I don't think I have changed much on the inside since I was a child. (This paragraph is a key shift in the writing. He is commenting on his life; he is now the editor, analyzing his choices, seeing with a new perspective. He likes what he is, problems and all.) I'm not sure if I regret turning anti-establishment, picking up social work and shutting off my material needs. The consciousness and experiences of that period of my life is worth it. I have a life ahead of me to build and enjoy. The future sure looks bright. Doing my best is what I firmly believe in. It's the ultimate source of my happiness. I know I'm asking a lot out of life. I'm giving a lot. I will get what I want. There are many people in this world who will benefit from my success. Giving certainly is more fulfilling than only receiving.

The development of character begins early for all of us. In David's case, his cumulative experiences taught him about his own judgment. His judgment was correct in many cases, except in regard to his mother, father, former wife, in-laws — and himself. He pays more attention to his feelings now, and acts directly when necesary rather than retreat or play the Victim, like his father.

"I always did well at whatever I tried. I'm disciplined and I finish what I start. I was proud of my social work. I am proud of my sales career. I always gave everything my best," he said.

DAVID'S JOB-SEARCH METHODS

For competitors like David, self-correction is subtle. Remember the earlier tennis analogy? A tennis player may be coached to turn the wrist an eighth of an inch. That slight shift may make the difference between winning and losing. David was trying to "close the sale" before he defined the problem. His approach was, "Here I am. Where can you use me?" He distributed resumes which usually landed on desks in the Personnel Department only to be filed away later. When his resume and letter were circulated, they met with little interest. A conventional resume is an ineffective marketing tool because it does not address specifics — the specific needs of the organization and of the person who has the problems. A job is created as an attempt to solve business problems. It is the ability to identify the problem which leads to the effectiveness of the proposal resume (see Chapter Eight). A special job which is your passion can be created just for you. David followed the process and found that he too "created" his own dream job.

International sales, David's area of interest, is a touchy market for many American businesses. For most businesses, international involvement comes second to domestic emphasis. Especially if domestic markets are providing good return, there is a natural resistance to become involved with the uncertain markets and politics of other countries. Stockholders want return on investment. The heads of multinational companies know from experience that it takes unusual political, economic, and social savvy to obtain and keep business. American technological know-how is strangely coupled with international naivete. We are a productive, capable nation and we are growing in our familiarity and orientation to the nuances of internationalism. David's task was to convince an American company that profits could be made by using his international knowledge.

David's New Way

David stopped mailing resumes and began to use the advice call approach. He selected people in his area who had an interest in international marketing. He contacted the Arab-American Chamber of Commerce, trade representatives, and other businesses, large and small.

The approach letter technique worked. David started having meetings that became extremely productive. He learned that several businesses could use his talents and even received two offers. Neither was the right niche but the success of the process raised his self confidence.

"I see now that I was trying to 'close' people too soon. I wasn't listening; I was trying too hard. People have been so helpful in these advice calls, and I think I've located the company I want, headquartered right here in the city. I'm sending a letter to the vice-president of international marketing. His name was mentioned in one of my meetings with the Arab Consulate. I was told his company had considered expanding its Middle East activities but had run into some difficulties. I need to learn more. Their products would have a huge market in the Middle East," David told me.

The meeting went very well. The vice-president was open to hearing about David's goals and spent considerable time explaining his company's position.

"Only three percent of our market is in the Persian Gulf area.

With so many recent political developments, we're not sure our staff understands all the social, political, and economic problems. We've drawn back from expansion until we can figure out the best approach. We know the market is there but corporate strategists are more comfortable with domestic markets," he told David.

David listened carefully and asked several questions. The vice-president's response encouraged him to ask for a chance to meet with other people in the division. Their perspective would provide him with more pieces of the puzzle, and at the same time he could get a feeling for the personalities involved. Their cooperation and enthusiasm for expanding the market in the Middle East was vital to any proposal David would make.

After many meetings that were spread out over a number of months, David was ready to make his proposal. During that time he had become familiar with not only his target company, but had kept himself informed on the latest developments in the Middle East. His proposal included an orientation time that would allow him to become thoroughly conversant with all the products and marketing strategy of the corporation. His final letter to the vice-president, written after the job offer was verbally extended, summarized what he could do for the company. David went on to the next step in his career. He had "arrived." By making a subtle correction in his attitude, he achieved his objective. You may need to shift your thinking in order to allow your self-correcting mechanism to go to work for you as David did. David limited himself when he depended on traditional methods to gain entrance into companies. But when he tried a new approach, he found that it worked.

Since David's story was first written, he has made another move. After two years he accepted a position as regional manager of the Middle East for a large hospital supply firm. This is a major step forward, financially and personally. He is coming full circle. He is coming back to his roots. I believe David's story will climax when he combines his social conscience with his marketing skill. Before he left for Athens, he told me of his dream.

"Nancy, it's the nuances in business and political relationships that are important. I want to become a master in liaison between major government figures in the Middle East and American businesses. The culture of the Persian Gulf countries demands a study of nuance. I want to help create mutual understanding and respect," he said.

Naive? Idealistic? I think not. The faith and energy of people like David are a hopeful force for change and international understanding. He is learning patience, and becoming the best he can be. The world changes from the influence of focused personalities who do what they love and do it well.

CYNTHIA'S STORY

A thoroughly discouraged woman came in my office, with so much negativity in her personality that I wondered if I could help her at all.

Cynthia was a high school teacher who had had a successful career in education. However, she was seriously disturbed with the continuing lack of interest by her students, fellow teachers, and (especially) the administrators. She felt her enthusiasm waning, and her normal commitment to her classes and her career was at the lowest point in her life.

"I have to exert great effort to get out of bed in the morning, and I dread the start of each day. The students are apathetic, especially about the subject I teach, Social Studies. I feel as if no one appreciates me. The other teachers have given up, just putting in their time, and the administrators only do what is required to keep their jobs. Education is a losing battle," she said, her whole face a study in frustration and fear of the future.

"Cynthia, how long have you felt this way?" I asked.

"For years, really. I knew five years ago where public schools were headed but I couldn't think of an alternative for myself. I've been teaching seventeen years; it's all I know. What else can I do?" she asked, nearly in tears. (Here was the evidence of a big challenge being set up, something that can be painful, but will lead to the opportunity for change and fulfillment.)

Cynthia had worked for days on a resume, had sent it to several companies and even had met with a few people, all with no results.

"I'm more confused than ever. My friends tell me I'm crazy to want to leave a secure position. I'm a good teacher but I want to explore other areas, especially the business world," she said.

I explained to Cynthia that any career shift would take months to pursue, and asked if she could bear up under the uncertainties that are part of a job search. I was concerned about the years of security that teaching represented and how that part of her life would weigh against an unpredictable future.

"I have to try," she said. "If I don't change now, I know I never will," she assured me, saying that with my help she could do it.

"Cynthia, I'm not a magician. You will do most of the work in this process and that's as it should be. I won't let you become dependent on me, for then we will be reproducing the past. From what you've told me, I see that you're trying to become independent, to grow in new directions. That is not so easy when you've had a life of relative certainty for seventeen years," I said.

Cynthia's completed assignments revealed that she was group-dependent, that she was not sure about her ability to make decisions, and that she preferred a team setting in work. I knew the process of finding a new job would be painful for her, but during that time she would gain enough knowledge to make her own decisions and feel confident about them.

During our discussion of her assignment, I pointed out her strengths as well as the areas where more internal work was needed.

"Your scores show you to be outgoing, assertive, venturesome, and fairly stable. You are intuitive, bright, and forthright. You are also dependent on a group for decision-making. To me, this means you don't trust your own judgment — you doubt yourself," I explained, adding that working with her would be a balancing act for me.

"What do you mean, don't you think my chances are good?" she asked, looking worried.

I laughed. "Yes, Cynthia, your chances are excellent. The balancing act I speak of is my ability to encourage you to think for yourself. That means I have to refrain from giving you answers, since responsibility and personal choices go hand in hand. I want you to know I'll enjoy working with you even on those days when I tell you what you don't want to hear."

Cynthia would remember that statement months later when her resolve was shattered from a week of disasters. Everything had gone wrong. The job she thought she had did not come through. She was not sleeping well, her health concerned her, her money was low, and all her advice calls seemed a total loss. She was even thinking that she should go back to teaching.

"Was the experience with the business world so unpleasant?" I asked.

"No, I loved meeting so many interesting people. Everyone did what they could to help, but no one wanted to hire me in sales — which is what I want to do. I know I can sell but I've been told I don't have enough experience. That's not true. I sell education, so any other product should be a cinch," she said.

Cynthia had interviewed for a good sales position. The sales manager liked her, but his supervisor did not want to risk the training cost on an unknown. She was still feeling the bite of disappointment.

"If you want a sales career you have to be able to take rejection. I realize you're discouraged and want to conclude this search. Remember, you only focused on sales as an objective just two months ago and you have come very close to a firm offer. Since you're worried about your finances, how about a stop-gap position to give you some money and thinking time?" I asked. I felt that Cynthia needed a respite from the pressure, an alternative.

She listened and then asked, "What kind of position?"

I told her that a friend of mine, Les, had called the day before and asked if I knew someone who could help him manage his office. He supervised the field sales staff in a financial planning services firm.

"I need someone who is mature and bright — able to handle prima donnas," Les had said, laughing. I had replied that I would think about it and call him back.

I knew Cynthia's personality matched Les'. He would be an excellent boss — dynamic, firm, sharp, with a good sense of humor. Cynthia was very much at ease with this type — a man very similar to her father, with whom she had an excellent friendship.

Cynthia called Les and scheduled an appointment with him to interview for the office manager position. Les called me the same day and said he was so impressed with her he wanted to hire her, but not to manage his office.

"If she's what I think she is, I'd like her on my sales staff. The financial planning field needs sharp, hard-working women. She expressed herself well, and she really knows her strengths," he said excitedly.

I was delighted and Cynthia was amazed. I asked her how she had handled herself in the interview.

"I did what I always do on advice calls. I tried to find out about him and the business. After an hour talking non-stop, we took a break, had coffee, and got back to discussing his business. I was fascinated *(passion clue!)* with what they do for people. What a great service, helping people manage their finances and investment needs!" She was more excited than I had ever seen her. This is a good example of someone experiencing a previously unrecognized passion. Sometimes the career search happens like this. All the research and advice calls seem fruitless. You feel like "giving up" and, suddenly, you find your niche!

As with many companies, even though the boss liked her, it was necessary for Cynthia to meet with other department heads before a final decision was made. After six more interviews she was hired. Les sent me a personal note of thanks and Cynthia came in two months later to see me. Her eyes were bright, her step was light — she looked great.

"I made my first big sale, Nancy. It was to another teacher, a friend whose inheritance had put her in a precarious tax position," she said.

During the training program with her new company, Cynthia had called on her old friends in teaching. (See the importance of maintaining contacts?) Her first sale, a friend, trusted her enough to allow the company staff to analyze the problem. Their solution finalized the sale. Cynthia will in time be able to analyze the financial problems herself. She is now in training and plans to return to school for a graduate degree in financial planning.

Cynthia's story illustrates that we sometimes lose our perspective and cannot see that we *are* "making it." I gave Cynthia some suggestions, but her own self-awareness and natural abilities got her the job. In her meeting with Les, she focused on him and his company, and forgot her own personal concerns. She had the same attitude that all high performers have — "the show must go on" no matter what. Cynthia's power was released when she trusted herself and communicated openly and honestly. Her years of teaching had served her well. All the times she had gone into the classroom perhaps not feeling her best, she still gave her best. Cynthia's written self-image (Chapter One) changed into a balanced image. Following are both images so that you can see the subtle shifts that were created. Cynthia kept her balanced image realistic.

How I See Myself

I see myself as a person desirous of getting more from life in the sense of personal achievement and fulfillment. Because I can be very disciplined and determined when I decide upon a course of action, I feel that I am capable of facing new challenges and willing to undergo the necessary hard work. Even though I am enthusiastic and hopeful, I do harbor self-doubts and concern about my real abilities, which perhaps have never really been tested. I can be more of a romantic than a realist and recognize that I need to become more pragmatic if I am going to be successful in a role other than that of a teacher.

I have learned to be self-sufficient and independent. I can be happy by myself and don't feel lonely when I am. I learned many years ago that loneliness is a state of mind, not a state of being. However, I hope to have a satisfying relationship with a man someday, for despite the fact that I can function on my own, my life certainly would be enhanced by a caring relationship.

Physically, I feel attractive and sexy. I try to keep in shape by jogging and watching my diet. I am conscious of my appearance and sometimes worry about growing older. But then if I were younger, I might not be as wise! I feel really healthy and energetic.

My Balanced Self

My balanced self would be far more confident and less cautious. Perhaps I could acquire these characteristics if I learned how to channel my energies and focus on some specific goals. With more confidence, I would be more decisive and willing to take risks. I would like to learn how to develop my psychic abilities and use them constructively. Also, I would like to associate with more people who are successful, that is, people who make real contributions to society. With this kind of exposure, I might have fewer negative thoughts — being critical and jealous, for example — and put more energy into constructive projects, things that will lead to a happier me. In summary, I want to learn how to be in full control of my life and destiny.

All of us want to be more in control of our lives. Cynthia expressed this need as she began the process. Months later, she achieved it. So can you.

We often express the desire to have control over our lives and destiny. The cosmic irony is that our paths *are* self-chosen; you will know you have *really* made it when you realize that you created your life plan very early. At the moment of birth you were an aware being, a part of an exquisite, intricately woven tapestry. This universal tapestry is enormous in its scope, and yet your thread is vital to the overall design. In fact, your individual life is a tapestry itself, rich with color, pregnant with meaning. You choose your design, changing it at will with your imagination. If you think long enough about what you truly want ("heart dreams," not "head dreams") and focus your picture-making mind on the result as if it already exists, the new tapestry is created.

The master of life lives his or her daily life with courage. Courage is not the absence of fear; rather, it is the ability to take action in the face of fear. You will experience disappointments as well as rewards when you follow the process outlined in this book. Changing jobs, meeting new people, and finding your right niche can be difficult. If it were not, everyone would be doing it! It is difficult in the beginning because it is such a personal journey, one that involves only yourself. Once you have started the process, you will find that you have mutual support from many of the people you will meet. You will not only receive support — but you will also give support to others.

When my clients are feeling low, they complain to me. That is part of my work, hearing about failures as well as successes. One day a client, Burt, came in to see me, totally frustrated.

BURT'S STORY

"Your system sounds wonderful, but it's not working for me. My letters are being sent to the Personnel Departments. One guy even told me not to bother him, that he had no openings," Burt said, ready to explode with anger at his treatment.

When we calmly analyzed his ratio of letters sent and subsequent meetings held, he was averaging fifty percent success! Even so, I was not pleased. When done well, the average is usually around eighty percent. I discovered that Burt had mailed two-thirds of his letters to the advertising field, a highly visible target. Many people are attracted to the glamour of advertising.

"Why did you send such a high proportion of your letters to advertising agencies? I have a feeling your niche is in a company, where your function would be to work with the ad agencies on your company's account. Let's contact more people within companies who do that," I said.

Burt's average rose, and at the same time he realized that the high-pressure atmosphere of an ad agency was not for him. People under pressure usually are not very receptive. Burt was "pushing the river," trying to break into a field that resisted his efforts. Because he was off target, his results were fewer than he expected. With a change of direction, his ratio improved dramatically. He sent more letters, did further research, and enjoyed good rapport in his meetings.

"I'm amazed at the reception I'm getting. I have so many people to call, so many referrals from my meetings, that I'm not sure I can keep up!" he said, enthused and delighted.

The end result was a job offer inside a company where he acted as liaison between the company and its advertising agencies. Burt made a subtle shift in his approach and found that he could follow his passion — advertising — in a niche that he had not anticipated.

MASTERY OF LIFE

Mastery of life is based on *faith*, *belief*, and *imagination*. Faith is the strongest and most productive of all your emotions. Faith is a state of mind. Skepticism, its opposite, is part of our internal warning system. Used properly, skepticism keeps you from making mistakes of judgment. If you will believe in the effectiveness of the ten passion secrets in this book, you will replace any unnecessary skepticism with belief and faith.

You first must have faith that you *deserve* to have a life that works. As your beliefs change, your sense of yourself begins to change. As you develop new attitudes about yourself and your life, and develop a greater awareness about yourself, you observe daily events with a keener eye. In time, you are ready to take action to move toward your goals. Unless you *act*, you remain a passive receiver, living a vicarious existence. But that is not what you were designed to do. That is like having a Porsche and only driving it to and from the grocery store once a week! You are designed to perform at a very high level. Your mind is a rich, unending resource, the creator of reality in all its forms. You have what no machine has: *imagination*, the creative source of art, music, science, business, and all ideas. Remember that your thoughts are things, powerful forces that you control.

In one very important sense, *all* your choices are good ones, for they are all directed by an invisible guidance mechanism within you that is leading you to ever greater self-awareness. You *are* in control, even if your life appears to be something a lot less than what you desire. Your life experience corresponds to your deepest beliefs about yourself and life.

For example, if you believe, as Cynthia did, that you may not have real ability, then your choices in a career will be made to minimize exposure, to eliminate risk. You will go for what is safe. But inside you is the creative self that wants to experience newness, as Cynthia found. The push for self-expression may take its toll in emotional turmoil, self-doubt, or anxiety. You may choose an inner landscape (where no one can see you) to work out the conflicts, rather than reaching out into the world to make your imprint. If you truly believe that your abilities, your skills and strengths, are limited, then they will be. However, if you believe they are unlimited, the future is yours!

The stories of Cynthia and David illustrate how we can limit ourselves with our beliefs. David believed that he must always be ready to fight for what he wanted, that competitors always lurked around the corner, ready to attack. His defensive posture was useful in his early years to get him through a repressive system. But as an adult, in a different environment, he learned to overcome this belief and move forward with a more cooperative and trusting attitude.

Beliefs are subtle. In order to identify the ones you have, examine them by thinking about the present state of your life. You may feel trapped, wanting something different, but doubting your ability to create the desired change. Like Cynthia, you may be in a job or business that you have done so long that you cannot imagine being hired into another field. Feeling trapped is a good motivator. Do not fight what you feel. Your feelings are the key that will lead you to your beliefs, allowing you to solve the puzzle.

POSITIVE AND NEGATIVE EMOTIONS

Emotions — both positive and negative — are integral to directing our choices. Take a look at both the positive and the negative emotions listed in Napoleon Hill's book, *Think and Grow Rich.*[4] See how they affect your ability to focus and take action.

The Seven Major Positive Emotions

1. The emotion of desire.
2. The emotion of faith.
3. The emotion of love.

4. The emotion of sex.
5. The emotion of enthusiasm.
6. The emotion of romance.
7. The emotion of hope.

The Seven Major Negative Emotions

1. The emotion of fear.
2. The emotion of jealousy.
3. The emotion of revenge.
4. The emotion of greed.
5. The emotion of suspicion.
6. The emotion of anger.
7. The emotion of hatred.

Both states or sets of emotions cannot occupy your mind at the same moment. One state of mind will dominate, depending upon how much you practice it. The world is full of people who work very diligently at negativity. Think about how many thoughts it takes to maintain a depressed state of mind. Experts have estimated that we think at least 50,000 thoughts a day!

How many of your 50,000 thoughts a day focus on the seven positive emotions? How much of your life is given over to passivity, acceptance of the status quo? How many of your thoughts are trapped in negativity?

YOUR STORY

The powerful and successful people that I have known, met, and served have similar attributes. They control what they think about, and what is more important, they take action. (Remember that the definition of power is the ability to take action, to influence.) You have that same ability to take action, to shape the course of your life.

Begin to take action with your thoughts, and use your imagination to write your story *exactly the way you want it to be*. Just fill in the blanks below and see what happens! (This is the affirmation technique, first used in Chapter Three.)

I, ____________________, have an exciting and rewarding career. I make $_______________ a year with_______________ benefits. I live and work in ____________________, my ideal geographical location. I provide a service to my company and/or customers/clients that gives them ___________________ and __________________. I am recognizedas a doer and a reliable _________________ in the ___________________ field. I have fine relationships with my co-workers and supervisors. I am seen as likable, warm, strong, and competent. I grow daily in self-awareness, in mastery of my life and chosen work. I truly have combined my livelihood with my passion. My work is fun and life-giving. My private life is fulfilling and joyous. I, _________________ , am highly pleasing to myself in the presence of others. I have supreme confidence in ________________ (statement of faith or spiritual beliefs, if you wish).

I like your story. It is real. Congratulations! *Celebrate!*

CELEBRATE!

When my clients complete the process, we celebrate the courage that healthy choice requires. The old life (and self), with all its learning and pain, is only a dim memory. We laugh, remembering the struggle together, how we were not sure we would make it. We tell each other the story, savoring every step that got us where we are.

Celebration is a vital part of a passionate life. Savor your triumphs with a celebration. Open the wine, have a party, ring the gongs, blow the whistles. Let everyone in earshot know about you. Your achievement is music to the ears of the discouraged and to those who love you. Now you know your passion in life and how it connects to others. You are here to do what you love for a living, in the way I have described in the book. You are here to give heart to the world, through your work and your passion.

SUMMARY

Passion Secret #10: Powerful people know when they "get there."

1. Be open to your full destiny; do not set limits.
2. Look for the vividness of life, the rich tapestry of your existence.
3. Adversity is a necessary ingredient in development of leadership. It is the tension that motivates change. Challenge is an integral part of a fully lived life.
4. *All* of your experience has meaning. All.
5. Rebellion is a healthy precursor to change: social, political, and personal. We must revolt against the tyranny that represses freedom, whether it comes from outside, or within ourselves.
6. Few companies have the time and funds to manage *your* career; you must take charge of self-management. First, try internal methods, inside yourself, inside your company. Second, try external methods, outside yourself (workshops, therapists, advisors), outside your company. Locate the source of the problem.
7. Practice "productive self-indulgence," avail yourself of all sources of help in getting the job or business you want.
8. After you have found your new career, continue the process of self-management. Do not be lulled into complacency with the tempting cushion of salary, benefits, and the company umbrella. *Be* the change you want to see happen, instead of trying to change everyone else.
9. We all live in the most exciting time in the history of the planet. The future can be summarized in two words: alternatives

and newness. Train your mind to be open to all the possibilities.

10. Consider the possibility of starting your own business, alone or in tandem with others.
11. Avoid "closing" your sale too soon. Take your time finding what your heart desires.
12. Always give your best. Stretch your capacity to give of yourself.
13. When you are discouraged, be honest about why "things" are not going well. When you are in harmony with your genuine interest — one that matches your skills, strengths, and values — "things" will go well.
14. You are designed to perform at a very high level. Use your personal power, take action.
15. Make a tally of your daily thoughts. How many include the seven negative emotions? How many include the seven positive emotions?
16. Write your story *exactly the way you want it*. Then, live it!
17. Always celebrate your achievements. Buy yourself something you have always wanted, go away for the weekend, spend a day puttering around your garden or pampering yourself — anything that gives you pleasure. Do not discount your achievements! Stop, pause, and celebrate with those who love you.
18. You are here to give heart to the world, through your work and your passion.

REVIEW

TEN STEPS TO DISCOVERING HOW TO DO WHAT YOU LOVE FOR A LIVING

1. Write your autobiography. This process may require professional help, particularly if you have never done any therapy or other personal growth work. Allow several months for the process of integration to occur.
2. Discover your strengths and values. This step follows the self-knowledge gained from your work on the autobiography.
3. Make a list of your ten most-wanted goals for the next six months. Update as time goes by. This list follows knowledge of your values. Make a collage — these images reflect your values.
4. Research your areas of interest using the Yellow Pages Index. Some of these interests will be personal, not professional. Break your list down to the top six — rewrite as insight comes as to whether or not the category is personal or professional.
5. Discover your personality type: partner, team, or solo. It is extremely important that you know your type, or what combination of the three reflect your personality. People often misunderstand their type, resulting in much unhappiness at work and home.
6. Research the marketplace to pick the company or activity that suits your personality: a large, medium, or small company, or solo work.

7. Contact the people who are doing what you want to do, either by telephone or letter. *Each situation has its own rules*, so use your instincts. Practice makes perfect; your self-knowledge grows as you meet people and gain information.
8. Hold advice calls (also called informational interviews, or networking) with experts or individuals in the field in which you have an interest. If you are changing positions or careers, you may need to upgrade your skills, or you may find that you already know how to do what you want to do, but did not know the terminology or how to use your resources.
9. Consider entrepreneurship as a partner, team, or solo. Start with local businesspeople — the chamber of commerce is a good place to begin. Use the advice call approach, and attend meetings and seminars to learn about present and future possibilities and problems.
10. Integrate your learning — mastery requires constant fine-tuning. As you gain experience, the path becomes easier, the hills become smaller. Then you are ready to teach what you know to others coming along behind you. You know the journey is the important thing in life, not the goal; your love and competence are your gifts to your world. Celebrate!

THE TEN PASSION SECRETS

1. The first step to power is clarity.
2. Powerful people do not want to be like anyone else.
3. Powerful people know that getting there is all the fun.
4. Powerful people always have other powerful people help them achieve their goals.
5. Powerful people know how to find their niche. They follow their passion.
6. Powerful people enjoy the process of research; then they act and move ahead on the information they have.
7. Powerful people know how to make and keep lasting relationships (contacts).
8. Powerful people trust their instincts.
9. Powerful people know that freedom is the result of self-discipline.
10. Powerful people know when they "get there."

ENDNOTES

Chapter One

1. Jane Roberts, *The Nature of Personal Reality* (A Seth Book) (Amber-Allen Publishing/New World Library, 1994).
2. Napoleon Hill, *Think and Grow Rich* (New York: Fawcett Books, 1960), pp. 222-240.
3. Robert E. Firestone, Ph.D., *The Fantasy Bond, Effects of Psychological Defenses on Interpersonal Relations* (New York: Human Sciences Press, 1985), pp. 273-75.
4. C. G. Jung, *Modern Man in Search of a Soul* (New York: Harcourt Brace & World, Inc., 1933), p. 122.
5. David Kiersey and Marilyn Bates, *Please Understand Me, Character and Temperament Types* (Del Mar: Prometheus Nemesis), p. 16.
6. Napoleon Hill, *Think and Grow Rich* (New York: Fawcett Books, 1960).

Chapter Two

1. Jane Roberts, *The Nature of Personal Reality* (A Seth Book) (Amber-Allen Publishing/New World Library, 1994).
2. Alvin Toffler, *The Third Wave* (New York: Bantam Books, 1991).
3. *Ibid*, pp. 44-45.
4. D. G. Zyfowsky, "15 Needs and Values," *Vocational Guidance Quarterly*, Vol. 18 (1970), p. 182.

Chapter Three

1. Srully Blotnick, *Getting Rich Your Own Way* (New York: Doubleday and Company, Inc., 1980).
2. Gaylon Greer, "How Did the Rich Get That Way?," *AAII Journal*, (March 1984), pp. 23-24.

Chapter Four

1. Napoleon Hill, pp. 105-106.
2. Konstantin Stanislavsky, *My Life in Art* (Moscow: Foreign Languages Publishing House, 1928).
3. Kenneth Branagh, *Beginning* (New York: W.W. Norton, 1990).

Chapter Five

1. Richard White, *The Entrepreneur's Manual* (Radnor, Pa.: Chilton Book Company, 1977).

Chapter Seven

1. Jean Renoir, *Renoir, My Father* (Boston: Little, Brown & Co., 1958), p. 144.

Chapter Eight

1. Richard N. Bolles, *What Color Is Your Parachute?* (Berkeley: Ten Speed Press, 1992).
2. Kahlil Gibran, *The Prophet* (New York: Alfred A. Knopf, 1972), p. 29.
3. Michael Phillips, *The Seven Laws of Money* (Menlo Park and New York: World Wheel and Random House, 1974), pp. 8-9.

Chapter Nine

1. J. Krishnamurti, *The First and Last Freedom* (New York: Harper & Row, 1954), pp. 102-3.

Chapter Ten

1. *Selected Letters of John Keats*, ed. Lionel Trilling (New York: Farrar, Straus & Young, 1952), p. 127.
2. *The Autobiography of William Butler Yeats*, (New York: Macmillan Company, 1928), p. 300.
3. Victor Frankl, *Man's Search for Meaning* (New York: Simon & Schuster, 1970).
4. Napoleon Hill, p. 201.

ACKNOWLEDGMENTS

"The chief idea of my life, I will not say the doctrine I have always taught, but the doctrine I should always have liked to teach, that is the idea of taking things with gratitude, and not taking things for granted."

— G. K. Chesterton, autobiography

Mary Maniscalco was the ideal sixth grade teacher, patient and encouraging. She told me I would be successful because I was hard-working and industrious, words that stayed with me in difficult times.

Helen Fowler, my college journalism teacher, gave me the privilege of editing the college paper, and the freedom to say what I thought. Her faith in me many times surpassed my own.

Marjorie Robinson was the English teacher every college student should have. Her humor and love of her subject made her a model of learning.

Milton Danielson and his Logic class made me think; his praise water for a thirsty mind.

Professor of English John Vickery said I should write psychological novels for a living. While not a novel, I'm sure he'll agree *Work with Passion* is an in-depth analysis of an old human problem.

Roy Maloney, author of *Real Estate, Quick and Easy*, saw my writing one day.

"That's good, that's a book, write it!" he said.

Carol Miller was a friend and business partner whose support was invaluable to me, as was the insight of Jungian analyst/astrologer, Jessica Murray.

Carol LaRusso, formerly of New World Library, worked with me until we were both satisfied with the first edition of the book. Her exactness and geniality were a writer's best friend. Gina Misiroglu's insightful editorial comments helped bring the second edition of the book into the twenty-first century.

Becky Benenate's editorial precision created a visual presentation that matched the contents of the book, as did Stephanie Eichleay's typographical skill.

Marc Allen, president of New World Library, had the eye of the master typographer and good business sense. He gave the book the treatment it deserved.

Finally, *"The Lord is my strength and my shield; my heart trusted in him, and I am helped; therefore my heart greatly rejoiceth; and with my song will I praise him."* (Psalms 28:7)

ABOUT THE AUTHOR

Nancy Anderson was valedictorian of her class at Victor Valley Community College and a Regents' Scholar at the University of California, Riverside, where she graduated magna cum laude with an interdisciplinary degree in English and Political Science.

Following graduation in 1976, she worked with career counseling firms for five years before starting her own practice, at which time she wrote *Work with Passion*, based on her experience with clients.

She lives and works (with a great deal of passion) in Mill Valley, California.